DISTANCE EDUCATION

STATEWIDE, INSTITUTIONAL, AND INTERNATIONAL APPLICATIONS: READINGS FROM THE PAGES OF *DISTANCE LEARNING* JOURNAL

COMPILED BY

MICHAEL SIMONSON

EDITOR OF *DISTANCE LEARNING* JOURNAL
AND PROGRAM PROFESSOR
INSTRUCTIONAL TECHNOLOGY AND DISTANCE EDUCATION
FISCHLER SCHOOL OF EDUCATION
NOVA SOUTHEASTERN UNIVERSITY

ISBNs:
   Paperback: 978-1-62396-274-6
   Hardcover: 978-1-62396-275-3
   E-Book: 978-1-62396-276-0

CONTENTS

PART III:
INTERNATIONAL APPLICATIONS OF DISTANCE EDUCATION

Preface

Michael Simonson

*D*istance Education: Statewide, Institutional, and International Applications is a collection of the best and most important articles from the pages of *Distance Learning* journal, a professional publication written by practitioners for practitioners. *Distance Learning* journal is a premiere outlet for articles featuring practical applications of distance education in states, institutions, and countries.

During the 10 years of publication of *Distance Learning* journal there have been hundreds of articles published that explain the efforts of practitioners who are involved with implementing, operating, or evaluating distance education programs. This book of readings is a compilation of 24 of the most important articles published in *Distance Learning* journal. This book is designed for emerging and experienced practitioners who wish to learn from the efforts of others—efforts based on science and research with an emphasis on what is practical.

This book of readings is organized into three sections:

- Section 1: State-based and Statewide Approaches to Distance Education:

    The seven articles in this section explain distance learning efforts in Iowa and feature its statewide fiber-optics network. Next discussed in this section is the celebrated Florida Virtual School. Finally, papers explaining distance education efforts at Western Governors University, in Georgia, Nebraska, Alabama, and California, and included.

- Section 2: Institution-Based Applications of Distance Education:

    The 10 articles in this section explain distance teaching and learning in colleges, schools, governmental institutions, and the military:

- Section 3: International Applications of Distance Education

    There are seven articles in this section. Articles are included that present distance education initiatives in Cyprus, the Caribbean, Belize, and Italy. Also featured are three articles dealing with distance education in Africa's Republic of Congo.

Distance education is defined as institutionally-based formal education where the

Michael Simonson, Editor, *Distance Learning*, and Program Professor, Programs in Instructional Technology and Distance Education, Fischler School of Education, Nova Southeastern University, 1750 NE 167 St., North Miami Beach, FL 33162. Telephone: (954) 262-8563. E-mail: simsmich@nsu.nova.edu

learning group is separated and where interactive communications technologies are used to connect students, teachers, and resources for learning. *Distance Learning* journal supports this definition by publishing manuscripts that concentrate on distance education practices where this definition is appplied.

The field of distance education—inclusive of distance teaching and distance learning—has matured to the point where research-based best practices are now available in the literature of the field. While research provides a foundation for any field seeking the status of a profession, it is also important to understand the successes of those who are implementing research. This book of readings is a compilation of 24 success stories that demonstrate the impact of science on the practice of a field. Articles were selected because they have direct impact on not only the present status of distance education, but also on its future.

Part I
State-Based and Statewide Approaches to Distance Education

Meeting the Shifting Perspective
The Iowa Communications Network

John Gillispie, Joseph Cassis, Tami Fujinaka, and Gail McMahon

The educational world operates in many dimensions. Population, learning expectations, resources, and technology all contribute to today's shifting perspectives on how to deliver curriculum to students. In 1989, when the Internet was unheard of and "global economy" was not in our regular vernacular, the state of Iowa was already starting a giant technology shift. With the creation of the Iowa Communications Network (ICN), our predominantly rural state was ahead of its time by using fiber optic telecommunications to bring video distance learning opportunities across the miles to Iowa students.

Today, over 6,400 miles of fiber cable, 3,100 owned by the network and 3,300 leased, allows Iowans to access education, health, and government through the network's authorized users—secondary and postsecondary schools, libraries, hospitals, National Guard armories, state agencies, and federal offices (see Figure 1). Standard

John Gillispie, Executive Director, Iowa Communications Network, Grimes State Office Building, 400 E. 14th Street, Des Moines, IA 50319.
Telephone: (515) 725-4707.
E-mail: john.gillispie@iowa.gov

Joseph Cassis, Deputy Director, Iowa Communications Network, Grimes State Office Building, 400 E. 14th Street, Des Moines, IA 50319.
Telephone: (515) 725-4600.
E-mail: joseph.cassis@iowa.gov

IOWA COMMUNICATIONS NETWORK VIDEO CLASSROOMS

Figure 1.   Almost 75% (518) of the classrooms are in the education system.

Tami Fujinaka, Government Relations Manager, Iowa Communications Network, Grimes State Office Building, 400 E. 14th Street, Des Moines, IA 50319. Telephone: (515) 725-458. E-mail: tami.fujinaka@iowa.gov

Gail McMahon, Public Relations Manager, Iowa Communications Network, Grimes State Office Building, 400 E. 14th Street, Des Moines, IA 50319. Telephone (515) 725-4713. E-mail: gail.mcmahon@iowa.gov

ICN video classrooms are based on Asynchronous Transfer Mode (ATM) connectivity with Motion Picture Experts Group-2 (MPEG-2) video compression.

Those who had the bold vision to think outside brick-and-mortar met the ICN with open arms. Some who did not see the need, now have a new perspective, while those who had the vision, now need and want more; and the ICN is shifting its perspective to deliver.

TIME SHIFT

Any time, anywhere—a unique concept just a few years ago—is now an expectation among much of society. Today's traditional students have grown up in the instantaneous world of technology, where time is based on how long it takes to upload or download information from the Internet, not how long it takes to travel somewhere.

A constant challenge facing the ICN throughout its young life has been the issue of school bell schedules. With over 350 school districts, and an almost equal number of differing bell schedules, the need for a shift in perspective regarding time and education is ever increasing.

Bell schedules are often cited by school districts as an obstacle to using the ICN, but the fact remains that where there is a will, there is a way. Some Iowa K-12 administrators look past bell schedules and work together to bring classes to their students. For example, Brooklyn-Guernsey-Malcom (BGM) High School Principal Rick Radcliffe faced losing a Spanish teacher and another foreign language option for students. So, he created a model to entice the Spanish teacher to stay and, as word spread about BGM Spanish classes over the ICN, requests to participate came in from other districts. Conflicting bell schedules posed a challenge, but nothing insurmountable. One school even changed its schedule and calendar to match that of the BGM district. With flexibility and a shift in perspective, four school districts retained the possibilities for almost 200 Iowa students to meet foreign language requirements by using the ICN video services.

The ICN is not just video; the network also provides bandwidth to authorized users. A growing trend toward time-saving online and hybrid courses, a desire for

Figure 2.   BGM HS Spanish instructor Nicki Maestre teaches to her students and others via a traditional MPEG-2 ICN video classroom.

more access to online curriculum content, and increased movement of content via Internet Protocol (IP) have all created a dramatic increase in the need for bandwidth.

Through a strong collaborative effort forged by the network and Iowa Public Television (affiliated with the Iowa Department of Education), pre-K-12 students, teachers, administrators, and school personnel benefit from distance learning opportunities delivered over the ICN. During the 2006-07 school year, more than 50,000 students and teachers came together "virtually" through *K-12 Connections*. This IPTV project, designed to provide curriculum-enhancing opportunities for students, educators, and school personnel, provided almost 7,000 hours of full-motion, interactive video learning sessions to Iowa students, teachers, or schools.

One university professor sees *K-12 Connections* as a way to educate and spark students' interest in science and teaching in a field where demand is high. Iowa State University professor Dr. Larry Genalo is the host of the "Science Fun: What's Hot and What's Not" ICN sessions, which focus on the atomic structure of materials and the effects of changing these structures through heating and cooling. His ICN sessions are full of activity and lively demonstrations. Metal, glass, and rubber objects are melted, frozen, bent, broken, and shattered by using fire and liquid nitrogen. In addition to the demonstrations, Dr. Genalo has constant interaction with the students and explains real-world examples, such as the space shuttle Challenger and the Titanic, which bring home the lesson.

Current *K-12 Connections* sessions are scheduled via a reservation system, as are all ICN video sessions, which provides little time flexibility. With a shift in perspective, *K-12 Connections* is progressing into online streaming and more video rebroadcasts of popular ICN sessions, for easier access by teachers, students, and administrators, via Internet connectivity made possible through the ICN.

PLACE SHIFT

The "anywhere" mentality of today's distance learner is a shift from the centuries-old face-to-face delivery of classes. The ICN's MPEG-2 infrastructure calls for video classrooms at most public school districts and certified public schools that were willing to purchase the classroom equipment, as well as community colleges, regent universities, and private colleges. Today, ICN video classrooms are within 15 miles of every Iowan.

The American mindset no longer accepts the excuse that if you live in rural Iowa you have to give up the opportunity for advanced classes or a field trip to the capital in exchange for valued rural culture. The ICN was built on the premise of equal access to educational opportunities for all Iowans—in 1994, one of the first classes shared was a high school Russian class. The mantra for many of today's parents is, "If it's there, I want it for my child." If course content is available, a student should be able to access it, no matter where he or she lives. Parents and their children expect to be able to access curriculum like Chinese, Russian, statistics, and physics. Busy schedules, including academics, sports, jobs, and family activities underscore the need for nomadic learning.

However, the debate over virtual versus face-to-face classes still plays a part in distance education and for the ICN. Some educators, administrators, parents, and others believe that the most effective way to learn is with face-to-face communication between the student and the teacher. Even in today's technological world, some still consider online classes, with electronic interaction via e-mails and chat rooms, to be less effective than face-to-face interaction. The ICN helps bridge the two factions. The traditional ICN video high school course, offers MPEG-2 broadcast

Figure 3. ILO physics instructor Terry Frisch demonstrates a concept to students over ICN from the Johnston High School video classroom, which is Voice over IP capable.

quality video, providing many of the elements that educators believe are missing in online courses. Students can access classes not available at their location, there is live interaction with an instructor, and the push-to-talk microphones are similar to having students raise their hands to ask a question. Students can ask questions and instantaneously receive an answer.

Online offerings have surpassed the traditional video classroom courses; however, the ICN video classroom remains an important tool for Iowa's small schools and communities. The ICN delivered more than 184,000 hours of video to K-12 districts and higher education institutions

around Iowa in fiscal year 2006-07. High school students continue to benefit academically from high school, college-credit, and Advanced Placement classes offered over the ICN, which was the original intent of the network. Foreign languages outweigh other topics in the number of session hours, coming in last year at just over 5,000. On the college level, traditional and nontraditional students also have opportunities to participate in videoconferencing classes. Some community college consortiums have as many as 13 high school locations with students joining via video in career-focused coursework. Northeast Iowa Community College had

Figure 4. Jim Christensen (right) of Northwest AEA and Sioux City Police Officer Chad Sheehan visit over the ICN with Wales Police Officer Lucy Bennet and Welsh students.

more than 200 students in the fall of 2007 taking classes through a health careers consortium. The University of Northern Iowa led the higher education usage last year and offers 15 programs over the ICN, including undergraduate and graduate programs, and one certificate program, to nontraditional students around the state, along with two online graduate programs.

Iowa Learning Online (ILO), an initiative of the Iowa Department of Education, offers several hybrid online/MPEG-2 videoconference classes, allowing the conflicting beliefs to come together while serving students. Location and accessibility factors are addressed, but the face-to-face factor remains. ILO offers classes to school districts for free or at a discounted rate. During the current school year, one ILO chemistry class has 31 students participating from South Page, Russell, Mormon Trail, Schaller-Crestland, Ankeny, Belmond-Klemme, and Waterloo School Districts. Students explore the central ideas of chemistry through online discussions, readings, online and kitchen labs, and problem-solving scenarios. Teachers use the ICN video classroom to discuss and view classroom demonstrations and laboratory experiments and to hold regular office hours. Students spend considerable time working on real-life problems in chemistry, and required regional labs are an integral part of the learning experience. Each student also has a student coach in his or her school. The districts participating in just this one chemistry class represent a diverse geographic and demographic populace of the state, further adding to the learning experience.

Today, we assume that students in a geographic area want to learn together. With the power of the Internet, geographic boundaries disappear and allow students to collaborate anywhere around the world. However, this is nothing new to the ICN, which has carried Iowa students to worlds outside their school corridors since 1995.

After his sixth grade class in the Galva Holstein School District (population just over 1,000) became the first elementary students to use the ICN in the fall of 1993, Jim Christiansen was hooked on using the network, and was determined to take his students to all corners of the world and then some. He created an interactive project linking middle-level students in schools across the state with NASA planetary exploration experts. Christensen then developed his Virtual Interaction Project Planning Model from which projects such as the AstroVIP emerged—interactive videoconferences conducted between Iowa students and astronauts at Johnson Space Center. He conducted the first videoconference between students and the crew of the International Space Station. Iowa students continue to connect to astronauts in flight and under water today.

During this time, Christensen also developed an international program linking students across the United States with students in the United Kingdom. To this day, oceans apart, enthusiastic third graders in two school communities regularly come together thanks to this project and ICN technology. Students in Sioux City, Iowa, and the country of Wales have created a tool for collaboration and international understanding by using the ICN. Their visits include topics such as holidays, sports, the cost of living, and the weather in Iowa. The Sioux City students even participated in a question and answer session with an American astronaut and Russian cosmonaut who were guests at the Welsh school.

Wales Halfway School Principal Colin Evans says the students play an integral part in the success of the program, helping decide the content of the conference at least 3 months in advance, allowing plenty of time for practice. In 6 years, they have streamlined the international exchange to involve two yearly ICN videoconferencing sessions, an "e-pal" program, and report sharing.

Another video session over the ICN brought together 29 students and faculty from four community colleges in Florida, Wisconsin, Illinois, and Washington, as well as one in Ecuador, so they could meet before a "Transcultural Nursing" study-abroad program, sponsored by Community Colleges for International Development. Headquarters for CCID are at Kirkwood Community College, in Cedar Rapids, Iowa, which hosted the meeting.

Numerous other sessions have crossed borders and brought students of all ages together, such as the 2006 National High School Mock Trial championship team from Valley High School in West Des Moines. The team was honored by their school in a celebration with their peers over the ICN, while the team was still in Oklahoma. The championship team beat 43 competing schools at the national competition in Oklahoma.

The anywhere concept does not just apply to K-12 or higher education students working together in the name of distance learning. Professional development and training have been prevalent over the ICN, and the network's role in the community has become even stronger. In telemedicine, the Midwest Rural Telemedicine Consortium (MRTC) is successful in educating health care professionals and specific patient groups across the ICN. The MRTC reaches out to hospital administrators, employees, patients, and the general public through accredited and nonaccredited programs and education classes, such as diabetes, pain management, and coping with cancer. The group reaches a wide audience, while saving time and mileage for all involved. The consortium has also sponsored international educational opportunities, such as connecting a doctor in Des Moines with a dermatological society in the Philippines.

The state library system relies heavily on the ICN to educate librarians and the public. Some examples include local and city government representatives learning how to help the U.S. Census Bureau prepare for the 2010 census, Public Library Management 1 and 2 courses, required for public librarian certification, and satellite downlinks of teleconferences provided by the College of DuPage in suburban Chicago. The state library also relies on the network as the backbone of its Web sites providing Iowans access to a wide range of learning resources, including library catalogs, databases, census data, patent information, and consumer health information.

In Iowa's far northeast corner, the ICN video classroom at Waukon High School has become an integral part of the community. The school led the way in room usage in fiscal year 2007, providing additional learning opportunities for the community. For 6 to 7 hours a day, high school students and adult learners took college credit classes ranging from medical related to statistics to entrepreneurship and marketing. Younger children participated in educational, interactive sessions offered by IPTV and educational and community professionals received training without the high costs of travel. The room has been so successful for the school and community that district officials asked Northeast Iowa Community College to include an ICN classroom in their satellite campus being built across the street from the high school.

MENTAL SHIFT

The days of students sitting in classrooms is rapidly changing. Student learning methods can be customized to their specific learning patterns with current technology advances. The adoption of new technologies by students is almost an innate process, but administrators and instructors struggle to keep up the pace. The next generation of tools allows collaboration without the need to be a technical wizard. Video over IP, Wikis, chat boards, discussion groups, and social networking sites—all are tools in the public domain making a rapid crossover into the educational arena and making time and place even less important factors in the decision process students and teachers use to seek out learning. All of these tools require non-blocking bandwidth, something the ICN has had to do since its early days.

Observing the social patterns of the multithreading next generation learners promotes the viewpoint that collaboration using technology is a more natural process for them than any preceding generation. These tools, with their ease of use, make collaboration a natural for even the most technically challenged person, and creating a mental shift that can push aside the factors of time and place.

The call for collaboration resounds throughout Iowa. More schools are coming together to offer courses in a collaborative manner as teaching resources become an increasingly scarce commodity. In the case of the BGM School District, Principal Radcliff used the ICN as a way to provide a monetary incentive for the teacher and maintain an academic option for his students and those in four other districts. More districts are looking at collaborative class sharing with other districts for fall 2008, as they grapple with the challenges of high fuel prices, teacher shortages, and meeting students' needs in rigor and standards.

For the ICN, collaboration in creating formats to deliver content created by partners that are valuable to students has been a priority over the last 4 years. A partnership with IPTV ensures the *K-12 Connections* virtual field trip program continues to operate and provides valuable professional development opportunities for all levels of school personnel. The innovation shown

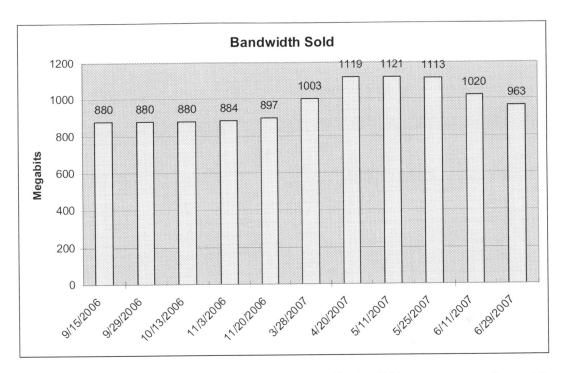

Bandwidth Sold

Figure 5. Educational entities use 74% of the Internet provided by the ICN. Downward trend reflects K-12 school year ending for the summer.

by the partnership has resulted in reaching large-scale, diverse audiences not reached before, such as school nurses and school food service professionals.

Iowa Learning Online continues to gather momentum, but increasingly uses Video over IP and Internet-based course software to deliver on the promise of distance learning. These initiatives use a mixture of technologies to deliver their content, and the ICN remains an essential piece of the whole solution delivered.

The shift in the expectations of students, parents, and the next generation of teachers is not happening; it has already happened. A mental shift among administrators and educators is slowly, but surely, kicking into gear. Time, space, soaring fuel costs, and financial resources have schools rethinking access to technology, and the rapidly evolving marketplace brings resource constraints to the forefront. Many Iowa school buildings do not have ICN video classrooms,

cannot afford a dedicated classroom, some of the rooms are already fully booked, and some have rooms being used for other purposes.

For the ICN, the shift from the video classroom to streaming content is taking place rapidly. The growth of Internet services has happened exponentially in a very short period. This shift is putting pressure on the ICN to adapt and adopt with its own mental shift. While the traditional video classroom usage has remained about the same over the last few years, the demand by schools for big Internet "pipes" has increased dramatically (see Figure 5).

IP has dynamically changed the way people interact in education, business, social networking, safety, and in health. Videoconferencing is one of those capabilities that is significantly changing through IP; providing a greater number of people access to communicate interactively as an alternative to face-to-face. ICN recognizes the need for a shift in delivery to provide schools, and other authorized users, greater access to videoconference—not as a replacement of its current video classroom MPEG-2 service, but one that compliments this service and, in the end, benefits students and educators by filling the voids felt in technology, budgets, and space.

In the early 1990s and before the commercialization of Internet, over 750 classrooms truly gave ICN the "WOW factor." Videoconferences using the legacy ICN video classrooms remain hallmark with broadcast-quality connections and reliability consistently averaging five 9s or higher. The quality of Video over IP does not equate to broadcast MPEG-2; however, users are adapting to their expectations over convenience, similar to cell phones versus landline phones. With the sleek, multipurpose, credit card-sized phones of today, do we still expect to have a call drop or to hit a dead spot, once in a while? Absolutely. Nevertheless, the benefits of convenience, access, and mobility outweigh those occasional frustrations with quality, lack of cell towers, and multitudes of plans. So much so, that many people have dropped their landlines completely. Such is the conundrum of tradition (ICN MPEG-2 video) versus advancement (Video over IP).

Students at Edgewood-Colesburg Elementary School can not learn from IPTV's *K-12 Connections* programs. They are 12 miles from the ICN video classroom at Edgewood-Colesburg High School—same district, different town, which is often the case in Iowa. Participation would mean transporting young children to the high school to participate. With Video over IP, the mobility and access of the equipment means a teacher can use it anywhere there is an Internet connection via a laptop or mobile PC. There is no dependency on a specific classroom.

A high school in northwest Iowa has an ICN video classroom, that is a "receive-only" site. However, they want to originate sessions, too, so they can have their teachers teach to other schools, possibly boosting a course or department struggling to stay afloat due to low enrollment. The costs of upgrading their current ICN classroom could significantly outweigh the cost of adding a Video over IP system in the building. Mobility and access come in to play again, as the equipment can move throughout the building, allowing more teachers the ability to use it for teaching curriculum enhancement or class sharing.

Connecting sites by using Video over IP takes a well-coordinated effort, since IP addresses and availability of participants need to be known. Congestion of Internet traffic may further impact the quality and sound of the videoconference. Various forms of equipment among schools might cause problems with the connections, and local Internet service providers may have different levels of quality of service that might affect the sessions. All that being noted, the fact remains that Video over IP addresses the void that schools face, given their constraints in access to technology, budgets, and space resources, while reflecting the world's shift in technological expectations.

SHIFTING GEARS

A high school principal receives a phone call from a seventh grader's parent, wanting to know if the student will have access to Chinese in 5 years when he reaches high school. A college freshman laments to her former high school counselor about the lack of access to advanced science and math classes, which would have better prepared her for college. Teachers request to teach in their school's ICN video classroom because it has more technology available to them than their regular classroom … including something as simple as a CD or DVD player. New teachers yearn for more accessibility to the latest and greatest technology.

Technology continues to whittle away at the arguments of time and place in the Iowa classroom, where students and upcoming teachers have already shifted into high speed and are cruising in overdrive. The ICN is shifting, too, bringing these new technologies to current and future generations, with a focus on the new expectations and standards of today's educational world—mobility, access, and collaboration.

Just as technology has supported the increasing globalization of business, the ICN remains, and will continue to play, an integral part of the shifting solutions delivered for the globalization of Iowa education—transporting knowledge, instead of students.

Florida Virtual School
Growing and Managing a Virtual Giant

Kay Johnson

I n central Florida, Kaila Julia wants to be a nuclear physicist. In order to follow her dreams she needs an advance placement (AP) calculus course. When she could not fit the course into her schedule, she opted to take it online through Florida Virtual School (FLVS). David Marz, a junior in Volusia County, turned to FLVS when he was diagnosed last spring with bone cancer. By taking classes online, David can keep up with his classmates while he receives monthly chemotherapy treatments.

 is shown above the caption below.

Kay Johnson, Marketing Manager, Florida Virtual School. Telephone: (941) 341-9725. E-mail: kjohnson@flvs.net

Stories like these are becoming common among K-12 students who now enjoy online learning options through their school, district, or state—and those options are growing rapidly. Though distance education has been offered in colleges and universities for quite some time, it has been slower to catch on in the K-12 sector. Happily for students, this is no longer the case.

Ten years ago, K-12 online learning options were reserved largely for remote areas, such as the Western provinces of Canada. There were very few K-12 initiatives in the United States, and funding or legislation to support distance learning was practically nonexistent.

Change came in 1997 from a southern state that, until recently, did not exactly conjure ideas of bold and progressive educational initiatives. Two counties in Florida were awarded a "Break the Mold" grant from the state. Designed to encourage innovation, the grant allowed Orange and Alachua counties to explore online learning as an option for K-12 students. Such was the beginning of Florida Virtual School, now one of the country's largest virtual and most widely lauded virtual initiatives for middle and high school students.

That first year, Florida Virtual School served just 77 enrollments. In 2005-06, it served more than 55,000, and it projects to reach almost 80,000 in 2006-07. Today, the school stands as a remarkable success model on many fronts, including funding, legislative reform, professional development and, most important, student achievement. But FLVS has also provided something that educators across the nation need in order to create similar options in their area—a successful precedent.

How does an organization see such growth and success in such a relatively short time frame? "The organization is constantly pressuring itself to improve and innovate," notes Susan Patrick, president and chief executive officer of the National Council for Online Learning (NACOL), "It is inspiring in the sense that as FLVS realizes success, it puts effort into redevelopment, creating a constant cycle of innovation and improvement. That makes the program stand out."

Julie Young, president and chief executive officer of Florida Virtual School, believes that the ability to create policy rather than live within the bureaucratic structure of the school system gave FLVS the freedom to innovate. "Having the latitude to … be driven by standards and student needs" versus a textbook was the fuel for innovation. The twin demands of standards and student needs continue to fuel the self-challenging ethic that is so much a part of the organization's cultural ethos.

Indeed, FLVS has raised the bar on itself several times. "In the early years, our completion rate was about 50%, and we thought that was pretty good because it was consistent with rates we heard from universities who were, at that time, much further into the online learning game," notes Phyllis Lentz, director of Global Services at FLVS. "The state, however, let us know that they really expected something different from us. They didn't need an option that was just like those that already existed. They needed something better."

So Florida Virtual School did something that schools don't often do: They asked students for input. In fact, student feedback has since become integral to the way FLVS conducts business. "What we learned from that feedback was invaluable in shaping our program," says Lentz. Over the

course of the next few years the completion rate climbed to percentages in the 1990s. The rate fluctuates from year to year, but remains steadily above 80%.

Changes in expectations for teacher-student interaction came as a direct result of the student and parent surveys and eventually shaped the performance-driven funding model that now sustains the school.

PEOPLE, POLITICS, AND PARTNERSHIPS: RAISING FLVS

THE RIGHT PEOPLE

While a stubborn, student-centered focus is the "single direction that everything else can fall around," according to Young, it requires an equally focused staff to maintain that heading. Young believes that one of Florida Virtual School's biggest advantages was the ability to build rather than inherit a team. It allowed FLVS to hire teachers from the get-go who were passionate about change in order to reach students better.

Bruce Friend, vice president of NACOL, agrees. "When comparing FLVS to other programs, I tell people that the real difference is the instructional model and the quality of the staff. People make the difference. You can have the best online course, but the course isn't going to teach itself."

Finding the right people for a rapidly growing school, however, is a challenge. "We've provided a great deal of innovative opportunities and perks for our teachers," notes Pam Birtolo, chief learning officer. Indeed, while administrative jobs are the usual option to the classroom, at FLVS teachers can move into online content development, training, mentoring, and more. Birtolo and Jennifer Whiting, chief academic officer, note that the next generation of e-learning will see new levels of individualized content that can actually morph depending on the interactions and learning needs of the student. These

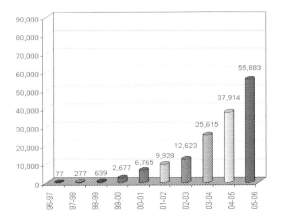

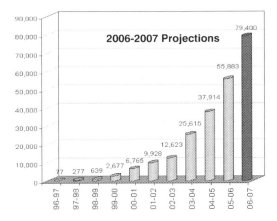

Figure 1. Growth at Florida Virtual School. Since 2001, FLVS has experienced triple-digit growth in course enrollments. In 2003, when FLVS became the first public school in the country to be funded purely on student performance, course more than doubled with successful completions remaining at 80% or better. Since inception in 1997, over 60,000 individual students have taken course with FLVS—a number that also continues to grow by double-digits annually.

changes provide exciting opportunities for innovative teachers who love to find new ways to reach students.

Teachers at FLVS also enjoy new levels of recognition for their accomplishments. Since the school itself is funded upon successful student completions, teachers who successfully reach students beyond the minimum requirement are rewarded monetarily in the form of a per-student bonus.

While financial rewards are certainly appealing, the chance to grow professionally is perhaps equally attractive. An extensive professional development and teacher support program has even veteran classroom teachers cheering. Veteran AP instructor Dianna Miller notes, "I find the support offered by the full-time mentoring staff invaluable to my ongoing growth as a virtual teacher." A "just in time" mentoring program that trains new staff for a full year provides new hires one-on-one daily support as they ramp up to the online environment. Thereafter, a combination of teacher-specific data feedback, teaming, and ongoing training keeps teachers at the top of their game. Teachers are very much in a fish bowl at FLVS in that instructional supervisors can view everything from when the last paper was graded to when the last call to a student was made. The idea, though, is to support teachers who may be struggling in order to ultimately help students succeed.

Interestingly, teachers seem to welcome the challenge. "Teachers are willing to give up tenure, go to an annual contract and be evaluated on performance," says Young, noting that this and a turnover rate of less than 3% is the greatest testimony to a fully committed staff that has jumped into the deep end and is actually enjoying it.

THE RIGHT POLITICAL TACTICS

Another factor in Florida Virtual School's success: political savvy. "Julie [Young] had the foresight to see that you not only have to manage your staff, but you have to manage up," notes Todd Hitchcock, vice president of FLVS Global Services. He notes that Young's remarkable ability to "navigate the political waters" was foundational to the school's success.

Indeed, funding and legislation are often noted as the top two barriers to the growth of online learning. It is particularly difficult to realize the benefits of online learning without stepping on sacred beliefs about local control. When the time came to move from line-item to a per-pupil funding model, Young and other FLVS leaders lobbied to be the first school ever to be funded strictly on performance. If the students don't succeed, the school isn't paid. Young's ability to meet challenges like this head-on has likely paved the way for other programs across the nation.

As Director of Global Services, Lentz works with many virtual programs across the country. "When I talk to other initiatives, there are two main factors that prevent success: lack of funding and no legislation that prevents schools from denying access to students." Lentz notes that the State's decision to provide free and guaranteed access to FLVS to all Florida students was a critical success factor.

THE RIGHT PARTNERS

Another component of success for FLVS was the adoption of a business management model. Equally important were partnerships created to nurture the model. FLVS has seen three notably successful partnerships: with IBM, Jones Education, and UCompass. Young believes the key to those successes was mutual dependence. "I always looked for partners with a shared vision, not just someone interested in selling us something, but also looking at moving our industry forward."

In the IBM partnership, the two organizations were aligned in a mission to take a leadership role and make a significant contribution to the industry. FLVS contracted with IBM at varying levels for the first 4 years and, according to Young "they were giving back to us the same amount in soft services. Each [side] had an equal voice into where we were going." The IBM partnership provided FLVS with business expertise, a critical need for an organization filled with educators. The same was true with Jones Knowledge, who owned

the e-education platform that FLVS used at the time. Jones also provided business insights, marketing guidance, and sales support as FLVS made inroads into the national e-learning arena.

For UCompass, the company that owns and provides the current learning management platform, *Educator*, for Florida Virtual School, the win-win is in smarter product development. "FLVS provided intellectual capital and product feedback from practitioners in the K-12 e-learning field to Ed [Mansouri, owner of UCompass]," says Young. In return, Mansouri created a platform replete with customizations for FLVS.

When considering a business partner, Young looks for leadership within the partner organization, a shared vision for student-centeredness, and an opportunity for give-give and win-win for both sides. "At the end of the day, we need to have an asset if we are going to develop something with someone." That asset could be tangible—as in a product or service to be sold—or intangible, such as market insights or increased reputation.

Hitchcock, vice president for global services adds that a "long haul" focus is critical. "If [both parties] know it's a long-term relationship, you'll both be more likely to respond to one another." He also recommends looking for partners with "a track record for being innovative in their products or their people."

FLVS thrived in the early days on the zeal of passionate educators. But as the organization grew, these same educators recognized the need for business partners to maintain the market-driven approach that has made the school successful. Young's advice to schools looking at similar partnerships? "Do your homework on the business you intend to partner with. Do not assume anything. Have a significant dating period prior to the engagement. Use an attorney no matter how much you like each other."

MOVING FORWARD: FACING THE GIANTS

THE GIANTS OF SUCCESS AND STABILITY

Being hailed as a top leader has its challenges. When you reach the summit, it's naturally tempting to sit down and simply enjoy the view. It becomes imperative to adopt a set of performance indicators that can be measured and tracked. That input, along with solid business instincts, will provide for strong decision making.

FLVS uses a slew of data measurements to track grading turnover, teacher-student contact, or overall progress. Progress is tracked by students, courses, and teachers. Of course, the most important performance indicator for Young is always successful completions. But "soft" data are also collected and considered in the decision-making process. Young pays particular attention to daily e-mails from parents filled with "passionate gratitude," but even negative e-mails provide input for future decisions.

One question on the annual customer satisfaction surveys that Young likes to track is where students respond negatively or positively to the statement: "My teacher cares about me." Young also looks at things like feedback from students who drop courses. She wants to know why and would they recommend an FLVS course to a friend anyway?

In an organization where "change" is almost a mantra, knowing where to focus energy and resources becomes critical. Data management measures like these allow leadership at FLVS to keep the student as their focal point while making the areas needing change more obvious.

THE GIANT OF CHANGE

Change is a double-edged sword. On the one hand, it is critical to an organiza-tion that desires to morph itself to student needs. On the other hand, a growing organization needs to establish policies and procedures, often the death-knell to innovation, to support growth and scalability.

"There's a big risk in a large organization that the organization will begin to create policies for employees rather than for front-line customers," notes Birtolo. Hitchcock agrees, saying he hopes FLVS will maintain a "dating without getting married" approach to policy. "Schools get so mired in policy.... We need to never write another policy. Write plans, procedures—guidelines that we can modify and adapt at any time, so if it doesn't work eight weeks from now, we can change."

Lentz adds that it is important to stress that change is a given. "Having the mental set is part of the battle. Then when things happen, you can just accept it for what it is. You just know it, and expect it." Young concurs, adding that the staff must understand that FLVS is a technology organization as well as an educational one. "We have to change to remain at the forefront. No one can get too comfortable, and they have to be okay with that."

Florida Virtual School expects to quadruple enrollments over the next few years, so it is indeed a juggling act to calm fears of change, create stable and scalable models, while at the same time working like mad to fan the flames of innovation. Whiting argues that being such a large organization can also be a curse to innovation, "We see ourselves in the press as being the biggest and first, but I want to be known as being the most innovative. And we're going to have to constantly reexamine what it will take to be the leader."

For Young, the challenge is to keep pushing everyone to reach higher. "I really do believe that good is the enemy to great. No matter how good you are—if something is working well, how can you make it better?"

FEARS AND PASSIONS

So if these leaders are not afraid of change, what *does* scare them? Internally, a loss of progressive thinking is a concern. Due to FLVS's tremendous growth and need to hire so many teachers so quickly, Whiting worries about bringing old ways of thinking into the FLVS culture. Birtolo concurs, "When you import hundreds of new teachers every year, you are importing all those practices that we wanted to get away from in the classroom."

And it is the disenfranchisement in America's classrooms that worries Young. "Many students indicate that they are tolerating [going to school] as a means to an end. In a recent student panel of what I would consider very successful students, they agreed that they are only engaged about 20% of the time and that they have to 'power down' to go to school."

Susan Patrick, whose role at NACOL provides an international viewpoint, is haunted by drop-out statistics. "We need to help people understand that it's not ok to have a third of our kids drop out. It's not okay to use tax dollars to support schools that are not providing quality learning. There are twenty-first century models of education, powered by e-learning, that are accelerating education in places like Singapore, Africa, Asia, and Europe. Singapore has 100% of its high schools online. It's not just about distance learning. It's about improving *all* of education. While we debate change—other countries are just moving forward."

Friend also worries about global competition. "I'm concerned when parents talk about online courses being 'too rigorous.' We know they are rigorous, and that's kind of the point. How do you take the fact that jobs are going to China, India, and Ireland from just being a news story to students seeing the reality of what that is?"

On the flip side, the leadership at FLVS is passionate about the promise that online learning affords. Young believes Florida Virtual School's role is to be an advocate for *all* students and for the entire online learning industry. "We were so supported in Florida. We were appropriately funded to do the research; we had the ability to take time to make mistakes and adjust. I've always felt that we have a responsibility to … to make this a quality industry, to be at the policy table, to be an example."

The impact of online learning on individual students is also a powerful motivator for the staff at FLVS. "Students can go for a lifetime through school believing they aren't competent or capable," notes Lentz, "but for them to be able to work at their own pace and then realize that they *are* competent—how that changes their concept of themselves and their abilities—that really jazzes me when I hear a student make a comment like that."

Friend echoes this sentiment, noting the power of choice afforded by online learning—choices independent of having more money or moving to a better neighborhood. "I think that's awfully powerful for parents." In the broader scope, Friend argues that online learning meets every twenty-first century skills requirement "probably better than any educational venue in the country right now. Virtual schools have the ability to fundamentally change the way we deliver education and what it means to go to class. If you really believe that learning is all around you … having the ability to reach students at any time, I don't think there's anything that can do this like online learning, and certainly FLVS is a leader."

Education Without Boundaries

The Western Governors University Story

Daniel Eastmond

INTRODUCTION

The Western Governors University (WGU) graduation held on Saturday, February 10, 2007 in Salt Lake City, Utah, was truly inspiring. At this celebration, the university awarded 495 degrees, with over 57 diplomas handed to graduates who converged on the city from more than 20 states. WGU faculty members also gathered from across the United States and arrayed in their academic robes,

Daniel Eastmond, Director of Learning Resources, Western Governors University, 4001 South 700 East, Suite 700, Salt Lake City, UT 84107-2533. Telephone: (801) 993-2328. E-mail: deastmond@wgu.edu

were meeting with their distance students for the first time in person. However, their voices were familiar to them, having spoken by phone and e-mail to each student several times monthly over the years.

President Robert Mendenhall greeted the assembly of family, friends, and WGU staff in Abravanel Hall, a large auditorium and home of the Utah Symphony (WGU having outgrown previous venues). Mendenhall explained that those graduating during this most recent 6 months represented about a third of graduates from the rapidly expanding university. He reflected on WGU's remarkable growth—from roughly 600 students in eight degree programs with 33 graduates at regional accreditation in 2003—to more than 7,500 students, more than 40 degree programs, and 1,581 graduates today.

Commencement speaker Bess Stephens, vice president of corporate philanthropy and education at Hewlett Packard and a WGU board member, exemplifies the struggles of an African American leader to advance her education and career. She boasts advanced degrees in chemistry and education, rising to her position as global director of HP's Foundation. Stephens spoke on lifelong learning. Applauding WGU, she remarked, "Students can work school into the flexibility of their schedules. They aren't limited by time and place but

WGU President, Robert Mendenhall, addresses the February Commencement audience.

their own willingness to commit and meet the requirements" (McFarland, 2007).

For me, the highlight was graduate speeches, particularly that of Joel Ellington. His father, a dirt-poor farmer in the Ozarks in Oklahoma, had no more than a third grade education. Joel, the sixth of 10 children, was one of the few to finish high school. A watershed experience happened in his senior year, when a high school counselor asked Joel whether his future plans included college. That possibility had never entered his mind. When he learned that it was doable, Joel improved his grades to enter and graduate with two associate's degrees from a junior college in Idaho where he also met his wife. He entered the workforce, began raising a family of his own, and the years went by. In 2000, Joel enrolled at Missouri Western, earning a bachelor's degree in education

and was able to begin teaching, a lifelong dream.

Joel entered WGU a couple of years ago, meeting major requirements, taking learning resources and passing assessments to almost complete his degree. One hurdle, the capstone project, remained, and Joel's situation had become particularly acute just then—as he had just rejoined the military full-time. Joel's mentor, Jennifer Smolka, called him, saying, "Joel, I know you; you can do this!" During an early morning run while struggling up a particularly challenging hill, Joel planned to stop at a speed limit sign ahead, only to discover upon arrival another short 80-yard stretch to the summit. With Smolka's words ringing in his mind, rather than walking, Joel picked it up and ran to the summit. From there he could see the whole valley and snowy tops of surrounding mountains. Similarly, girded with her faith and confidence in him, Joel found the power within to press on to the academic summit, completing the capstone requirement of his master's degree. He soon received another call on a field phone from his mentor exclaiming, "Joel, you've done it!"

Here on the stage of this large auditorium far from Missouri, Joel Ellington shared his tale of how WGU kept its promise to him and made his dreams come true—a dream nurtured by his father, though his parents never had the means or circumstances to gain such education themselves. He declared, "Without the help of my mentor, it never would have happened.... [She] called and stayed with me."

In September 2006, experts from higher education institutions, foundations, and accrediting bodies completed their investigations and deliberations about the future of American higher education, culminating in the Spellings Report (U.S. Department of Education, 2006). They concluded that higher education needs to become more accessible, affordable, outcomes-oriented, innovative, and accountable. WGU's President, Robert Mendenhall (2007), a member of that commission stated, "Ideally, distance learning will help to move all of higher education to better measures of learning—what students know and can do—rather than focusing on measuring time" (p. 13). WGU sets a course to accomplish these objectives as a unique competency-based institution of higher education, firmly committed to providing quality educational opportunities that fit the needs of underserved Americans as well as the competitive workplace of the twenty-first century.

MISSION AND PROMISE

Western Governors University's mission remains as originally conceived in 1996: "to improve quality and expand access to post-secondary educational opportunities by providing a means for individuals to learn independent of time or place and to earn competency-based degrees and other credentials that are credible to both institutions and employers." Likewise, the university's leadership formulated this "Promise" which it freely shares with students, setting an employee service standard: "We help our students achieve their dreams for a degree and career success by providing a personal, flexible, and affordable education based on real world competencies." The university strives to build a culture quite contrary to that of traditional campuses—one that focuses on students first, is data driven to measure and improve performance, is innovative and nimble, is high quality with high performance expectations, and is responsive and supportive.

Several aspects of the university make it an especially attractive value proposition for students. WGU is affordable—its tuition ($2,790 per 6-month term) is far lower than most private institutions, and scholarships, financial aid, and tuition reimbursement programs are in place for a majority of students. WGU is flexible—as an online institution, students have tremendous independence and convenience to choose the time and place of their studies. Because WGU is competency-based, it is relevant to the career choices and workplace opportunities of its students, and the constant communication, support, and assistance of a mentor/progress manager make its education personal. WGU is credible—demonstrated through state approvals, accreditation, governors' endorsement, corporate partners, and support from state and national government agencies (e.g., U.S. Department of Education, Congress, Veteran's Administration, and Department of Defense). Finally, the university becomes a good choice for students who wish to accelerate their education—based on the extent of their prior competencies and their determination, commitment, and dedication to exert the effort to move faster through their programs.

THE FOUNDING OF A NEW INSTITUTION

WGU was conceived at a Western Governors Association meeting in Park City in 1995 (C. Johnstone, 2006). With the growing numbers of citizens in the West, the governors determined not to build new "brick and mortar" institutions, but rather to harness the new technology of the World Wide Web in providing quality distance education to underserved populations, especially those living in rural areas. They determined that this education needed to be geared to the workplace needs of employers. A year later, the governors drew up a charter with 10 sponsoring states, and in fall 1996 began seeking regional accreditation for WGU. With governors Mike Leavitt (Utah) and Roy Romer (Colorado) leading the initiative, the fledgling institution eventually received start-up monies of $100,000 from each of 19 western states (the only direct state funding it would receive). Founding governor Roy Romer spoke of the vision he had for the institution:

> We wanted a university that was available through modern communications, and we wanted it based on performance. And, that was the essence of the experiment.... We wanted to be sure that we created a system in which you didn't get credit for a degree based just upon hours of exposure but based upon proven competence that you demonstrated. (Witkowsky, p. 1)

By 1998, the governors had worked with various corporate sponsors and higher education institutions to open the doors of the new private, nonprofit university. WGU initially did not offer its own degree programs—rather, it was a portal for students to choose distance courses and programs from dozens of participating postsecondary institutions and educational enterprises. After much hype about how the institution would remake the face of higher education and be swamped with enrollments, the initial results were disappointing. Very few students appeared at this nonaccredited upstart institution, as many students determined it was advantageous to go directly to colleges and universities in their locales that were launching their own distance education programs via the Internet. Institutions within states, likewise, banded together to form collaborative distance course and program sharing consortia as a counter response to the WGU initiative in an era ripe with innovation and the prosperous economy of the dot.com boom (Duin, Baer, & Starke-Meyerring, 2001).

ACCREDITATION AND GROWTH

WGU realized that its credibility and survival depended upon becoming an autonomous institution fulfilling an important alternative higher education niche by offering its own degree programs and achieving its own accreditation. The university began the accreditation process in 1996, but was instantly seen as an anomaly, since its footprint covered states accredited by several regions—a new situation for regional accrediting agencies that were geographically bound. To address accreditation needs of this new online competency-based university, the regional associations founded a special task force, the InterRegional Accrediting Committee (IRAC). It had representatives from the Northwest, North Central, Western Senior, and Western Junior regional accrediting commissions. C. Johnstone (2006) outlines the issues and events of the 6-year scrutiny of WGU by IRAC in its rigorous review process, progressing from *eligibility* (1998), to *candidacy* (2000), to *initial accreditation* (2003). Because of the need for more immediate credibility, the university sought national accreditation in 2001 and was awarded it a year later by the Distance Education and Training Council (DETC), a process that was "much shorter ... but its standards were equally high and its evaluation every bit as probing and thorough" (p. 5). With initial regional accreditation in 2003, WGU received an unprecedented accreditation by four commissions simultaneously for a 2-year period, with responsibility shifting after that to the Northwest Association.

Some key milestones in its brief history follow. The university began offering degrees in 1999. In 2002, WGU became nationally accredited by the DETC, which was followed by regional accreditation in 2003. The U.S. Department of Education awarded the university a $10 million Star Schools grant in 2001 to develop teacher education programs in shortage areas, and in 2003 helped launch the university's teachers college. The university began to flourish. Financial support shifted from corporate, foundation, and government assistance to the nonprofit, private university being funded almost entirely through tuition revenues. In 2006, the university launched its College of Health Professions.

Also in 2006, WGU's Teachers College completed a multiyear review to achieve accreditation by the National Council for Accreditation of Teacher Education (NCATE). NCATE stated, "In 2001, NCATE modified its standards in part to anticipate the accreditation of non-traditional providers, and WGU is the first to engage the opportunity" (Castaldi, 2006, p. 1). WGU President Mendenhall stated, "WGU is rapidly becoming one of the largest teacher education programs in the country, and we have teacher education graduates seeking licensure in all 50 states." Further, "Today, WGU graduates can apply directly to more than 40 states for teacher certification, and WGU students are eligible for reciprocity in most of the remaining states" (p. 1). The university has stated that what its teachers college "offers is no different from what teacher education programs at traditional institutions aim to provide: a solid foundation for beginning teachers to enter the classroom" (Honawar, 2006, p. 1).

WGU MODEL AND FEATURES

The learning experience at WGU is entirely at a distance wherever a student can access the telephone and Internet within the United States. Students start every month of the year, taking a short introductory course, "Education Without Boundaries (EWB)" before moving ahead on an individualized program of study. EWB prepares students for WGU's model of education and develops their skills to use various tools, such as participating in learning communities or conducting searches for full-text articles at WGU's virtual library. Students are expected to spend between 15 to 20 hours a week on their studies—and can move forward more quickly if they already possess many competencies of their degree program and are willing to devote more time and energy.

Competency-based education (CBE) rests on the premise that candidates should demonstrate their knowledge, skills, and abilities at the level of objective standards to receive the credentials, diplomas, or the licensure of a graduate. CBE particularly appeals to adult learners who already possess capabilities developed through prior work, education, or community experience—and to employers who want evidence that their workers possess the required abilities to perform in the workplace upon graduation.

A promise of CBE is that students won't have to retake courses in subjects in which they are proficient, thus accelerating the time to degree completion (while reducing expenses). WGU allows applicants to transfer in higher education credits at the lower division level where there is a match with required competencies. Certifications they possess, likewise, if part of the degree (such as in information technology) waive requirements. However, WGU affirms most prior learning by determining students' prior capabilities through preassessment, and then enables them to move rapidly to final, high-stakes assessments in their areas of competence.

From its inception, the university has been committed to using the latest technology to deliver quality distance education. Students entering WGU are expected to be adept at using telecommunications technologies, and WGU strives to incorporate technology into its competencies, assessment procedures, and learning resources to meet twenty-first century workplace demands. Not only are almost all of the university's services delivered at a distance through technology, but there is a continual commitment to keep pace with the best appropriate instructional technology available.

WGU's degrees are practical, career-oriented diplomas. The university seeks to produce graduates who meet the needs of employers for today's competitive global economy; it constantly reviews degrees to ensure that competencies fit current workplace demands. The university received special funding to create programs in areas of teacher shortage—science and math education, elementary teaching, English language learning, and social science. Business, information technology, and health professions programs similarly seek to match graduates with the needs of these sectors of the economy.

WGU's programs are tailored to address individual needs, suited to students' abilities, schedules, and interests while maintaining academic rigor. WGU assigns a mentor to advise and support students throughout their degree program. A first task is developing an academic action plan (AAP) that schedules out the sequence and dates of assessments with associated learning resources for competency development. This online AAP dynamically allows students to enroll in learning resources, schedule assessments, and continually see their own progress. Mentors maintain constant communication with each student— by telephone and e-mail at a minimum of every 2 weeks, revising the AAP for every 6-month term. Of WGU's roughly 350 employees, over 150 of them are men-

tors—the majority working throughout the country from home offices.

STUDENT ENROLLMENTS AND DEMOGRAPHICS

WGU President Mendenhall reported on the "skyrocketing" enrollment the university achieved after its 2003 accreditation, which increased more than tenfold from all states by 2006. "And enrollment is projected to double to 10,000 within the next 2 to 4 years, increasing to 15,000 by 2013" (Witkowsky, 2006, para. 23). With its expansion, WGU's enrollments roughly follow national demographics with its students coming from the most populous states: California, Texas, Florida, Georgia and Illinois, while Utah and Nevada still have large numbers based on founding connections of government partners.

The university accepts most adult students, particularly focusing on working adults who have competencies derived from life experiences of the workplace, prior education, and through community service. Not of surprise, the average student age is 37 years old. WGU particularly targets underserved students and prides itself that approximately 83% of its student body come from one or more of these categories: minorities, rural, low income, and first-generation college students. More precisely, 41% of students have household incomes of less than $35,000 a year; 31.5 percent of students live in a rural community; 42% of students did not have either parent attend college; and 22% of students belong to an ethnic or racial minority group.

GOVERNMENT, FOUNDATION, AND CORPORATE SUPPORT

In its early years before regional accreditation, WGU was sustained through major corporate and foundation donations as well as government grants. The university's nearly 25 member National Advisory

Board (NAB), is comprised of corporations and foundations that contribute money and advice to WGU. NAB members (including AT&T, BearingPoint, Consonus, Convergys, Dell Computer, Farmers Insurance, Bill & Melinda Gates Foundation, Google, Hewlett-Packard, Hospital Corporation of America, J. Willard and Alice S. Marriott Foundation, Microsoft, Oracle, Qwest, Sallie Mae Fund, Simmons Media Group, Alfred P. Sloan Foundation, Sun Microsystems, SunGard Higher Education, Thomson Corporation, Wasatch Property Management, and Zions Bank) each made substantial initial contributions and have given yearly dues, also. Wasatch Property Management, upon joining the NAB, donated premium office space in a high rise with an extended, low-cost lease arrangement. The Bill and Melinda Gates foundation, another NAB member, matched a "T-Plus" grant from the State of Utah to prepare school administrators in

the use of technology. The Federal Government contributed financial support through FIPSE grants and wrote the university into legislation to offer federal financial aid (FFA) to its distance students at a time when many institutions were hamstrung when using primarily distance delivery.

Perhaps the most significant of the early grants received by WGU came from the U.S. Department of Education. Besides USDOE's award of a $10 million Star Schools grant to build out the curricular programs of WGU's Teachers College for high needs teaching areas identified in the "No Child Left Behind" legislation, the USDOE offered an important scholarship grant. WGU applied for and was awarded a $3.7 million "Transition to Teaching" grant that enabled highly qualified paraprofessionals in the university's partnering school districts (Clark County, Nevada, Region IV of Houston, Texas, and later El

A national online institution, WGU's administrative offices are in Salt Lake City, Utah.

Paso, Texas) to receive half-tuition scholarships to gain teacher licensure through WGU's new programs. These important curricular and enrollment supports enabled WGU to successfully mount its highly successful teachers college.

Since regional accreditation allowed WGU's enrollments to burgeon, reliance on outside support has tapered off so that now more than 90% of operating expenses come directly from tuition revenues. It is worth noting that WGU has worked hard to maintain its FFA awarding status, to make its programs reimbursable to the employees of several companies (especially those on the NAB), and to become a player in Veterans Administration and Department of Defense (DOD) reimbursed postsecondary institutions. WGU also is able to award "Troops to Teachers" scholarships because of DOD and USDOE support. WGU estimates that 65 percent of its students are on FFA, and with another 18% receiving at least some assistance from their employer or the military.

Support in recent years has included: Hospital Corporation of America's sizable contribution to the design and launch of WGU's College of Health Professions; the Sorenson Legacy Foundation's donation of $150,000 toward the new College; the Tenet Healthcare Foundation's donation of $100,000 toward the new College; a major donation of 60 laptop computers from the HP Company Foundation (bringing total support to roughly $750,000); Sun Microsystems's $500,000 in-kind contribution of IT equipment and services; and the sizeable donation of equipment, servers, and space in Salt Lake City from Consonus as WGU moved its IT operations from Sunnyvale, California. Also notable among the current grants was the award of $400,000 from the Lumina Foundation for the university to conduct research to improve its outreach to underserved populations—a major strength and vital part of its mission. Another was the Department of Labor's award of a $3 million grant in February

2007 to award scholarships to rural teachers. This grant will also allow the university to conduct a study with the American Association of Colleges of Teacher Education (AACTE) to develop and disseminate a new model for addressing rural teacher workforce development. Obviously, many contributors throughout the years have made significant donations to WGU's success.

GOVERNANCE, PROGRAM DEVELOPMENT, AND COUNCIL MODELS

Guiding the overall course of the university is the board of trustees, comprised of governors, educators, and industry leaders. Currently, the former governor of Wyoming, Jim Geringer—a moving force behind the founding of WGU—chairs; current governors Jon Huntsman, Jr. (Utah), and Janet Napolitano (Arizona) also serve. The university continues to garner support (though no monies) from governors of its founding states, and it often holds its meetings in conjunction with the Western Governors Association.

The university's day-to-day operations rely on the decisions and initiatives of its senior leadership team. Very early on, WGU adopted an internal governance structure that is more akin to that of a corporate enterprise than most of higher education. It features: an executive management structure; promotion based on competency; the valuing of all employees equally; a single university structure; the solicitation and valuing of input from all employees, students, and other stakeholders; and academic program councils as major force behind curricular oversight.

WGU develops programs internally by both relying upon the expertise of senior qualified experts in each program area and relying on external standards. Nationally renowned academicians and corporate experts serve on program councils that oversee the development and maintenance of each program's curriculum. However, in several programs, such as teacher education, state and national standards, as well as those from accrediting bodies, dictate program content and candidate qualifications.

Program councils have oversight responsibility for the quality, currency, and effectiveness of the programs within their charge. They consist of six to nine subject matter experts drawn from other academic institutions, private enterprise, school districts, and state or national government agencies, and are the university's most senior faculty members. There is a council for each major curricular area—liberal arts, business, information technology, education, and health professions. They meet in person at WGU offices several times a year to monitor program effectiveness, evaluate learning resources, and provide advice on program planning issues. Speaking of the academic integrity created by councils in formulating competencies, former Provost Chip Johnstone wrote:

> The coherence of the degree is ensured by ... the comprehensive nature of degree competencies. These are not the result of a single faculty member's point of view, nor are they derived from course equivalencies. They are designed as complete structures—the body of knowledge, skills, and abilities that a broad cross-section of experts judge necessary for a student at a given degree level to possess. (D. Johnstone, 2005, p. 28)

In addition to approving all new degree structures and competencies, Councils conduct formal reviews of program effectiveness at least every two years, and more frequently for newly launched programs. During program reviews they make sure that competencies still align with current academic and professional standards. They review assessment performance to be sure they effectively measure the competencies and learning resources to be sure that they properly align.

MARKETING AND STUDENT SERVICES

Appealing to the right audience who will especially benefit from WGU's distance programs is the crux of marketing and recruitment efforts. As a nonprofit institution, the university does not have a large budget to spend on mass marketing. Word of mouth helps, but lead generation from interested applicants through Internet brokers—as well as through partnering organizations or grants—is WGU's preferred source of applicants. It especially seeks working adult students from underrepresented populations—rurally located, first generation college, lower income, and ethnic minority students whose work experience has outpaced their credentials.

The university employs a cadre of enrollment counselors to respond by e-mail and telephone to those who express interest in attending the university. Counselors in some ways parallel the mentoring process that goes on once the student matriculates. Each prospect works with an enrollment counselor who specializes in the degree field that he or she has chosen; the counselor assists the prospective student through the entire admissions process (e.g., financial aid, application, admissions testing, and scheduling to attend the introductory course, "Education Without Boundaries").

Given its missions of "expanding access," WGU is more open-enrolled than its traditional counterparts; however, student selection is still important to winnow out those who will likely succeed at its model of distance education. WGU requires all applicants to complete an admissions test that measures academic competency, and considers each applicant's situation, technology skills, and commitment toward their educational goals before allowing entry. Of course, a high school diploma or equivalent (and TOEFEL scores for nonnative English speakers) are required for entry into baccalaureate programs. A bachelor's degree from an accredited institution is the minimal requirement for entrance into the university's graduate programs.

WGU accepts lower-division undergraduate credits in transfer, waiving those relevant competencies. However, in upper-division or graduate work, transcripts will not suffice; the student must demonstrate those competencies through assessment (which should be expedited if there is successful prior college work in that area).

WGU's own transcript is somewhat unique but readily accepted at other institutions. All competency assessments are taken as "pass/fail" with a "pass" meaning that *the student has demonstrated competency at a grade equivalent of B or better."* Transcripts also list the competencies by "courses of study" (assessments) with the number of competency units (credit equivalents) each one represents.

WGU has an office devoted to retention and student success. These employees contact "at-risk" students to see how the university can assist them to make it through each term. They may assist with minor purchases (e.g., textbooks) if that becomes a major obstacle. These counselors coordinate with various university offices to address any problems these students face. The liaison works with any student complaints in a like manner, also making arrangements for students with disabilities. The Student Success office organizes incentives for student achievement of milestones and administers scholarships for students in underrepresented populations to attend and succeed at WGU.

As its graduates multiply, WGU is committed to their ongoing success. Rather than ask for contributions back to the university, WGU affords them continued mentoring, peer-networking through a special portal, and career services. The university measures its own success by the success of its graduates—such things as their performance relative to others on standard tests and certification exams; their placement, promotion, and pay; employer evaluations; the relevance of the degree to their career; and their recommendation to others to attend WGU.

ASSESSMENT

Students demonstrate competency through assessments. WGU uses various measures in combination, relying on external graders to determine competency. For each domain (typically four to eight in each degree program) WGU has established multiple measures to ascertain competency. These typically include objective and essay exams in proctored testing centers, and performance tasks done online to apply skills and knowledge to realistic work requirements and portfolio development—turned in electronically for grading. For initial licensure, students in the Teachers College are also "observed," during their student teaching experiences using a grading rubric administered by a qualified clinical supervisor and arranged for and trained in the student's school district, wherever located across the nation. Degrees culminate in a capstone project that synthesizes the knowledge from several domains into a culminating product, usually written and presented online via Web and phone conference to graders.

Students occasionally must travel to proctored sites (such as test centers) that WGU arranges near their homes—the only site-based requirement for most programs. Also, WGU arranges for independent grading of its essays, performance tasks, portfolios, and capstones. (Online testing software automatically grades objective tests). The assessment department contracts with roughly 150 qualified graders, training them and continually monitoring their performance and interrater reliability. Graders also give important feedback on student work, especially if it must be reworked if "not passed."

In addition to its program councils, the university established an assessment council, comprised of experts who oversee and advise on measuring the competencies in each program area. In cases where programs use industry-recognized assessments in their programs, such as Praxis, SHRM, CMBA, or IT certifications (e.g., MCSE, iNet+, Security+, MySQL, etc.), the university compares its students' average scores with the industry average to achieve a standard of excellence above the mean. WGU builds most of its assessments in-house, through rigorous psychometric practices approved by the assessment council. In other cases, like its business and IT programs, WGU uses industry certifications as a component of the degree requirements. This practice assures that graduates from its programs have demonstrated competence within their fields as defined by the industry itself.

LEARNING RESOURCES

While enrolled at the university, students use a variety of learning resources (LRs) to brush up on existing competencies and develop new ones. From its inception, the university determined not to duplicate the online offerings of other institutions of higher education but instead to bring in suitable, aligned courses as needed to assist students. Since no students come fully competent, they spend the bulk of their time at the institution becoming proficient through interaction with a variety of LRs. These include textbooks, Web sites, Web-streamed e-learning, learning community discussions with peers and mentor experts, CDs and videos, virtual library resources, and online courses taken from other institutions. WGU makes sure that its LRs are available at any time or place, modular, low cost (since funding comes from student tuition revenues), open or available frequently, self-paced (especially for acceleration), interactive, and feedback-providing (Eastmond, 2006). Each course at WGU has an associated "course of study" (an annotated syllabus) that directs student learning.

WGU arranges for all of its LRs from third-party providers, through contract. These include online courses from accredited institutions of higher education, such as University of North Texas, Rio Salado College, and Chadron State College and nonaccredited enterprises, such as Abromitis Online Learning and Wasatch E-learning. Increasingly, however, the university arranges access to independent learning resources—e-learning, videos, simulations, and websites—through commercial providers such as NetG, SkillSoft, Teachscape, and MindEdge. All of these LRs are integrated into WGU's catalog to automate the enrollment process and assure that students get immediate access to most LRs online. The university also has contracted for tutoring services in math, writing, and other content areas where students may struggle (Eastmond, 2006).

Students learn to use WGU's virtual library, arranged by contract with the University of New Mexico, in their first introductory course at the university, "Education Without Boundaries." Then they use various library services such as database searches for full-text articles, reference desk, e-reserves, and interlibrary loan throughout their study at the university. WGU's librarian supplies most of these services directly while interfacing with the full services of the University of New Mexico library.

WGU has moved from operating a virtual bookstore through a third-party vendor toward getting more precise textbook content electronically. The university is working with several major publishers for specific chapters and sections of its adopted textbooks to be made directly available online for students—with e-reading capability to search, bookmark, highlight, and make individual notes in those copies. This e-content is integrated with other types of LRs within WGU's "courses of study" so students can seamlessly move from one LR to another.

WGU GOALS AND FUTURE DIRECTIONS

The university's provost and vice president of academic affairs, Craig Swenson, reflected recently about WGU's role in American Higher Education:

> I believe that WGU is the most innovative higher education institution in the United States, with a single-minded focus on improving the cost and quality of higher education.... Many people say that higher education is all about teaching, but it is really about learning—helping students become learners, gain competencies, and measuring and credentialing those competencies. That is what WGU does and it is why this institution is so important as a model to our higher education system. (Osmond, 2006, p. 2)

WGU considers itself successful through achievement of its purpose and mission. That is to develop and promote *competency-based* education; provide effective, *high quality* education programs; create a more efficient, *lower-cost* model for higher education; expand *access* to underserved populations; develop programs to anticipate and *meet significant needs* (public and private); and *use technology* to deliver more effective, efficient, and quality education.

Success really depends on the accomplishments of the university's students and graduates. That means maintaining and constantly improving WGU's retention rate, academic progress rate, graduation rate, and student satisfaction. These metrics are constantly monitored and have become performance objectives tied to compensation for everyone in the university. That success is captured in these recent vignettes:

- Penny Allison, a parent and teacher, reported: "I am able to work when it is convenient for me ... Sometimes that is 2 a.m., because I work three jobs and have a family" (Osmond, 2006, p. 2).

- During Hurricane Katrina, an online group of student friends, one in Utah and another in Michigan, were able to give moral support and even recreate some of Sara Miller's work. The student was living in Mississippi when her home (including textbooks, papers, and computer) was destroyed (Osmond, 2006, p. 2).

- Angie Lambert, a 2006 graduate, stated "I loved the WGU program—It didn't waste any of my time like other college classes have" (Witkowsky, 2006, para. 47). It saved her from a several-hour commute to the nearest university campus, and her degree landed her a new job, teaching fourth grade.

Western Governors University's challenges include reaching out to adult and underrepresented populations who will benefit most from these credentials, and gaining recognition of the validity of this alternative education model. Having the endorsement of national, regional, and association accrediting bodies has substantiated the model within the higher education community. The university holds the promise of extending affordable, quality higher education to deserving adults in a manner convenient to their life situation, enabling them to realize their educational dreams and progress within the workplace or pursue further educational goals.

REFERENCES

Castaldi, G. (2006, November 1). Western Governors University Teachers College receives NCATE Accreditation. *NCATE Press Release*. Retrieved March 8, 2007, from http://www.wgu.edu/about_WGU/press_releases.asp

Duin, A. H., Baer, L. L., & Starke-Meyerring, D. (2001). *Partnering in the learning marketspace. Educause Leadership Strategies* (Vol. 4). San Francisco: Jossey-Bass.

Eastmond, D. V. (2006). Learning resources in a competency-based university. *Distance Learning, 3*(2), 24-29.

Honawar, V. (2006, December 6). Accreditation makes virtual teachers college "real thing." *Education Week, 26*(14).

Johnstone, C. (2006). Odyssey of an innovation: The regional accreditation of Western Governors University. *CAEL Forum and News. The Council for Adult and Experiential Learning (CAEL).* Retrieved March 8, 2007, from www.cael.org/forum_and_news/odyssey-innovation.htm

Johnstone, D. (2005, July/August). Competency alternative: Western Governors University. *Change,* 24-33.

McFarland, S. (2007, February 19). Western Governors U. sees its student enrollment boom. *Salt Lake Tribune.* Retrieved March 8, 2007, from www.sltrib.com/education/ci_5257903

Mendenhall, R. (2007), Challenging the myths about distance learning. *Distance Learning Today, 1*(1), 1, 4, & 13.

Osmond, A. (2006, September/October). Western Governors University. *Zions Bank Community Magazine,* 19-20.

U.S. Department of Education. (2006). *A test of leadership: Charting the future of U.S. higher education.* Washington, DC.

Witkowsky, K (2006). Remote access: Western Governors University offers "competency-based" higher education, at a distance. *National CrossTalk, 14*(2), Retrieved March 8, 2007, from: http://www.highereducation.org/crosstalk/ct0206/news0206-wgu.shtml.

WESTERN GOVERNORS UNIVERSITY
2003 = 33 GRADUATES
2007 = 1581 GRADUATES

Constructing the 39th Statewide Network
The Story of Network Nebraska

Brenda Decker, Tom Rolfes, Walter Weir, and Rick Golden

INTRODUCTION

This article is the story of one of the youngest statewide networks in the United States: Network Nebraska. After reading the title, one could hardly imagine what would be newsworthy or printable about the development of another state network. It is obviously not the first; and almost certainly will not be the last. It's definitely not the largest and almost assuredly is not the smallest.

What this is, however, is a story of determination and vision; about how a relatively small group of persistent people brought about tremendous change in the way that public policy and funding and network services are administered on a statewide basis. It is a story of finesse, risk taking, trust, and bumpy roads along the way. It is a story of heroes and heroines and, if you read to the end, you will

Brenda Decker, Chief Information Officer, State of Nebraska, 501 S. 14th, P.O. Box 95045, Lincoln, NE 68509-5045. Telephone: (402) 471-3717. E-mail: brenda.decker@nebraska.gov

Tom Rolfes, Education I.T. Manager, Office of the Chief Information Officer, 501 S. 14th, P.O. Box 95045, Lincoln, NE 68509-5045. Telephone: (402) 471-7969 E-mail: tom.rolfes@nebraska.gov

get to meet some of these incredible people.

If you are from one of the 40 states that claim a statewide network and you have lived through the growing pains of developing an organization where none existed, you may chuckle and nod your head about reading these personal accounts. If you happen to be from one of the 10 states yet to achieve statewide public networking, you may read with interest the "lessons learned" and "if we had it to do all over again" to avoid similar pitfalls. Network Nebraska is only midway through a 3-year development plan that will interconnect over 330 public K-12 higher education entities and up to 100 nonpublic education systems across the state, all of whom had well-established distance learning relationships and existing telecommunications providers prior to the start of the project.

IN THE BEGINNING...

After reading numerous accounts of the origins of statewide networks across the United States, it was determined that no single template for change or model of network exactly fit the environment and forces that were at work in Nebraska in 2003.

What was discovered through research was that large-scale public telecommunications networks are much easier to develop if the following components or features are present: A public sector champion or champions (e.g., governor, university president, state senator, commissioner of education); an upfront funding source (e.g., legislative appropriation, federal grant, bonded investment); a public policy mandate (e.g., a gubernatorial initiative, legislative bill, campaign promise); a trusted business unit (e.g., state agency, college or university department, consortium of public entities, 501(c)3); a sustainable funding source (e.g., public services fund, legislative appropriations, user fees); the onset of a disruptive event (e.g., loss of provider, legacy technology extinction, sudden cut in funding, natural disaster) and, to a lesser extent, having a history as an early, estab-

Walter Weir, Chief Information Officer, University of Nebraska, 3835 Holdrege Street, Lincoln, NE 68583. Telephone: (402) 472-2862. E-mail: wweir@nebraska.edu

Rick Golden, Assistant CIO, Networks and Systems, University of Nebraska, 901 North 17th Street, 327E Nebraska Hall, Lincoln, NE 68588-0521. Telephone: (402) 472-7626. E-mail: rgolden@nebraska.edu

lished service provider (e.g., Internet services, Web hosting, dial-up connectivity, IP [Internet protocol] networking).

THE IMPETUS

What was unique about Nebraska's network development story is that almost none of these factors existed to get the original network off the ground. There were no huge or sudden disruptions, nor any over-the-top crusader making educational broadband a top priority. However, back in 2003, then-Lieutenant Governor Dave Heineman (now Governor Heineman) and L. Dennis Smith, president of the University of Nebraska, agreed that the State of Nebraska and the University of Nebraska would work together on telecommunications projects for the common good. That single suggestion did create the original impetus for the state's two largest telecommunications resellers (state government, University of Nebraska) to begin collaborating, along with Nebraska Educational Television. Within months, the State Division of Communications and the University of Nebraska entered into the world

of competitive Internet provision for the state's K-12 and nonuniversity higher education entities. They also began cooperatively procuring contracts for aggregated backbone transport to serve state agencies and university facilities. And so the Collaborative Aggregation Partnership (CAP) was born, and it exists to this day.

Meantime, in the K-12 world, there existed a dozen or so decentralized distance learning consortia comprised of school districts and neighboring colleges who had banded together originally to exchange synchronous video distance learning classes. The earliest of these formed in 1992 and the most recent in 2002, with 45 late-adopting school districts added in 2003. These 12 consortia were using a variety of incompatible, aging audio/video technologies and were rapidly approaching the end of their long-term (10-year) telecommunications contracts, so something had to be done. The school districts had used lottery monies, federal grants, and local funds to purchase their original analog, motion JPEG, and MPEG2 video equipment over high bandwidth (45Mbps, 100Mbps) circuits, but virtually

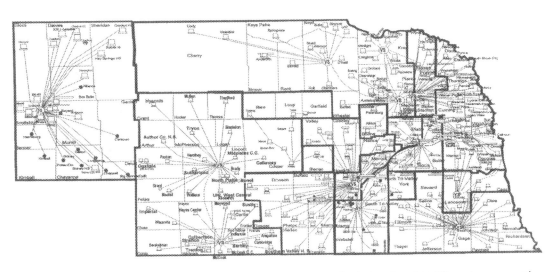

Figure 1. Nebraska's original distance learning consortia were divided up into 12 different groups with disparate technologies.

no escrow funds were ever set aside for technology replacement. Also, the consortias' incompatible video compression technologies and localized and regionalized infrastructure did not lend itself well to statewide distance learning exchange.

Partly in response to the heated debate between the adoption of analog versus motion JPEG technology in the 1990s, the state legislature created the Nebraska Information Technology Commission (NITC) in 1998. Comprised of nine members appointed by the governor (with the lieutenant governor as chair) and confirmed by the legislature, this commission is assisted by five advisory councils (state government, community, education, eHealth, and GIS) and a technical panel. The role of the technical panel is to review requests for technology funding and to set standards and policies to guide the state's future investments in information technology.

The NITC developed nine strategic initiatives in 2004, two of which directly affected educational networking. The first was the Statewide Synchronous Video Network and the other was Network Nebraska. In essence, the Synchronous Video Network was to bring about the unification and interconnection of video distance learning applications, and Network Nebraska was to provide the conduit or transport to interconnect the distance learning classrooms and more cost-effective Internet.

The first legislative appeal to provide funding for the aging distance learning equipment was brought forward in January 2005. Facilitated by a determined group of distance learning coordinators with little experience in legislative lobbying or advocacy, a $30 million video equipment and wide area networking "train wreck" image was painted before the unicameral legislative body. When the debate settled, the legislature denied funding but did agree to launch a 6-month Distance Education Enhancement Task Force to study the issue and to come back before

the body in January 2006 with recommendations. As a result of the next session, "LB 1208" was passed by the legislature in April 2006 by an overwhelming margin and signed by the governor to become law, with an effective date of July 2006.

CARROT OR STICK?

Legislative Bill 1208 set out a number of policy, funding, and coordination changes across the state. This legislation tasked the state chief information officer (CIO) with providing access to every public school district and public higher education institution in the state, but it did not require participation. The bill also required the University of Nebraska to assist in this effort.

Since participation was not mandatory, the legislation provided a number of financial incentives or "carrots" for participation. First, it recognized the importance of equipment upgrades by allowing each high school building and educational service unit $20,000 in equipment reimbursements from lottery funds if they joined the statewide network and participated in distance learning. The bill also provided 8 years of lottery funding for distance learning incentives of up to $1,000 for each video course sent, up to $1,000 for each video course received, and additional incentives for sending asynchronous courses or reaching "sparse" or "very sparse" districts with distance learning courses, when delivered over Network Nebraska. The total amount of lottery funds attributed to this project through 2015 is estimated to be about $34 million and is administered by the Nebraska Department of Education.

In order to offset the potential increase in cost of full IP, flexible wide area networking, the legislature also introduced a new telecommunications allowance within the state aid formula that allowed any "equalized" (high need) school district to be compensated for 85% of the post E-rate cost of telecommunications. In effect, with the average state E-rate reimbursement at 67%, the final net cost of telecommunications for these 207 school districts is approximately $5 of every $100. For the 47 school districts that are unequalized, their only benefit is E-rate. Nonpublic school systems may also participate in Network Nebraska but do not receive state aid; only E-rate. Higher education entities do not receive any direct itemized support for telecommunications.

The legislature also provided approximately $1.3 million to a newly formed Distance Education Council to purchase a statewide clearinghouse and scheduling system. This Web-based Renovo Software system allows any school district or college to list their distance learning courses on a statewide clearinghouse and allows any eligible entity to register for the courses. Once the tentative schedule of send and receive courses is finalized, the software system is programmed to become the daily calendar of device control; turning on and off codecs all over the state for every multi-point, recurring videoconference.

WHO'S IN CHARGE?

As mentioned earlier, the state CIO was deemed responsible for providing access to every public education entity in the state by July 1, 2012, but the law did not require any entity to participate. Also, the statute did not provide for any direct funding to the network for development or administration. It specifically required that any administrative costs incurred in building and maintaining the network be paid for by the participants. This presented an accounting challenge early on because there were over 16 months between the time that staff began working on network development and the first revenue appearing from the Network Nebraska Participation Fees.

These provisions challenged Network Nebraska to be customer-centered and economically minded. If the cost of partici-

pation became too high, the entities would not join. If only a few entities joined, the network would not achieve its goal of economies of scale of less expensive Internet access through aggregated purchasing or affordable statewide transport through shared backbone costs.

Qualified staff members of the Educational Service Units, or ESUs, as they are called, also responded to the project by assisting with network design and RFP review. ESUs also offered to become the rebilling entities to their member schools for the State of Nebraska. By using the ESUs' standard rebilling mechanisms with schools, the central finance division of the state was able to keep its costs down, consequently keeping the Network Nebraska Participation Fee as low as possible. Without the collaborative assistance of the ESU and college staff helping with network design and support, this project would not have succeeded.

SUCCESS OR LACK THEREOF?

The authors are happy to report that, at the time of this writing, 100% of the south-central Nebraska institutions (83 school districts/ESUs and 6 colleges) are in the process of joining the network in the summer of 2008. The Phase I upgrade, summer of 2007, saw 100% of the northeast region (92 school districts/ESUs and 2 colleges) join the network. The third and final phase, consisting of over 100 schools and colleges in southeast Nebraska and the panhandle, will join the network in the summer of 2009 (see Figure 2). At project's end, Network Nebraska is expecting to have 100% of all its public colleges and public K-12 districts connected with high bandwidth fiber transport.

It's important to understand that "joining" the network is composed of three main obligations. First, each education entity must commit to a connection of 30Mbps or greater optical fiber for public school districts and 10 Mbps or greater

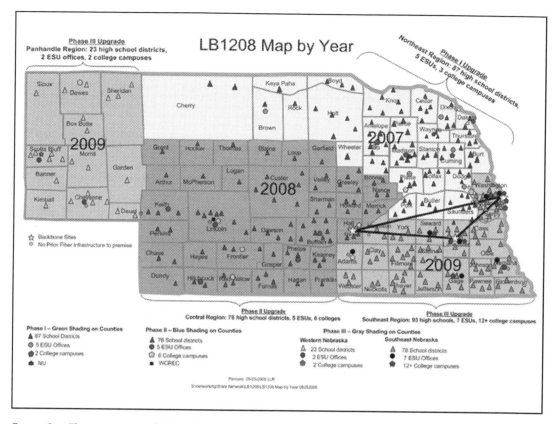

Figure 2.   The conversion of 336 schools and colleges to a high bandwidth, IP network will occur over three summers.

fiber or fast copper Ethernet for nonpublic education systems and smaller colleges. This connectivity can be bid either by the CIO or the local entities, with specifications provided by Network Nebraska as taking them to a certified network aggregation point, one of three in the State. Second, each participant, regardless of size, must agree to assume its share of the Network Nebraska Participation Fee, about $200/month. And third, each participant must, regardless of geographic location, agree to assume its share of the Interregional Transport Fee to help interconnect the three LATA regions of the network, about $95/month (before E-rate). In comparison to other similar statewide networks, these costs are very modest and also represent a fully sustainable funding

plan, with no outside or upfront assistance by any state entity.

In addition, individual colleges or school district consortia may purchase Internet access off of the statewide contract, currently at $38/megabit/month for 2008-09. This per unit cost has decreased steadily and substantially since the first aggregated Internet access purchase in 2003.

What originally was considered by the network constituents as a funding weakness and lack of support by state government is now considered by the network organizers a determinable strength and more reliable funding model by not being dependent on unpredictable state general funds. With the network management and administrative functions fully funded by participation fees, the focus remains on the

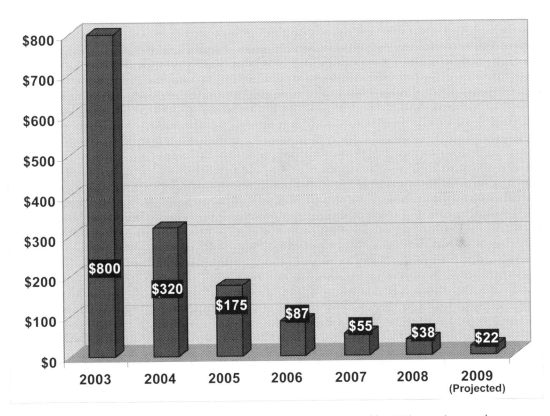

Network Nebraska Internet Access Cost
(Average $$ per Megabit/month)

Figure 3. Network Nebraska Internet access unit costs have decreased by 97% over 6 years due to aggregated purchasing.

services and needs of the customers, partners, and end-users. The measure of success since the beginning of the network has always been "better services for the same or lower prices."

WHAT MAKES IT ALL WORK?

Network Nebraska, as Figure 2 suggests, is not a completely unique infrastructure. There are three large network aggregation points located in Grand Island (308 LATA), Lincoln (402 LATA) and Omaha (402 LATA), that act as the core routing and "choke points" for the Layer 2 network. All 300+ district and college entities belong to

one of the three regional Ethernet clouds and are then routed through one of the core network nodes. The three-segment backbone, consisting of 500Mbps to 1000Mbps, then interconnects the three regions. The 28 Nebraska telecommunications companies all play a part in either the backbone transport or wide area Ethernet network. The Network Nebraska engineers, together with their public education partners, have collaboratively decided the approved routers and switches acceptable on the network; IP block addressing schemes; Quality-of-Service (QoS) routing protocols for different types of data; and

Figure 4. Frau Elaine Bruning, 7-year veteran distance learning teacher from Humphrey Public Schools, works on German vocabulary with students from Schuyler and Twin Rivers.

an informal approach to network trouble-shooting and problem resolution. As intented, the network has been extremely reliable since its first days of operation. ESU, college and Network Nebraska staff all share in the monitoring of individual sites' traffic and can, on a moment's notice, shut down a rogue location, if overtaken by viruses or malware. Videoconferencing traffic is prioritized from end to end through the various routing devices and regions to make sure that all multipoint conferences interact with very high quality audio and video with no degradation.

WITH AN EYE TOWARD THE FUTURE?

As with any technical innovation, it takes time for humans to adapt. Even with a statewide, IP-based network infrastructure, it will take time for end-users to discover its power and flexibility. For instance, it is still common for school districts to use only their one former static motion-JPEG room, even though they could be adding several more IP video devices at a fraction of the bandwidth. They will soon discover that they have bandwidth for many more uses and applications. Dan Hoesing, superintendent of four school districts in northeast Nebraska, may be one of those pioneers. In the first year of operation, Hoesing has purchased an additional 17 mobile IP video carts to exchange distance learning courses with his small rural school districts. He reports that they are on schedule to add an additional six carts for the fall of 2008, making a total of 27 distance learning rooms divided among four districts. Hoesing and his four high school principals report that they reached over 860 students each day of the 2007-08 school year with 57 different distance learning classes, and an additional 270+ college credits being earned through dual enrollment classes. Several of the high school seniors were enrolled in enough college courses to be considered full time. It's no wonder why Hoesing was selected as one of eSchool News' Top 10 Tech Savvy Superintendents for 2007. Hoesing's teachers all use Angel Learning Management to augment each of their video courses, which allows students and teachers to interact, exchange assignments, and conduct electronic assessments. The four districts are also experimenting with portable white boards on their codecs' data channel to fur-

ther enrich the teaching and learning experiences. Dr. Hoesing reported that his four school districts recouped over $200,000 in distance education incentives in the 2007-08 school year to help facilitate further program growth and equipment investments.

Although Nebraska has a rich video distance learning heritage, the Partnership for Innovation (a K-16 consortium of Nebraska instructional officers) recently committed $150,000 in discretionary Perkins grant funds to purchase a 3-year institutional license from the National Repository for Online Courses (NROC). This promises to be Nebraska's first statewide venture into a virtual, online curriculum. The Nebraska Information Technology Commission and Network Nebraska are eager to partner with the

Figure 5.   Superintendent Dan Hoesing and Principal Craig Frerichs discuss woodworking projects with Coleridge Public Schools upperclassmen, whose class is being taught over Network Nebraska.

Partnership for Innovation to help guide the technical deployment of these content servers. If done strategically, the National Repository for Online Courses courses can be joined by other commercial content on a very robust digital content repository, thereby storing, cataloguing, and retrieving teacher-produced learning objects.

LESSONS LEARNED?

So, when asked "What would you do differently if you had to do it all over again?", The Network Nebraska organizers would contend that the public partnering of K-12, higher education, University of Nebraska, and Office of the Chief Information Officer has gone about as well as it could possibly go. When all the involved entities have such a large stake in the game (i.e., network reliability, increased Internet demand, and finite financial resources), it's easy to stay focused on the ultimate goal; a statewide federated network. While the original LB 1208 legislation offered much in the way of incentives for participation, it did not allow much in the way of top-down control. Therefore, much of the development had to be participative and democratic. This worked well when deciding on a single make and model of router for each site on the network; it did not work so well when the same entities had to decide on a single codec make and model or even the same codec equipment configuration to be deployed. Setting up a multi-tier centralized help desk and trouble-ticketing system was resisted by the K-12

entities and dismissed as unnecessary. Still, school districts and ESUs have begun to trust Network Nebraska to act on their behalf. Success has bred more success.

WHAT'S NEXT ON THE AGENDA?

At the time of this publication, the Phase II conversion will have been completed and the Phase III Letters of Agency (Erate permission to enter into a consortium) will have been submitted. The interregional transport (backbone) bandwidth will need to be increased for 2009-10 and the statewide Internet access contract will have to be rebid. More work needs to be done to give the customers and partners a formal voice into how Network Nebraska is managed and maintained. And, once all the entities are on board and the network is fully deployed, more attention can be placed on new and emerging technology applications on the network and developing even more collaborative content relationships within and outside the Nebraska.

For more information, visit the following Web sites:

- Network Nebraska:
  www.networknebraska.net
- Distance Education Council:
  www.nebdec.org
- Nebraska Information Technology Commission:
  www.nitc.nebraska.gov
- Nebraska Office of the Chief Information Officer:
  www.cio.nebraska.gov

Georgia Virtual School

Melanie W. Goss

INTRODUCTION

The purpose of this article is to trace the creation and evolution of Georgia Virtual School (GVS) and to discuss the reasons that Georgia students are participating in the program. The program details and offerings and what GVS students and teachers are saying about the program are also discussed.

The Georgia State Board of Education approved a plan endorsing online Advanced Placement (AP) courses as well as core curricular courses in August of 2001. The Virtual Learning Business Plan was approved in order to address a need for online courses in Georgia schools to provide special curricular opportunities

Melanie W. Goss,
Teacher, Crisp County Middle School,
1116 24th Avenue East, Cordele, GA 31015.
Telephone: (229) 276-3460.
E-mail: mgoss@crisp.k12.ga.us

and options for schools that had problems with providing complete course offerings, that were experiencing scheduling conflicts, and that had a shortage of highly qualified teaching staff (Georgia Department of Education, 2007).

In October of 2001, Georgia's virtual learning program was turned over to Technology Services. Georgia had qualified for a 3-year federal grant Advanced Placement Test Fee Program offered by the U.S. Department of Education that targeted low-income and disadvantaged Georgia students who take AP courses. Georgia qualified for the grant based because more than 50% of its students qualified for free or reduced-price lunch (Georgia Department of Education, 2007).

AP Nexus was the official title of the grant, which was a collaboration among Georgia, Tennessee, and South Carolina. The objective of the grant was to make online courses available to those students who were the target of the grant, the low-income and disadvantaged students. Apex Learning was hired to provide the courses online. At the time of the contract, Apex Learning was the largest online AP course provider (Georgia Department of Education, 2007).

The AP Nexus program became known to Georgia schools and interest was expressed by many schools systems to participate in the program. Many of the schools that expressed interest in the program did not qualify for the grant, and the Georgia Department of Education began to hear of a need for more online AP as well as regular core curricular courses to be offered. This led to an expansion of Georgia's online offerings with other vendors and new contracts (Georgia Department of Education, 2007).

Several Georgia school systems had already been interested in online learning and met in Atlanta to address the need for a state-sponsored virtual school. The response to creating a statewide virtual school was great, and all of the system representatives in attendance at the meeting agreed to collaborate and assist with the creation of Georgia Virtual School (Georgia Department of Education, 2007).

GEORGIA VIRTUAL SCHOOL

Georgia's governor signed the GVS bill on May 4, 2005, establishing Georgia's first virtual school. GVS offers courses to public students as well as private and home-school students. Each of GVS course meets Georgia's standards for Quality Core Curriculum and Georgia Performance Standards. GVS also meets College Board standards, and offers a variety of scheduling options to meet the needs of all local school systems. GVS is expanding continuously and refining and adding course offerings (Georgia Department of Education, 2007).

WHAT GVS STUDENTS ARE SAYING

I just think it's really cool that I can talk to students who are in the same class across the state. This was a great way for me to take a class because other science classes didn't fit with my schedule. (Toon, 2007, para. 2)

In college, the teacher's not going to be on you telling when things are due every day or reminding you, so I'm really learning that from this class. I think other students could get a lot out of this. (Toon, 2007, para.)

It allowed me to do my work on my own time. During school you have to wait for the teacher. On the internet you can do

all the work in advance. I like going at a fast pace. (Reinolds, 2005, para. 9)

I'm taking Mandarin Chinese. It's always been a dream of mine to travel to Asia and be a English as second or other language teacher. I feel that Mandarin would help me in a way securing my place at that job. (Benton, para. 5, 2010)

It's really different. It's very exciting, and it's a new way to challenge yourself (Benton, 2010, para. 6)

You've got to be on your p's and q's to pass an online course, because you've got an actual teacher somewhere out there monitoring what you're doing. (Benton, 2010, para. 11)

WHAT GVS TEACHERS ARE SAYING

I'm still teaching students, I just go about it totally different. I like to do online chats and get to know the kids too. While the courses offer students more flexibility and opportunities, they're not for everyone. (Reinolds, 2005, para, 9)

Generally a C-student in a building is a C-student online. And an A-student in the building is an A-student online. (Reinolds, 2005, para. 22)

Usually they start out slow and then they catch on and get the same grades as in the classroom. The ones who do very well tend to be just organized people anyway. (Reinolds, 2005, para. 24)

WHO ARE GVS TEACHERS?

GVS's faculty includes retired, former, and full-time teachers. Some of GVS's teachers have made the choice to stay at home to teach due to personal reasons (Reinolds, 2005).

TRAINING FOR GVS TEACHERS

GVS teachers must complete a ten-week online training course. They become familiar with the pedagogy and teaching of virtual learning. They receive training in the technical aspects of online teaching and get hands-on training by a mentor teacher. They complete a student teacher training period, which is facilitated by experienced online teachers (Georgia Virtual School, Teacher Training Section, 2010).

All GVS teachers are highly qualified. They must complete the online training course. They must be cognizant of the special policies and procedures that are unique to the virtual learning environment. The mentoring process for GVS teachers assures quality and consistency throughout the program. GVS teachers who teach AP courses must also complete a special training course before teaching AP classes. Sixty of the 165 highly qualified instructors with GVS have become certified to teach AP courses (Georgia Department of Education, 2007).

MEETING STUDENT NEEDS THROUGH GVS

Twenty-two percent (77) of Georgia's high schools do not offer AP courses, and 19 of them do not offer more than one AP course. When students apply for college, they are at a disadvantage over other Georgia students if they have not taken AP courses. Since AP courses help students prepare for the college-level work, these students are not on a level with the students who were able to have access to the AP courses. The size of the school systems, along with staffing problems, hinders these systems from being able to offer the types of course offerings that they would like to offer. Georgia has 180 school systems, 35% of which have less than 2,500 students. Over 33% of Georgia's school systems have one high school. Ten percent of Georgia's high schools have a population of less than 500 students. This limits these systems in course offerings and properly qualified staff to teach the desired

specialty courses (Georgia Department of Education, 2007).

Students have scheduling conflicts, want to add to their current course choices, move faster in their program of study, make up failed courses, have illness which renders them homebound, or may have moved in from another state and need to catch up on Georgia's high school requirements for graduation (Georgia Department of Education, 2007).

ENROLLMENT IN GVS

In the fall and spring, GVS allows students to take one Carnegie unit during their regular state-funded school day. Students who are homebound due to medical reasons are allowed to enroll on a case-by-case basis. Public school students are given priority over students who attend private schools and those who are home school students (Georgia Department of Education, 2007).

There is a two-phase process to registration in GVS. Phase I consists of allowing public school students a period of time to register for the limited number of seats before private and home school students are allowed to register. Phase II allows the private and home school student to register for the full-time employee-funded seats, if available, after Phase I (Georgia Department of Education, 2007)

TUITION FOR GVS

GVS offers a half Carnegie unit courses for $300 and one Carnegie unit for $600. The tuition only applies to nonstate-funded seats in GVS (Georgia Department of Education, 2007).

GVS INSTRUCTORS' SALARIES

The instructors at GVS are paid on a per student basis by the Department of Education: $130 per student for a half Carnegie unit course, $155 per student for a half Carnegie unit AP course, $260 per student for a one Carnegie unit course, and $310 per student for a one Carnegie unit AP course (Georgia Virtual School, careers section, 2010).

GVS Credit Recovery Program

GVS offers students credit recovery for courses in which they have been unsuccessful in meeting the course requirements for graduation. The academic seat time has been satisfied, but the content standards have not been met. The credit recovery program's goal is to increase the graduation rate and to help struggling students remain in school (Georgia Virtual School, Credit Recovery section, 2010).

Georgia students who were previously unsuccessful in attaining credit towards graduation and who are enrolled in a public school in Georgia may participate in the online credit recovery program. It is encouraged that these students be determined to achieve their goals, be independent, and be self-motivated (Georgia Virtual School, credit recovery section, 2010).

GVS's Course Options

GVS offers 20 AP courses to Georgia students. AP courses are college-level and approved by the College Board. They help prepare Georgia's students for the AP exams required of each AP student in the spring of each school term. College credit is often awarded to students who pass the AP tests (Georgia Virtual School, Advanced Placement Courses section, 2011).

GVS offers the following courses: computer science, French, Spanish language, English language, English language and composition, calculus, statistics, European history, government and politics, human geography, macroeconomics, psychology, U.S. history, world history, biology, chemistry, environmental science, physics, art history, and music theory.

GVS offers the following regular courses, among others: Banking and investing, broadcast video, computing in the modern world, fundamentals of web design, financial Literacy, Chinese, Japanese, French, Latin, German, Spanish, advanced composition, journalism, speech, geometry, trigonometry, and astronomy.

In 2009, the language courses were the most popular with GVS students. Latin, Spanish, French, German, Chinese and Japanese were among them (Benton, 2010).

Conclusion

Georgia is one of many states that have established virtual schools to enhance the educational choices for its students. In its second year, GVS doubled its enrollment (Starkman, 2007). By the end of the second year, GVS had increased its enrollment from 1,500 students to 4,600 students (Christensen & Horn, 2008). Georgia is expanding its course offerings and training more teachers with each new school year. Georgia purchases some courses from other online schools and also trades courses to widen the course offerings to its students (Starkman, 2007). Funding for GVS comes from both state and corporate grants which includes BellSouth, which granted GVS over $20 million dollars in its first three years (Starkman, 2007).

According to the GVS program director, online learning is definitely on the ascent and is not a wave of the future; rather, it is here—and to stay. She states that she truly believes in online learning (Starkman, 2007), and that GVS benefits students in both rural and urban areas. She notes that if an AP course does not make at a particular high school, there is a solution online. She also gives the example that students need free periods in order to take connections or exploratory courses such as theater and band and offering an online course after school can solve this scheduling conflict (Reinolds, 2005).

GVS offers solutions to Georgia students in areas that were unsolvable before

2005. Students in rural areas have access to highly qualified teachers in specialty areas such as foreign language, AP math classes, high-quality business and finance courses, and computer courses not available in the many small rural school systems. Students who are hospital homebound have access to classes and can work at times when they feel well enough to work. This alleviates the extra pressure that these students feel by being away from the classroom for extended or regular periods of time. Formally or currently home-schooled students have options to go beyond the limitations of their home-school teachers in areas of specialization. Many of the GVS course offerings require highly specialized training for its teachers. Students who transfer to Georgia from out of state areas have choices in catching up with their peers toward graduation requirements. Students who have been unsuccessful in required courses can take credit recovery courses and get back on schedule for graduation. Students who feel stifled in the brick-and-mortar setting can expedite their graduation date by moving ahead of the regular students. Students who have special talents, such as in music, dance, and sports, can work their training and or performance schedules around their schoolwork. There are many areas of benefit to Georgia students with the establishment of GVS. GVS plans to continue to expand its course offerings, including those for middle grades (Georgia Department of Education, 2007).

REFERENCES

Benton, B. (2010, March 6). Virtual school extends courses across Georgia. *McClatchy-Tribune Business News.* Retrieved from ProQuest Newsstand. doi:1978332311

Christensen, C. M., & Horn, M. B. (2008). How do we transform our schools? Use technologies that compete against nothing. *Education Next, 8*(3), 12-18.

Georgia Department of Education. (2007). The history of Georgia Virtual School. Retrieved from http://www.gadoe.edu

Georgia Virtual School. (2010). Georgia virtual school. Retrieved from http://www.gavirtualschool.org/

Reinolds, C. (2005, July 23). Virtual schools offers expanded learning. *Atlanta Journal & Constitution*, p. B8.

Starkman, N. (2007). Going the distance: Offering benefits of convenience, independence, and even improved academic performance, virtual schools promise to be here for the long haul. *T.H.E. Journal, 34*(2), 18-21.

Toone, S. (August 29). Georgia Virtual School grows more popular. *McClatchy-Tribune Business News.* Retrieved from Proquest Newsstand. doi:1848968621

> "I THINK IT'S REALLY COOL THAT I CAN TALK TO STUDENTS WHO ARE IN THE SAME CLASS ACROSS THE STATE. THIS WAS A GREAT WAY FOR ME TO TAKE A CLASS BECAUSE OTHER SCIENCE CLASSES DIDN'T FIT WITH MY SCHEDULE."

Wired for Success
Alabama's ACCESS to Distance Learning

Sherry Stancil

INTRODUCTION

For high school students in Alabama, virtual classrooms are as ubiquitous as the 16mm movie projectors were for their previous generations. In a time frame of only 6 years, the state became the third largest virtual school in the nation and the first one to equip all high schools with both videoconferencing and web-based learning labs (Watson, Murin, Vashaw, Gemin, & Rapp, 2010). The statewide initiative is called Alabama Connecting Classrooms, Educators, and Students Statewide (ACCESS). When considering how such an incredible feat was accomplished so quickly, one must address the diffusion of innovation theory. Rogers (1995) describes the diffusion of innovation as the "process in which an innovation is communicated through certain channels over time among members of the social system" (p. 5). Some of the specific elements contributing to the ACCESS's diffusion included the following: a student-centered mission, the selected instructional modes of delivery, highly qualified e-teachers, state oversight, and periodic program assessments by an outside evaluator.

BACKGROUND

A Governor's Task Force on Distance Education, led by Governor Bob Riley, met in 2004-2005 to discuss strategies for launching a virtual school program designed to make education more equitable for every public high school student. In doing so, they focused on several deficiencies in the school system:

- Alabama's high school graduation rate ranked well below the national level.
- School administrators in small and rural districts faced challenges with recruiting and retaining highly qualified teachers as required by No Child Left Behind.
- Alabama ranked 14 out of 16 southern states in the areas related to Advanced Placement exams among juniors and seniors—administering only 99 exams per 1,000 students in 2003.
- Many schools in the state did not offer foreign languages and advanced mathematics and science courses which pre-

Sherry Stancil,
Speech Communications Instructor,
Calhoun Community College, Decatur, AL.
Telephone: (256) 713-4824.
E-mail: sstancil7985@calhoun.edu

pare students for college-level coursework and enhance workforce development skills.

- Many schools did not have the funding needed for technological upgrades.

From the aforementioned deficiencies, the task force members formulated a list of objectives to guide their vision. Objectives for the pilot program were to provide access to advanced diploma courses, provide access to additional course offerings, provide access to advanced placement or dual credit courses, provide access to remediation and supplemental resources, leverage existing resources and distance learning offerings, and provide teachers with additional multimedia and technology tools to enhance instruction.

Task force members decided on a strategic plan that would include an incremental process consisting of a year-long planning period, a pilot phase, and a gradual expansion through two final phases. Governor Riley announced the ACCESS idea in 2005, and the initiative was introduced to students in 24 selected high schools the next year. The task force's original plan was to equip all public high schools with distance learning technology by the 2010 school year; however, all 371 high schools were furnished with videoconferencing and web-based capability ahead of schedule in 2009.

THREE STRANDS OF INTERVENTION

According to Meredith and Newton (2003), three strands must converge to ensure the success of an eLearning intervention: learner capability, technology, and teacher pedagogy. This is an important finding because some institutions might be more concerned with the technology aspects of distance education, rather factoring in the student and teaching aspects of the model. Similarly, an institution that heavily focuses on the teaching pedagogy of distance education without considering how technology and the needs of students will

factor into the equation could also be detrimental to the program's success.

LEARNERS

Access to technology does not always guarantee successful learning outcomes. One of the most important factors for educators to consider is the students' previous experience with technology. Prieger and Hu (2008) surmise that people who live in rural areas and those in low-income families are not as comfortable with using technology as other groups who have had more exposure to technology. Thirty-two percent of Alabama's students live in rural and impoverished areas. In an effort to ease the comfort levels of such students and to also gain an assessment of their learning styles, advisors with the ACCESS program consult with all potential distance learning participants before they are allowed to register for courses.

Age is another factor to consider when conducting an analysis of e-learners. ACCESS's demographics consist of students in Grades 9-12. The program is now beginning to expand into middle schools, offering high school courses for advanced students. Some young or novice distance learners are not ready to assume new responsibilities "such as monitoring their own learning goals, setting priorities, and controlling the pace of learning" (Svinicki & McKeachie, 2011, p. 243). Although they might be academically capable and technologically adept, secondary students might struggle in distance learning classes due to certain maturity levels needed to manage the autonomous nature of being separated from their teachers.

ACCESS offers courses for traditional and nontraditional students. In 2010, "ACCESS provided 29,415 student enrollments in courses needed by students to meet graduation requirements and 11,746 additional enrollments in noncredit remediation modules for the Alabama High School Graduation Exam and Career Forward" (ACCESS, 2010, p. 5). Palloff and Pratt (2007, p. 8) identified characteristics typically associated with successful distance learners:

- Open-minded about sharing life, work, and educational experiences as part of the learning process
- Able to communicate through writing
- Self-motivated and self-disciplined
- Willing to "speak up" if problems arise
- Able to meet the minimum requirements for the program

Business teacher Sonya Kennedy serves as the ACCESS facilitator at Priceville High School, a small school in northern Alabama where students are experiencing the benefits of taking advanced courses. She said, "Two students took French I last year, and they are taking French II this year. This is something that would not have happened had it not been for ACCESS. That's what's so great about the program. Students are able to take courses that they wouldn't be able to otherwise." Beginning with the ninth grade class of 2009, all public high school students are required to complete at least one distance education course before graduation.

INSTRUCTIONAL TECHNOLOGY

Earlene Patton, ACCESS Registration Coordinator with the Alabama Department of Education indicates that more participants enroll in web-based classes than the video-conferencing classes. ACCESS's web-based participants use a course management system called Desire2Learn, or D2L, which offers a variety of tools to facilitate learning. Every public high school in the state of Alabama is equipped with web-based labs designed to allow students to work individually at computers during the school day. These classes are asynchronous environments that "allow participants to log onto the class or discussion at any time, think about what is being discussed, and

post their own responses when they wish" (Palloff & Pratt, 2007, p. 68). Students can view their instructors' lectures from any place and any time by logging onto the Internet, where lectures in the forms of video and audio are either broadcast live or archived for later retrieval. Meanwhile, teachers can post assignments, record grades, and consult with students from a distance.

There are several advantages to utilizing ACCESS's web-based courses:

- Students can log on when it is convenient for them to do so.
- Students have access to greater course selections.
- Students are exposed to technology that prepares them for college coursework and employment.

Unfortunately, there are several disadvantages to web-based courses:

- Some students are not independent learners.
- The lack of face-to-face interaction delays feedback between teacher and student.
- Some students might lack the technical skills needed to navigate through the coursework and to troubleshoot minor technical problems.

Videoconferencing overcomes the limitations of web-based learning "by bringing teacher and learners face-to-face virtually in real time, [which] enriches the distant learning process" (Martin, 2005, p. 398). These synchronous environments allow participants and instructors to communicate with each other "in different places at the same time" using technology such as satellite, compressed video, and fiber-optics systems" (Simonson, Smaldino, Albright, & Zvacek, 2009, p. 10). There are several advantages to the video conferencing modality as a means of delivering distance learning courses:

- Videoconferencing creates a better sense of community than computer instructed course offers, since teachers and students are able to see and hear each other in real time.
- Students in underserved schools are connected to teachers and students in other areas, giving them access to courses not available in their home schools.
- Due to video and audio cues, teachers can immediately respond to questions raised by remote students.

The disadvantages of videoconferencing include:

- Remote students must coordinate their schedules with the host school's schedule for class meeting times.
- Remote students might experience feelings of isolation since there is a lack of "real" human interaction with other classmates.
- Technological difficulties can result in student/teacher frustration and confusion.

Simonson (2000) noted that "the key to success in a distance education classroom is not which technologies are used but how they are used what information is communicated through technology" (p. 29). Similarly, Clark (2001) contends that effective learning is not primarily contingent upon the media (face-to-face versus e-learning, in this case) but rather upon the instructional methods. Clark (2001) states, "The choice of media influences the important outcomes of student access, and the speed or cost of the delivery, but not the learning impact of the instruction that is delivered to the consumer" (p. 302).

TEACHER PEDAGOGY

Effective pedagogy is the key to overcoming issues related to making students feel connected to the learning experience regardless of if the online class is synchronous or asynchronous (Palloff & Pratt, 2007). Effective learning takes place when active students and teachers collaborate with each other in appropriate instructional environments. A factor that emerges as the primary difference between the distance education learning (fully online and blended) environments and traditional learning environments is student-teacher interaction. Students who feel more connected to their teachers and classmates are less likely to withdraw from class. ACCESS facilitator Sonya Kennedy explained,

> My job is to make sure students are on task daily. I check their grades once a week (usually every Friday) to make sure they are not getting behind. I communicate with their online teachers. We [facilitators] are also in the system so we can collaborate with online teachers to make sure their students are not getting behind.

Throughout the state, more than 650 teachers are teaching distance learning classes to more than 40,000 students who are enrolled in credit and noncredit remedial classes. Teachers are hired, trained, and supervised at one of three sites located at the University of Alabama, Troy University, and Madison City Schools.

While technology is convenient, a controversial topic revolves around the enormous growth of distance education and the challenges associated with its instructional methods. In strengthening the teaching pedagogy component of distance education, Meyers (2008) suggests that teachers use transformative pedagogy. It includes:

- creating a safe environment by valuing the opinions of students;
- encouraging students to think about their experience, beliefs, and biases which can be accomplished through discussion postings;

- using teaching strategies that promote student participation and engagement such as through the asynchronous discussion boards;
- posing real-world problems that address inequalities, which can help expand their awareness of how societal forces impact people; and
- encouraging action-oriented solutions by motivating them to participate in a democracy and become agents for social change.

ACCESS offers 70 courses, 20 of which were designed by the University of Alabama. Most of the coursework for students takes place during a set school period and not at home. This hybrid model gives students the best of both worlds, offering face-to-face interaction and e-learning opportunities tailored for their own individual needs.

LEADERSHIP

Management style can determine whether an organization's strategy of change will succeed or fail (Grant, 2008). Power is centralized in a top-down management. One of the key strengths of top-down change is evident when there are tight deadlines and multiple departments involved. Although input from others may be helpful, time constraints and practical concerns make broad-based input impossible. One of the weaknesses of top-down change is that these decisions are often limited in scope and not in the best interest of the organization because suggestions and feedback from lower management are not considered. Reduced productivity, broken lines of communication, and low employee motivation can result during top-down change. On the other hand, bottom-up management allows team members to participate in every step of the management process. One of the advantages of the bottom-up approach is that the planning process involves many people, which makes it

flow significantly faster. One of the weaknesses of bottom-up project management is the lack of clarity and control.

ACCESS's organizational structure is very similar to a machine bureaucracy, where "important decisions are made at the strategic apex; day-to-day operations are controlled by managers and standardized procedures" (Bolman & Deal, 2008, p. 80). The governor of Alabama and the Alabama Department of Education (ALSDE) oversee K-12 public schools and manage the budget of the mostly state-funded ACCESS program. The Technology Initiatives office, an entity of the ALSDE, manages and coordinates day to-day aspects of the program. Staff members at the three state's regional offices hire, train, and supervise ACCESS teachers. Additionally, designed ACCESS facilitators are located at each of the state's public schools to serve as a liaison between students and teachers.

PROGRAM EVALUATION

Assessment, accountability, and quality control measures are some of the key components in the operational tapestry of educational institutions. Multiple assessment tools quantify and qualify the effectiveness of curriculums, programs, and other services provided. Additionally, administrators collaborate with state, federal, and local governments in an effort to follow policies and laws that govern accountability. The International Society for Technology in Education (2010) evaluated the ACCESS program, and found that there are some areas of improvement.

- better technical preparation of students;
- engaged facilitators who supported students' needs;
- improved course materials;
- better two-way communication between students and teachers as well as between teachers and facilitators; and
- timely response to technology issues.

On a positive note, the International Society for Technology in Education report found that ACCESS had fulfilled its mission of providing equal access to students. Additionally, more than 75% of the ACCESS students reported their virtual school experience was equal or better than the traditional courses in the past. Graduation rates have increased, dropout rates have decreased, and the number of advanced placement takers has doubled as a result of the implementation of ACCESS and other state initiatives (Alabama Department of Education, 2010).

DIFFUSION OF INNOVATION

Alabama is home to one of the largest state virtual schools in the nation. Only Florida and North Carolina have larger virtual school enrollments (Watson, Murin, Vashaw, Gemin, & Rapp, 2009). How did Alabama's ACCESS leaders implement their program so quickly? Worthy of consideration is the diffusion of innovation theory which has four main elements: innovation, communication, time, and social system. As indicated by Rogers (1995), "Getting an idea adopted, even when it has many obvious advantages, is difficult. Many innovations require a lengthy period of many years from the time they become available to the time when they are widely adopted" (p. 1).

First of all, an innovation is anything that is "perceived" as being new to the potential adopter. Although educators in the state of Alabama had implemented technological innovations to improve academic achievement prior to ACCESS, such initiatives did not have the capability of delivering the state's goals. Classrooms throughout the state were wired with interactive videoconferencing and web-based learning innovations to expand course offerings to students, to provide alternative options to those seeking to retake courses needed to graduate, to alleviate schedule conflicts, and/or accelerate an academic program. Two characteristics of innovation are relevant to this case study including relative advantage and trialability. Despite the $10.3 million needed to fund the first phase ACCESS, the relative advantages of equal educational opportunities for every public high school student was greater than the hefty price tag, which enhanced the likelihood of diffusion. Another factor is trialability or the "degree to which an innovation might be experimented on a limited basis" (Rogers, 1995, p. 16). Implementation of ACCESS's program took place with only 24 schools during the pilot phase instead of equipping all 371 schools at the same time. This allowed ACCESS's task force to sample experimentally and to tweak technical glitches before full implementation.

Second, the information touting the promises of ACCESS was communicated via mass communications by starting with the governor holding media conferences that were broadcast on local television and radio stations and published in newspapers throughout the state.

The governor's messages and student testimonials resonated with stakeholders, teachers, students, and parents who then spread information to others via interpersonal communications.

Effective communication is circular in nature, meaning that feedback is required for an exchange of ideas, messages, and signals to take place. Noise is an enemy of communication and prevents the message from being perceived in the manner in which the sender had intended. Internal noise, possibly the most damaging to an organization's reputation, stems from the receivers' perceptions and attitudes toward the institution (i.e., "Is this program going to deliver on its program as ACCESS leaders proclaim?"). The credibility of the school system's message is not only measured by external evaluations and graduation rates, but also through testimonials communicated by students and other stakeholders.

Third, a combination of effective mass media and interpersonal communications hastened ACCESS's time from knowledge to implementation. However, continued program sustainability or confirmation will depend on how long the innovative measures are needed, how long funding will be available to support it, and if assessments from external evaluators continue to show improvements have been made in any areas of deficiencies. Symbolic approaches, such as making employees feel their personal input is important and meaningful, were advantageous for the governor's task force. Symbolic approaches include strategies that celebrate the smallest of accomplishments to increase the likelihood that positive behavior will be repeated in the future (Bolman & Deal, 2008).

Finally, the social system was influenced by a team of renowned experts in the field of distance education. Decisions are "made by relatively few individuals in a system who possess power, status, or technical expertise" (Rogers, 1995, p. 38). In the case study of ACCESS, several respected experts in the field of education participated in the governor's Task Force on Distance Education. Governor Riley was able to use his political influence to facilitate change outside the organization (i.e., getting the tangible resources needed for the initiative), the political realities that existed within the organization with satisfied ACCESS staffers, teachers, and students helped build his power base.

CONCLUSION

Nationwide, enrollment in state virtual schools is approximately 450,000 in 2010 (Watson et al., 2010). Thirty-nine states have state-led initiatives. For Alabama, ACCESS has opened doors to the state's underserved and "served as a catalyst to reverse statistics citing Alabama among the lowest?performing states for high school and college graduates" (ACCESS, 2010, p.

13). Remaining student-centered is of the upmost importance for these digital natives. Our very future depends on it.

REFERENCES

ACCESS. (2010). *A plan for continued excellence: 2011-2016.* Montgomery, AL: Author.

Alabama State Department of Education. (2009). *Alabama education report card.* Montgomery, AL: Author.

Bolman, L. G., & Deal, T. E. (2008). *Reframing organizations: Artistry, choice, and leadership.* (4th ed.). San Francisco, CA: Jossey-Bass.

Clark, R. E. (Ed.). (2001). *Learning from media: Arguments, analysis, and evidence.* Greenwich, CT: Information Age.

Grant, R. M. (2008). *Contemporary strategy analy sis* (6th ed.). Malden, MA: Blackwell.

International Society for Technology in Education (2010). *Alabama Connecting Classrooms, Educators, & Students Statewide (ACCESS): Year four evaluation Report.* Washington, DC: International Society for Technology in Education.

Martin, M. (2005). Seeing is believing: The role of video conferencing in distance learning. *British Journal of Educational Technology, 36*(3), 397-405.

Meredith, S., & Newton, B. (2003). Models of eLearning: Technology promise vs. learner needs. *The International Journal of Management Education, 3*(3), 43-56.

Meyers, S. (2008). Using transformative pedagogy when teaching online. *College Teaching, 56*(4), 219-224.

Palloff, R. A. & Pratt, K. (2007). *Building online learning communities: Effective strategies for the virtual classroom.* San Francisco, CA: Jossey-Bass.

Prieger, J. E., & Hu, W. (2008). The broadband digital divide and the nexus of race, competition, and quality. *Information Economics and Policy, 20,* 150-167.

Rogers, E. M. (1995). *Diffusion of innovations.* (4th ed.). New York, NY: The Free Press.

Simonson, M. (2000). Making decisions: The use of electronic technology in online classrooms *New Directions for Teaching and Learning, 84*(1), 29-34.

Smaldino, S. E., Lowther, D. L., & Russell, J. D. (2008). *Instructional technology and media for* learning (9th ed). Upper Saddle River, NJ: Pearson.

Svinicki, M., & McKeachie, W. J. (2011). *McKeachie's teaching tips: Strategies, research, and theory for college and university teachers.* Belmont, CA: Wadsworth.

Watson, J., Murin, A., Vashaw, L., Gemin, B., & Rapp, C. (2010). *Keeping pace with K-12 online learning: An annual review of policy and practice.* Evergreen, CO: Evergreen Education Group.

Getting Connected to the California K-12 High Speed Network

An Overview of Services and Applications

David Billett

INTRODUCTION

California, the most populous state in the union, is a state of innovation and promise. The size, population, and geography of California present unique challenges to equitable delivery of quality instruction to K-12 students. As a solution to the problems of getting all of California's K-12 students connected to learning and communication resources, the California K-12 High Speed Network

David Billett, Technology Resource Teacher, Henry T. Gage Middle School, Los Angeles Unified School District, 2880 East Gage Avenue, Huntington Park, CA 90255. Telephone: (323) 826-1500. E-mail: dbillett@lausd.net

(K12HSN, the network) was established under a grant provided by the California Department of Education. The K12HSN program connects to a statewide intranet supported by the Corporation for Education Network Initiatives in California (CENIC). The K12HSN provides support for California's K-12 public schools with network connectivity, Internet services, distance education and classroom applications for teaching and learning, in addition to videoconferencing support and coordination. With classroom and distance education resources, the K12HSN provides a number of technical support applications and diagnostic tools for school sites, districts, and county offices of education (COEs).

WHY THE K12HSN?

When properly implemented and capitalized, online technologies possible only with high-speed Internet access enable students to become more independent learners at increasingly advanced levels (Nicholas & Ng, 2009). Access to online resources and learning opportunities is only truly equitable when students are able to universally access high-speed Internet connections (North American Council for Online Learning [NACOL], 2007).

Services provided by the K12HSN align with recommendations proposed by State

Educational Technology Directors Association (SETDA, 2008). The goals of SETDA and the K12HSN include:

- access to online assessments, data and administrative tools;
- online and distance learning opportunities;
- individualized special education learning;
- Web 2.0 technology tools; and
- online and hybrid professional development opportunities.

Online assessments make data more accessible to administrators and teachers. Not only do online assessments measure what students have learned, but offer administrators and teachers access to information directly related to improvement of teaching practices while individualizing instruction for learners. Online and distance learning opportunities permit students without on-ground opportunities to study in Advanced Placement or elective classes through high-speed Internet access, where otherwise no courses or access would be available. Likewise for special education—a variety of available online resources make learning with experts and specialists a practical possibility.

High-speed Internet access is essential in providing professional development opportunities. Strategies endorsed by SETDA are available through the K12HSN. Education Portals, such as the California Learning Resource Network (CLRN), the California Technology Assistance Program (CTAP) and EdTech Profile enable teachers to search for standards-based instructional material and professional development opportunities designed to meet the diverse needs of all California teachers.

ACCESS AND EQUITY

By providing high-speed educational access in California public K-12 schools, the K12HSN assures equity by offering online high-quality delivery of educational resources without resorting to a tiered system of Internet connectivity. Private, commercial Internet providers have no legal obligation to offer affordable high-speed Internet access and can block or give preference to Internet resources and applications with no involvement or consultation from subscribers. Unfettered and no-cost access to distance learning applications and resources serves educational goals to raise literacy and student achievement (Windhausen, 2008).

BROADBAND CONNECTIVITY

The K12HSN fulfills a critical need for broadband connectivity in schools. With a commitment to providing broadband connectivity, the K12HSN offers access to emerging distance education applications for student learning, as well as online resources for professional development, school administration, and content sharing. The high-quality videoconferencing capabilities of the network facilitate meaningful two-way, interactive, and real-time educational experiences. More accessible, faster, and more reliable Internet means more access to and from school communities. Parents can videoconference with teachers, administrators, and support personnel, and students and teachers can collaborate on projects with counterparts in remote locations and receive expert-led lessons from virtually any location.

CENIC is a partner in realizing the need for broadband connectivity for all K-12 education institutions and students. The California Research and Education Network (CalREN) is the result of CENIC resources dedicated to cost-effective, high bandwidth networking to support the missions and needs of school faculties, staffs, and students. The CalREN was designed by CENIC to connect the majority of K-12 and higher education institutions to facilitate collaboration in education and research. A fiber optic network backbone

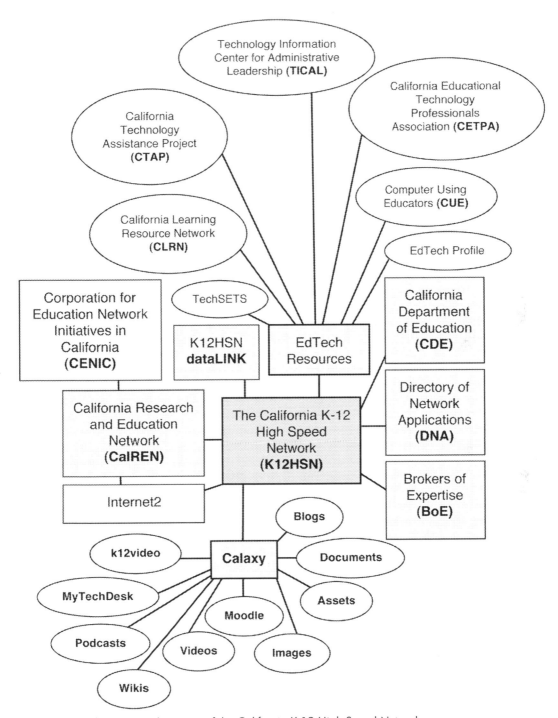

Figure 1. Applications and services of the California K-12 High Speed Network.

connects schools to county offices of education (COEs) in all 58 counties of California (CENIC, 2009).

A high-speed network for K-12 schools lifts constraints of educational opportunities imposed by a lack of or poor Internet connectivity. The K12HSN complies with recommendations made in the Final Report of the California Broadband Task Force (2008). The Final Report emphasized expansion of educational opportunities through increased access and use of broadband connectivity. By expanding broadband connectivity, the State of California and the K12HSN can "leverage educational opportunities" with a "robust technology support system" to provide appropriate curricular resources for students in meeting academic standards and developing skills to compete in the global economy.

PARTNERSHIPS, ASSOCIATIONS, AND AFFILIATIONS

The California Department of Education (CDE) initiated the K12HSN with a grant to the Imperial County Office of Education (ICOE) in 2004. Through ICOE, the California Department of Education (CDE) provides funding for the K12HSN in addition to facilitating collaboration between educational agencies and projects, financial and administrative services and technical oversight (CDE, 2008). As the lead state agency for K12HSN, ICOE received significant funding from the State of California. The K12HSN project shifted management from the University of California to the CDE to broaden the scope of services available to students at all public education institutions. The shift to the CDE, and ultimately to ICOE, was an effort to focus on technology and curriculum needs for the K-12 community. The CDE realizes that educators need to collaborate with one another to enable critical thinking about teaching practice, and provide effective tools to assist in closing the achievement gap and raising overall student achievement across the state (ICOE, 2009).

The Corporation for Education Network Initiatives in California, CENIC, and the California Research and Education Network (CalREN) are partners in combining

resources to implement the K12HSN with high capacity, high-speed connectivity to schools and research institutions in California. The CalREN infrastructure for K-20 California research and education users operates at the third tier of a three-tiered network service. CENIC owns and manages 2,700 miles of fiber optic connection supported by cutting edge networking technology components. The upper two tiers of the CalREN network are reserved for the High-Performance Research Network and an experimental/developmental infrastructure for network researchers (CENIC, 2009a).

CENIC and CalREN acknowledge the increasing significance of high performance connectivity to California K-12 schools. After a recent annual CENIC conference, the president of the organization revealed that results from a post-conference survey indicated that members and constituent organizations expressed increasing interest in online learning applications (CENIC, 2009). This unsurprising revelation bodes well for the ongoing development of increasingly sophisticated distance education applications accessible to K12HSN users. The CENIC organization has also made a commitment to use distance education applications to increase online participation for future conferences.

CalREN also links to the national Internet2 network as part of the Internet infrastructure dedicated to education. Internet2 is billed as one of the leading proponents of advanced networking, and is led by key members of the research and education communities. Internet2 supports the K12HSN with a split mission. As a partner in K12HSN, Internet2 "supports and enhances ... educational and research missions" in and is committed to sustaining advances in the Internet infrastructure (Internet2, 2009). As a partner in providing high speed, high capacity Internet connectivity to California K-12 schools, Internet2 services are able to actively engage the education community in the development of new communication and information technologies that support online learning and teaching.

The DataLINK service of the K12HSN was designed and implemented to directly connect connectivity data with related information from California K-12 schools. DataLINK is a database of K12HSN schools and districts and the types of constituent connections to the state infrastructure. Connectivity information is aggregated and provided by DataLINK primarily to gauge and assess at school site, district, county, region, and state levels. Future implementations of DataLINK promise to expand and allow correlation of collected connectivity data between other databases that include student performance and demographic information. The goal of facilitating access to multiple databases will be to ensure that K12HSN resources and connectivity are having a positive impact on student achievement statewide, in addition to providing data for making sound decisions towards student and school success.

The Directory of Network Applications (DNA) is another service delivered by the K12HSN primarily to provide access to locally produced content resources. Focusing on the practitioner, the DNA assists in locating electronic instructional support materials developed by institutions, agencies, and individuals in California. Limited to electronic materials that reside on the K12HSN, DNA assures fast and reliable access to the instructional material. Efficient access to DNA materials allows for a comprehensive search solution as well. The DNA custom search capabilities let users search by resource type, curriculum area, grade level and California subject area content standards. Most content is provided free of charge to schools and COEs. There are several fee-based services available through contracts initiated by the state, COEs, and districts, usually at extremely low or reduced prices.

The California Learning Resource Network is a component of K12HSN that provides a clearinghouse of electronic learning resources (ELRs) aligned to California state curriculum frameworks and standards. Resources are approved for inclusion in the CLRN through a review process that coves legal compliance, standards alignment, and minimum requirements set forth by the California State Board of Education. Operating as an evaluator of instructional content for California public schools, CLRN objectives are geared to teachers, instructional coaches, and others responsible for instructional delivery. The CLRN's stated objectives are to: (a) identify and review supplemental electronic learning resources such as software, video, and Internet resources; (b) identify learning units aligned to resources and the state academic content standards; and (c) maintain an interactive Web site to provide information about electronic learning resources through an online searchable database and links to state education technology projects and resources (California Learning Resource Network, 2009).

A third-party agency conducted an extensive evaluation study of the CLRN for the 2007-2008 school year. The evaluation process included surveys, self-assessments, interviews, and records of accomplishments to determine awareness and use of the CLRN, and whether the service "identifies electronic learning resources to meet instructional needs" (Cradler, Beuthel, Cradler, & Barline, 2008, p. 109). The CLRN evaluation results indicated that 91% of survey respondents from the population CLRN users agree strongly that CLRN is useful for identifying ELRs aligned to instructional needs.

The California Technology Assistance Program (CTAP) is another state funded initiative and K12HSN affiliate providing support to schools and districts to integrate technology into teaching and learning. California is divided into 11 CTAP regional offices that emphasize the integration of educational technology and provide support necessary to provide professional development opportunities in addition to sharing online educational resource information. CTAP support is focused into five areas: staff development, technical assistance, information learning resources, telecommunications infrastructure, and coordination and funding (CTAP, 2008).

EdTech Profile is a California Department of Education State Educational Technology Service (SETS) project, providing educational administrators with tools to guide their decisions about integrating technology into classroom instruction and how to create and evaluate effective teacher technology training programs. Information collected from the EdTech Profile is aggregated and used to plan professional development programs. Data are also used to monitor and evaluate state and federal technology grant programs (EdTech Profile, 2009).

TechSETS, an offshoot of the SETS project, operates an online interactive help desk for counties and districts to establish professional development programs and provide enhanced support for school site based instructional technology specialists. Technical support is contracted through the San Diego COE. The Technology Information Center for Administrative Leadership (TICAL) is another K12HSN partner providing professional development for district and site administrators focusing on digital school leadership with data-driven decision-making. TICAL programs are also offered to assist in integrating technology into all facets of school administration. These services are contracted through the Santa Cruz COE with funding provided by the CDE.

The K12HSN is also affiliated with two major professional organizations, the California Educational Technology Professionals Association (CETPA) and Computer Using Educators (CUE). Both of these organizations are concerned with improving student achievement through the use of instructional and communication technology. CETPA emphasizes the improvement of data access for administrative information processing in public education, with the goal of increasing "information sharing and communication among K-12 technologists on technology-related issues" (CETPA, 2009). The goal of CUE is to advance student achievement through technology in all disciplines, from preschool through college. CUE holds a widely anticipated annual conference that is among one of California's most well attended educational technology events.

To tie all K12HSN affiliates, associations and partners together, the CDE has developed the California Brokers of Expertise (BOE) project to connect teachers, schools, and districts with best practices. The BOE project is intended to become a knowledge management system collecting educational research. The body of information gathered would be examined for trends that lead to strategies to implement research for reform and improvement of California schools. BOE goals formed in collaboration with K12HSN include: (a) to provide classroom tools and resources aligned to California Content Standards; (b) to provide easily accessible research-based, instructional resources searchable by grade level, content area and demographic information; (c) to provide opportunities for creating and publishing high-quality content that has been proven effective for teachers; (d) to facilitate communication and dialogue with educators across the state who have similar questions (California BOE, 2009).

WEB 2.0 APPLICATIONS OF THE K12HSN

The K12HSN offers tools for California K-12 distance education and classroom teachers as part of a comprehensive suite known as Calaxy. Applications provided by Calaxy are appropriate for classroom and distance education purposes, anticipating instructional, communication, and technical needs of teachers. Distance education and other Internet-based applications are hosted on the reliable and robust state network, ensuring consistency in instruction with a minimum of technical interventions required by teachers and other users. One of the primary intents of the Calaxy suite of applications is to give California public school teachers knowledge of and access to what are referred to as Web 2.0 tools. Available tools for designing, developing, and delivering instruction include blogs, document sharing, video and photo sharing, podcasting, wikis, course and learning management, technical support tools, and videoconferencing. Calaxy tools for communication and collaboration include social network and messaging within a trusted community of California educators. Significantly, these services are available at no cost to California public schools.

Tools provided by Calaxy have come about in response to a general call in education for K-12 teachers to prepare their students for collaboration and communication in an environment that should increasingly reflect the ways in which students live and learn outside of the classroom and other instructional spaces. Web 2.0 applications give teachers the means to engage their students through learner-centered activities. Teachers creating learning networks for personal and professional use can expand their network to include teachers and colleagues, with enhanced abilities to access and share information. In addition to the instructional advantages of managing content and learning with Web 2.0 tools, Calaxy services can take the technical load off of school sites and technical support personnel with cloud computing capabilities. Using a cloud computing model, files and other electronic information are not stored and retrieved on local, school site-based computers, but from locations elsewhere on the Internet. Teacher-created learning networks available from any Internet-enabled computer is one way the K12HSN and Calaxy tools

meet the needs of evolving methods for engaging students and delivering instruction on student terms.

School principals, district support personnel, instructional coaches, and other school leaders can take advantage of Calaxy-provided Web 2.0 tools to encourage reform at school sites. Interconnecting with instructional leaders across California can positively affect instruction by demonstrating higher expectations from students and teachers by using social networking, blogs, wikis, and other collaborative tools. Leading by example, administrators taking advantage of Calaxy tools can set the way for others who have not yet seen the implications of Web 2.0 in education. Calaxy provides practical applications that demonstrate the ability and variety of methods to facilitate communication, collaboration and, ultimately, leadership (Higgins, 2009).

CALAXY TOOLS

Of all the applications and resources provided by the K12HSN, Moodle, the open source course and learning management system, has the most significant implications for K-12 distance education in California public schools. The financial implications are obvious—commercially available equivalents to the Moodle platform are well out of financial reach for most schools, districts, and COEs. Calaxy Moodle courses are available free to all California teachers following a brief verification process. By creating online courses, teachers can offer virtual learning environments for students in blended or completely online programs.

Calaxy offers blogging and wiki services, again at no cost to California teachers. These collaborative online tools let any number of users create Web sites. Blogs and wikis are relatively simple and highly accessible Web 2.0 tools that teachers and students can use for cooperative projects in which all participants can equally create and add relevant content. The blogging and wiki features of Calaxy offer enhanced functionality with the ability to moderate content added by students and other non-administrative blog and wiki owners. Alongside blogs and wikis, video and podcasting services are also part of the Calaxy suite of applications. These applications comprise a "new publishing revolution" (Hargadon, 2008). With the capability to let participants not just read the Web but meaningfully contribute to its content, Web 2.0 tools such as blogs, wikis, video, and podcasting turn students from passive participants to active contributors. Other Calaxy services intended for teacher and student use include image and document storage, retrieval, and sharing. These content sharing services are moderated by contributors and administrators for appropriate content.

The MyTechDesk and Assets features of the Calaxy suite are powerful, web-based systems for managing and tracking school work orders and inventory. These are yet additional K12HSN services provided to all California schools and districts at no cost. Either used as standalone applications or a joint solution, Assets and MyTechDesk have been implemented to allow local school and district sites to efficiently manage inventory from acquisition to obsolescence. These management tools let coordinators, administrators, and other school site personnel involved with instructional technology make informed decisions about services provided by the school to integrate and support instructional technology. Using MyTechDesk and Assets date in decision-making processes can lead to greater efficiency of support personnel and lower cost of ownership of instructional technology inventory (K12HSN Calaxy, 2009).

SUMMARY

The K12HSN is poised to become an increasingly vital resource to California K-12 schools. The diverse nature of partners and collaborators ensure that the K12HSN will stay abreast of innovations and developments in information and communication technologies. Working in conjunction with several other state initiatives, the K12HSN has garnered sustained support for technology to improve teaching and learning. Increasing broadband access, online services, and content under the aegis of the California Department of Education virtually guarantees the availability of K12HSN resources to teachers, administrators, and students who will progressively be turning to online services.

The challenge that lies ahead for the K12HSN is to inform its constituent COEs of its services that many districts and schools may already be supporting financially. Redundancy is beneficial to the quality and integrity of network systems and hardware, especially for systems routinely backed up with a set of secondary and other auxiliary resources. However, redundancy can be anathema to schools and districts expending resources to maintain services that the State of California and the K12HSN is already providing at little to no cost. The K12HSN has professional development and data analysis resources built into almost every online service offered. Whether for administrators, teachers, or school support personnel, the K12HSN offers relevant and valuable services that help schools do what they have to do: manage resources and raise student achievement.

REFERENCES

California Broadband Task Force. (2008). *Final report of the California broadband task force.* Sacramento, CA: Author. Retrieved March 18, 2009, from http://www.calink.ca.gov/taskforcereport/

California Brokers of Expertise Project. (2008). *California brokers of expertise project—State of education* (CA Department of Education). Retrieved March 30, 2009, from http://www.cde.ca.gov/eo/in/se/brokers.asp

California Department of Education. (2008). K-12 High Speed network (K12HSN)—State technology programs (CA Department of Education). Retrieved April 2, 2009, from http://www.cde.ca.gov/ls/et/st/highspeednetwork.asp

California Educational Technology Professionals Association (CETPA). (2009). *CETPA: Our vision statement.* Retrieved April 2, 2009, from http://www.cetpa-k12.org/about/.

California K-12 High Speed Network. (2009c). *DNA—California K-12 High Speed Network.* Retrieved March 3, 2009, from http://www.k12hsn.org/resources/directory/dna.php

California Learning Resource Network. (2009). *About the California learning resource network.* Retrieved March 10, 2009, from http://clrn.org/home/about.cfm.

Corporation for Education Network Initiatives in California. (2009). President's message: Looking back on Long Beach and the CENIC Annual Conference. *CENICtoday, 12*(3). Retrieved April 1, 2009, from http://www.cenic.org/publications/cenictoday/Mar09_CT.html

Corporation for Education Initiatives in California. (2009a). *About CENIC.* Retrieved March 19, 2009, from http://www.cenic.org/about/index.html.

Cradler, J., Beuthel, B., Cradler, R., & Barline, R. (2009). *California learning resource network: 2007-2008 Evaluation report.* Retrieved March 18, 2009, from http://clrn.org/advisory/2008_May/CLRN_2008_Report_v13.pdf

EdTech Profile. (2009). *EdTech Profile FAQ.* Retrieved March 29, 2009, from http://edtechprofile.net/faq.php

Hargadon, S. (2008, March 4). *Web 2.0 is the future of education.* Message posted to http://www.stevehargadon.com/2008/03/web-20-is-future-of-education.html

Higgins, C. (2009). What's so powerful about Web 2.0? *Principal Leadership, 9*(7), 60-64.

Internet 2. (2009). *About us.* Retrieved March 30, 2009, from: http://www.internet2.edu/about/

Imperial County office of Education. (2009). *K12HSN: California K-12 high speed network.* Retrieved March 20, 2009, from http://www.icoe.org/technology/projects-partnerships/k12hsn

K12HSN Calaxy. (2009). *Calaxy assets.* Retrieved March 30, 2009, from http://www.k12hsn.org/calaxy/assets/

Nicholas, H., & Ng, W. (2009). Engaging secondary school students in extended and open learning supported by online technologies. *Journal of Research on Technology in Education, 41*(3), 305-328.

North American Council for Online Learning. (2007, November). *Access and equity in online classes and virtual schools.* (Issue Brief). Retrieved March 28, 2009, from http://www.inacol.org/docs/NACOL_EquityAccess.pdf

State Educational Technology Directors Association. (2008). *High-speed broadband access for all kids: Breaking through the barriers* (Issue Brief). Retrieved March 28, 2009, from http://www.setda.org/

Windhausen, J. (2008). A blueprint for big broadband: An EDUCAUSE white paper (White paper). (ERIC Document Reproduction Service No. ED 499917)

Part II

Institution-Based Applications of Distance Education

The Global Campus

Examining the Initiative From the Perspective of Diffusion Theory

Kevin E. Johnson

The University of Illinois Global Campus is a rather new initiative with the mission to "become a national leader in online education, focused on innovation, quality, superior instruction, service, and accessibility" (University of Illinois Global Campus, 2007, p. 1). As a campus, The Global Campus itself is not accredited and relies on partnerships with other colleges and departments to design and develop its online programs and courses. Therefore, faculty senate buy-in and support at all three land-based campuses is essential.

Kevin E. Johnson,
CEO, The Cutting Ed, Inc.,
506 W. Florida Ave., Urbana, IL 61801.
Telephone: (217) 253-8670.
E-mail: kevin@thecuttinged.com

This unique structure has encountered its own challenges to the point of forcing The Global Campus to close its doors as a separate campus and return distance education programming to the individual campuses.

In September of 2005, a newly appointed president, Joseph B. White, made it clear in his inaugural speech that the University of Illinois should strive to become a leader in providing quality education in a more accessible and user-friendly fashion (White, 2005). Since that time, efforts ensued on creating a fourth campus: The University of Illinois Global Campus. In 4 short years, The Global Campus formed and developed distant programs, enrolled students, conducted virtual classes, and come full circle to closing its doors for restructuring.

The University of Illinois Board of Directors approved the creation of The Global Campus in March 2007. The board's decision was based on several market analyses and the president's vision for increasing the university's presence in the distance education field. The board approved the initiative based upon a proposal brought forth by a core team of professionals, headed by Chet Gardner, who was appointed special assistant to the president in 2006. The proposal included a strengths, weaknesses, opportunities, threats analysis, market analysis of initial programs, and processes and policies for registering students, designing quality courses, hiring faculty, and measuring success. Originally, it was intended that The

Global Campus would become a for-profit arm of the university as well, which ultimately was changed due to all three campus faculty senates expressing lack of support for a profit-based business model.

Once the board approved the initiative, the core team was provided with a budget and the green light to hire additional staff. The staff had less than nine months to establish its new virtual campus before going live with its first two programs in January 2008. For the next year, The Global Campus was criticized for the lack of enrollment numbers and continued lack of support by many faculty and academic units. It was decided that one possible solution was to become accredited so that the virtual campus could work toward academic independence. In November 2008, the board of trustees approved the request to seek accreditation, which was quickly added to the Global Campus project management schedule to be completed by Fall 2010. To help address faculty concerns, the board of trustees approved The Constitution for the Academic Policy Council of the University of Illinois Global Campus, which established a faculty oversight committee of Global Campus academic programs and educational policies. Despite these efforts, on April 15, 2009, the president and University of Illinois Senates Conference produced a document that outlined a redesign for the Global Campus that would return all academic responsibility over to each of the campuses and stopping all efforts of The Global Campus to become a separate campus.

So, what went wrong? Let's look at the initiative through the eyes of Rogers' (2003) elements of diffusion and try to identify components of the theory that may have helped The Global Campus initiative be more successful. According to Rogers (2003), *diffusion* is "the process by which (1) an *innovation* (2) is *communicated* through certain *channels* (3) *over time* (4) among the members of a *social system*" (emphasis added, p. 5). Let's first examine

these components one a time in order to get a picture of the entire system.

INNOVATION

Even though the University of Illinois is already comprised of three land-based campuses, only a few individual departments have implemented distance education courses within their program. For example, the Urbana-Champaign campus' Graduate School of Library and Information Science (GSLIS) offers a fully American Library Association accredited master of science degree program (http://www.lis.illinois.edu/programs/leep/). For the most part, program planning, instructional design, and delivery methods specific to distance education are foreign concepts to university faculty and college/department administration. Therefore, the innovation in our scenario is the construction of a new virtual campus that challenges the social structure of the members associated with the existing culture.

In order for faculty to adopt such an innovation, they must understand the five *characteristics of innovations*. These characteristics also help determine and individual's rate of adoption as well. They consist of *relative advantage, compatibility, complexity, trialability, and observability*. When we examine these one at a time relative to The Global Campus, we can begin to see where considering Rogers' (2003) theory in the initial planning stages may have encouraged a more successful implementation.

1. *Relative Advantage*: one's perception of how advantageous the innovation in terms of economics, social prestige factors, convenience, and satisfaction (Rogers, 2003). For a majority of the Global Campus adopters, the advantages of The Global Campus are indirectly related to the individual. Unless the individual became a course designer or an instructor, the benefit to oneself is minimal at best. One must

look at how partnering with The Global Campus benefits students, the department, and the overall university system. This is not to say this can't be achieved, but understanding this in the initial planning stages may have helped administration focus on approaches to getting more buy-in.

2. *Compatibility*: determines how compatible the individual perceives the innovation to the adopting society (Rogers, 2003). In the initial stages, The Global Campus was to be a for-profit arm of the university that relied solely on the idea of hiring subject matter experts to design courses and adjunct faculty to teach them. Faculty senates shared their concerns regarding content development and oversight of instruction being taken out of existing department and faculty responsibility. However, similarly speaking, faculty also expressed concern about their workloads and their inability to take on additional responsibilities.

3. *Complexity*: "The degree to which an innovation is perceived as difficult to understand and use (Rogers, 2003, p. 15). The starting of a new campus is always complex in nature. However, most people understand the nature of developing policies, procedures, and other technologies to create an on-ground campus. The creation of a virtual campus is something few can relate to and may be perceived as overly complex and technical simply due to ignorance. This in itself is a gap The Global Campus administration tried to close by conducting face-to-face meetings where field experts, administration, and faculty could discuss and answer questions.

4. *Trialability*: the degree to which an individual is able to practice the innovation before making a decision (Rogers, 2003). The Global Campus worked hard to meet with other successful programs such as University of Massa-

chusetts, University of Phoenix, and Capella University before deciding on a model. However, no faculty were a part of these exhibitions and demonstrations. Faculty and administration, however, were invited to participate in the proposal process for deciding on a learning management system.

5. *Observability*: the degree to which the results of an innovation are visible to others. Global Campus administration provided faculty and college administrators with economic projections specific to enrollment and university income (Rogers, 2003). Other than financials, the only measurable outcome for which adopters could observe progress was enrollment numbers. Unfortunately, The Global Campus was unable to meet project enrollment numbers within its first year of operation. One the same note, Global Campus staff had only 9 months to put a campus together, which was 4 months less than expected based on the time needed to get board of trustee approval. Timing affected not only initial startup plans but program approval and marketing efforts as well, which all contributed to the campus' ability to achieve enrollment numbers.

COMMUNICATION AND COMMUNICATION CHANNELS

Specific to diffusion, *communication* occurs when some method is used to connect those with expert knowledge and experience regarding the innovation with those without knowledge and experience surrounding the same innovation (Rogers, 2003). In 2006, White appointed Gardner to lead The Global Campus initiative. Gardner, at the time, was serving as the assistant vice president for academic affairs. His first task was to develop a core team of experts to develop a proposal to submit for review by the faculty senate at all three campuses before presenting it to the board of trustees for approval. Faculty and staff were invited to campus presentations and provided the opportunity to give feedback and discuss concerns. Though this strategy provided opportunities for faculty involvement, no faculty participated on the core team.

TIME

Time with respect to diffusion reflects three measurable components of the discussion process which include (a) the time it takes for an individual to be introduced to the innovation to the time it takes the same individual to determine whether to adopt or reject the innovation, (b) the timeframe in which the innovation is adopted relative to that of other adopters, and (c) the rate of adoption by those within the system (Rogers, 2003). With regard to The Global Campus, time was of the essence. However, in its lifespan of 4 short years, too many adopters determined to reject the innovation to the point of pressuring the initiative's administration to close the doors.

SOCIAL SYSTEM

Rogers (2003) defines a *social system* as "a set of interrelated units that are engaged in joint problem solving to accomplish a common goal" (p. 23). Innovation decisions can be made based upon one of three types of choices: (a) *optional innovation-decisions* where "choices to adopt or reject an innovation that are made by an individual independent of the decisions of the other members of the system" (p. 28), (b) *collective innovation-decisions*, which are those "choices to adopt or reject an innovation that are made by consensus among the members of a system" (p. 28), and (c) *authority innovation-decisions*, which are "choices to adopt or reject an innovation that are made by a relatively few individuals in a system who possess power, status, or technical expertise" (p. 28).

It was the decision of President White to move forward with developing The Global Campus, therefore, causing the initial choice to be one of authority. However, due to the political nature of a system as large as the University of Illinois, no one person has sole authority to implement such large initiatives in a manner that rejects the input, concerns, and voices of its members. Such authoritarian introduction of The Global Campus may have been the single greatest factor in its downfall.

In order for an authoritarian approach to be successful in terms of diffusion, the authoritarian figure must require implementation and have full authority to do so. The University of Illinois, like many institutions of higher education, shares operational power among tenure-track faculty, governing boards, and advising committees. Therefore, the successful creation of a separate virtual campus would have required full autonomy and administrative control or the overall support of the faulty senates and chancellors at all three campuses.

Without an authoritarian figure dictating adoption, change must happen through the use of *opinion leaders* who serve as respectable members of the society and are early adopters of the innovation (Rogers, 2003). With no opinion leader sitting on the initial core team The Global Campus initiative could have been perceived as an us against them (faculty against administration) scenario, causing resentment and negative attitudes toward change from the onset. Michael Lindeman (personal communication, October 21, 2009), director of program and course development for The Global Campus, feels that appointing a faculty member (or other opinion leader within the system) to lead the initiative rather than an existing administrator would have earned more initial respect by the adopting community. By doing so, faculty may have felt that the existing academic oversight and rigor would have been less questionable. However, one must still wonder if things had been different, how different would they actually be? Would the mission to reach more students be successful if the university's current model had simply transferred to an online delivery modality? Would tenure-track faculty rely on adjunct faculty to help ensure multiple sections of a course could be offered? No one knows. What we do know is that due to the administration's inability to get the faculty senates' and chancellors' support, The Global Campus closed its virtual doors on December 31, 2009. Individual campus units became responsible for the creation and implementation of any distance education adventures. May The Global Campus torch not burn out, but be passed, carrying reminders of past mistakes and successes, and may each campus stay true to the original mission of The Global Campus: "become a national leader in online education, focused on innovation, quality, superior instruction, service, and accessibility" (University of Illinois Global Campus, 2007, p. 1).

REFERENCES

Kolowich, S. (2009). What doomed Global Campus? Retrieved from the Inside Higher Education website: http://www.insidehighered.com/news/2009/09/03/globalcampus

Rogers, E. M. (2003). *Diffusion of innovations.* (5th ed). New York, NY: Free Press.

University of Illinois Global Campus. (2007). *The University of Illinois Global Campus instructor policies and procedures manual.* Champaign, IL: Author.

White, J. B. (2005). *Inaugural address.* Retrieved from http://www.uillinois.edu/president/speeches/20042005/sep22.Inaugural.Address.cfm

"THE UNIVERSITY OF ILLINOIS GLOBAL CAMPUS IS A RATHER NEW INITIATIVE WITH THE MISSION TO BECOME A NATIONAL LEADER IN ONLINE EDUCATION, FOCUSED ON INNOVATION, QUALITY, SUPERIOR INSTRUCTION, SERVICE, AND ACCESSIBILITY."

Online Learning Opportunities for K-12 Students in Florida's Nassau County

Kari Burgess-Watkins

INTRODUCTION

Research suggests that in approximately 4 years, 10% of all courses will be computer based and by 2019, 50% of all courses will be online (Christensen & Horn, 2008). In Florida, school districts must provide full-time virtual instructional programs to students in kindergarten through Grade 12.

Kari Burgess-Watkins,
Technology Integration Specialist, Nassau County School District, 1201 Atlantic Avenue, Fernandina Beach, FL 32034.
Telephone: (904) 491-9941.
E-mail: burgesska@nassau.k12.fl.us

While the Nassau County School District has been using Internet-based courses for high school credit recovery purposes, the district did not have an established full-time virtual school program. During the 2006-2007 school year, Nassau County public high school students earned 201 one-half credits through the online credit recovery program offered by the district (Rodeffer, 2007). The number of one-half credits earned increased to 614 during the 2007-2008 school year (Rodeffer, 2008). Due to budget constraints, the district reformatted the credit recovery program for the 2008-2009 school year and students earned 235 one-half credits through the online program (Burgess-Watkins, 2009). In addition to the online credit recovery courses offered by the district, Nassau County public school students have been enrolling in online courses offered through the Florida Virtual School.

In the 2009-2010 school year, Nassau County School District opened the Nassau Virtual School, which offers free online courses for eligible elementary, middle, and high school students residing in Nassau County. Nassau Virtual School provides online learning for current public school students, hospital homebound students, home education students, and private school students.

The implementation of the full-time K-12 virtual instructional program has been a daunting task. Fortunately, other innovative K-12 Florida districts have been offering distance education programs for a few years and have proven instrumental in establishing the necessary framework for Nassau Virtual School. The Nassau Virtual School team met over the course of a year to determine the mission, goals, objectives, programs, courses, budgets, policies, procedures, job descriptions, teacher pay schedules, website development, advertising, and other administrative tasks.

MISSION STATEMENT

The mission of the Nassau Virtual School is to extend educational opportunities for growth to all students through a flexible online environment, and thereby foster the development of each student as an inspired life-long learner and problem-solver with the strength of character to serve as a productive member of society (Nassau County School District [NCSD], 2010).

GOALS AND OBJECTIVES

The goals of the Nassau Virtual School are to:

- meet the legislative requirements for K-12 students as established by Section 1002.45 of the Florida Statutes;
- provide public high school students with an online opportunity for credit recovery, grade forgiveness, and supplemental or acceleration coursework;
- provide all eligible hospital home-bound students with the opportunity to take courses online;
- provide students in Grades 9-12 with an online opportunity to earn a high school diploma;
- provide online courses for Nassau County home education high school students; and

- Provide online courses for private high school students residing in Nassau County.

In order to meet the requirements of the legislation as well as fulfill other needs of students within Nassau County, Nassau County School District is using a multifaceted approach. Nassau County School District uses Florida Virtual School Full Time (FLVS FT) for students in Grades K-12, a franchise of the Florida Virtual School for students in Grades 6-12, EdOptions for students in Grades 6-12, and Florida Adult and Technical Distance Education Consortium (FATDEC) courses for adult education students.

FLVS FT FOR GRADES K-8

Florida Virtual School in partnership with Connections Academy created FLVS FT. By signing a contract with FLVS FT, Nassau County families and students have access to a high performing "A"-rated public virtual program (Connections Academy, 2011). The full-time, 180-day comprehensive program is offered to Nassau County kindergarten through 12th grade students. In order to qualify for the FLVS FT K-12 program, the student must reside in Nassau County School District's attendance area and meet one of the following criteria:

- the student has spent the prior school year in attendance at a public school in this state and was enrolled and reported by a public school district for funding during the preceding October and February for purposes of the Florida Education Finance Program surveys;
- the student is a dependent child of a member of the United States armed forces who was transferred within the last 12 months to this state from another state or from a foreign country pursuant to the parent's permanent change of station orders;

- the student was enrolled during the prior school year in a school district virtual instruction program under this section or a K-8 Virtual School Program under s.1002.415, Florida Statutes; and
- the student has a sibling who is currently enrolled in the school district virtual instruction program and that sibling was enrolled in such program at the end of the prior school year.

Through the FLVS FT program, students benefit from the flexibility of online courses, Sunshine State Standards curriculum, highly qualified Florida-certified teachers, regular communication, and personalized, instruction (Florida Virtual School Full Time, n.d.).

The majority of the FLVS FT K-8 curriculum is in print and supplemented through online content and resources. Once a student has applied and the district has verified eligibility, Connections Academy ships all of the required learning materials directly to the student's home.

FLVS FRANCHISE FOR GRADES 6-12

In order to provide FLVS courses to Nassau County students in Grades 6-12, Nassau Virtual School signed a franchise agreement with the FLVS. The franchise courses are taught by local Nassau County School District teachers. Nassau Virtual School teachers, students, and parents benefit from the expertise of the FLVS in terms of online instruction, instructional management, student management, support, and technology infrastructure. Teachers and students can login and work on their coursework any time and from any location with access to the Internet. In order to participate in the Nassau Virtual School franchise courses, the student must meet one of the following criteria:

- be enrolled in a Nassau County School District public school;

- be enrolled as a home education student with Nassau County School District; and
- be enrolled in a private school and whose legal guardian is a Nassau County, FL resident (NCSD, 2010).

HOME EDUCATION STUDENTS

High school home education students residing in Nassau County may retain home education status and utilize Nassau Virtual School courses to enhance their curriculum. Students have access to all offered courses and can take one or as many as six online courses per semester. The student's parent or guardian acts as guidance counselor to approve course selection (NCSD, 2010).

PRIVATE SCHOOL STUDENTS

Full-time private high school students residing in Nassau County can take one or as many as six online courses per semester with Nassau Virtual School. All private school students are required to meet with their guidance counselor in order to register for Nassau Virtual School courses.

HOSPITAL HOMEBOUND

High school hospital homebound students can take one or as many as six Nassau Virtual School courses with the approval of the hospital homebound facilitator and the guidance counselor from the student's home school. Course selection is determined by the student's guidance counselor (NCSD, 2010).

COENROLLED STUDENTS

Public high school students enrolled in a traditional Nassau County high school can take courses online with Nassau Virtual School as part of their schedule. A student's schedule may not exceed six courses between the schools. All public school students are required to receive approval from their guidance counselor in order to register for Nassau Virtual courses (NCSD, 2010).

FULL-TIME DIPLOMA-SEEKING STUDENTS

The full-time online program allows students to earn a regular high school diploma and complete their coursework online with Nassau County School District certified teachers. Students report to a campus for FCAT Testing and other assessments as necessary. Students are able to customize their education for accelerated learning or to accommodate their individual needs. In order to participate in the Nassau Virtual School diploma seeking program, a student should:

- have been promoted to the next grade the previous school year;
- have a 2.5 or higher grade point average;
- have scored at Level 3 or above on the FCAT Reading and Math during the previous school year; and
- meet all Nassau County Student Progression Plan Criteria (NCSD, 2010).

SELF-EVALUATION ONLINE LEARNING QUIZ

Online learning can provide opportunities for students to take courses any time and from anywhere; however, this style of learning may not be appropriate for every student (Florida Virtual School [FLVS], 2009). FLVS has developed a list of technical competencies, access, and learning style questions to help students determine if online learning is an option for meeting their educational needs.

In order to help a student determine if he or she will be successful learning in an online environment, he or she should carefully consider the FLVS "Is online learning for you?" questions (FLVS, 2009) prior to requesting Nassau Virtual School courses.

If the student can answer "YES" to ALL of the questions, online learning may be a viable option for his or her educational needs (FLVS, 2009). If the student answers "NO" to two or more, he or she will likely experience difficulty and should resolve these issues prior to attempting online coursework (FLVS, 2009).

TECHNICAL COMPETENCIES AND ACCESS

- Taking into consideration my personal, academic, work and extracurricular activities (sports, clubs, etc.), will I be able to devote as much or more time to my online class, as I do for my traditional studies?
- Am I comfortable using the Internet as a means of communication and research?
- Do I own or have access to a computer with Internet access and e-mail?
- Do I know or I am willing to learn how to copy, cut, and paste text/files between programs?
- Am I willing and able to learn and apply new software applications?

LEARNING STYLES

- Am I able to prioritize tasks, organize assignments and complete assigned work by the required date?
- Can I solve problems and work through difficulties independently?
- Are my writing, reading and communication skills above average?
- Do I prefer to work alone on assignments?
- Can I read and follow detailed instructions on my own without an instructor lecturing and giving verbal explanations? [Questions adapted from Florida Virtual School's Tips for Students signing up for FLVS classes (FLVS, 2009).

COURSES

Nassau Virtual School offers 42 middle and high school courses in the following subject areas: career education, critical thinking, English, Spanish, math, science, and social studies.

INSTRUCTION

The majority of the Nassau Virtual School policies are derived directly from the contract with FLVS. Nassau Virtual School teachers are required to speak via telephone with students and their parents at least once per month. In addition, the teachers and students interact regularly through e-mail, voice mail, and telephone. Students are encouraged to contact the teacher when there is any type of academic need. Teachers are required to respond to all e-mail and voicemail within 24 hours during the regular work week (Monday-Friday) and weekend communication (Saturday-Sunday) should be handled with integrity and professional judgment. All communication between the teacher, student, and parent is documented in the course management system. Unlike the traditional classroom where the student must move on with the rest of the class or physically attend their next class, in a virtual course, the student can call the teacher and work through the material until he or she is able to understand it (NCSD, 2010).

COURSEWORK

Students are expected to login to each course for active participation at least three times a week. All Nassau Virtual School courses have a pace chart. The pace chart outlines exactly what is expected to be submitted by the student on a weekly basis. Each student is required to submit a specific amount of coursework each week in order to maintain the appropriate pace. Teachers work with the student to modify the pace chart to reflect a traditional, extended or accelerated pace. Failure to maintain the required number of weekly submissions will result in warnings, grade penalties, and potential withdrawal from

the course. If a student will not be participating in a course due to travel or other commitment, the student must be on pace and notify the teacher in advance of the planned absence in order to discuss assignment completions and pacing (NCSD, 2010).

GRACE PERIOD

The grace period provides the student with an opportunity to "try out" the course while allowing the teacher to evaluate the student's performance. A student may drop a course without academic penalty by notifying the teacher before the 28th day in the course. If a student is not "on pace" with the coursework during the grace period, the teacher will contact the student and parent. If the student remains "off pace" by the end of the grace period, the student will be administratively dropped from the course without academic penalty. After the 28th day of the grace period, the student will earn a grade for the course regardless if the grade is passing or failing. Students must maintain pace in order to stay enrolled in the course (NCSD, 2010).

ASSESSMENTS

The teacher regularly conducts discussion-based assessments at certain points within the course with each student via telephone. During these assessments, the teacher discusses the student's coursework and the course content in order for the student to demonstrate mastery of the content while also verifying the authenticity of his or her work. Each student is required to take a final exam in all Nassau Virtual School courses. The final exam helps the teacher validate the student has demonstrated mastery of key course concepts and standards. The student is expected to take the exam as directed by the teacher. With the intention of maintaining the integrity of all Nassau Virtual School courses and grades, the teacher may choose to facilitate or require an oral or a face-to-face assessment at any point in the course (NCSD, 2010).

ACADEMIC INTEGRITY

In order to participate in Nassau Virtual School courses, the student must agree to the FLVS academic integrity policy. Academic integrity means:

- Your work on each assignment will be completely your own.
- Your collaboration with another classmate on any assignment will be preapproved by your teacher.
- You will not practice plagiarism in any form.
- You will not allow others to copy your work.
- You will not misuse content from the Internet.
- You will not give any assistance to students scheduled to take the course in the future.
- Your parent or guardian will attest that you completed the work on your own (NCSD, 2010).

TEACHER RESPONSIBILITIES

As outlined in the Nassau Virtual School teacher's job description, teachers are expected to (NCSD, 2010):

- instruct assigned classes based on the curriculum established by Nassau Virtual School/Florida Virtual School;
- identify, select, create, and accommodate the needs of students with varying backgrounds, learning styles, and special needs;
- assist students in accomplishing course/program objectives;
- establish an environment that is conducive to learning and active participation in learning activities;

- establish relationships with students and parents through e-mail and monthly phone conferences;
- monitor student progress and encourage students to maintain pace established by the virtual school pace charts;
- participate in professional development and faculty meetings;
- utilize all required and recommended Nassau Virtual School computer applications.;
- maintain accurate and complete records in accordance with laws, rules, policies, and administrative regulations;
- regularly check the usage logs to verify that students are active in the course;
- provide timely feedback to students on their assignments and assessment tasks; and
- follow the policies stated in the memorandum of agreement as required by the Florida Virtual School Franchise Agreement.

In order to ensure each teacher effectively performs his or her assigned teaching responsibilities, virtual classroom walkthroughs are conducted based on a model from Broward Virtual School. During the observations, the teacher and program manager simultaneously view various portions of the course management system and discuss instructional practice, student progress, and student-teacher communication to make certain quality teaching and learning are taking place within the virtual classroom.

PARENTAL INVOLVEMENT

While the student is responsible for all of his or her own coursework, parental involvement is critical component to the student's success in online learning. A parent or guardian should consider the following questions in order to determine whether online learning is a viable solution for the parent or guardian and child. As a parent, are you willing to:

- Know and use your child's username and password to access their grade book, announcements, assignment feedback, etc?
- Make sure assignments, tests, and quizzes have been completed?
- Check weekly to see submitted assignments and grades?
- Help your child determine and stick to a schedule?
- Encourage your child to ask questions, call the teacher, or e-mail the teacher when he or she needs help?
- Provide the teacher with your e-mail address to receive monthly progress reports?
- Discuss problem areas with your child and communicate with the teacher and guidance counselor as often as needed?
- Make yourself available to discuss your child's progress with the teacher?
- Provide a quiet study space for your child with access to the Internet, telephone, and printer?
- Contact technical support as needed? [Questions adapted from Marion Virtual School's Making Virtual Learning Work —Tips for Parents (Marion County Public Schools, 2009)].

Nassau Virtual School offers students and parents a choice regarding their educational options. Together they must decide whether the student should attend a traditional brick and mortar school or opt to participate in a flexible educational model. Students take online courses for a variety of reasons, such as the opportunity to learn at their own pace, the ability to work and go to school, rigorous training schedule, or to makeup credits from academic setbacks. The Nassau Virtual School bridges a gap for those students whose needs are not being met in the traditional classroom. Since the legislative mandates regarding online learning are still new, Nassau Virtual School has the chance to be a part of the development process for K-12 online learning in the state of Florida. As Nassau County School District strives to implement online learning in the K-12 environment, Nassau Virtual School will continuously evolve and work with other districts to meet the diverse needs of Nassau County students as well as the requirements of the legislation and Florida Department of Education.

REFERENCES

Burgess-Watkins, K. (2009). *Credit recovery overview.* Fernandina Beach, FL: Nassau County School District.

Christensen, C. M., & Horn, M. B. (2008). How do we transform our schools? *Education Next, 8*(3), 13-19.

Connections Academy. (2011). *Florida Virtual School Full Time.* Retrieved from http://www.connectionsacademy.com/florida-school/free-online-public-school.aspx

Florida Virtual School. (2009). *Tips for students signing up for FLVS online classes.* Retrieved from http://www.flvs.net/Students/Pages/TipsforStudents.aspx

Florida Virtual School Full Time. (n.d.). *Florida Virtual School Full Time.* Retrieved from http://www.flvsft.com

Marion County Public Schools. (2009). *Tips for parents.* Retrieved from http://www.marion.k12.fl.us/schools/mvs/parents.cfm

Nassau County School District. (2010). *Nassau Virtual School Policy Manual.* Retrieved from http://www.nassau.k12.fl.us

Rodeffer, J. (2007). *Evaluation of NEFEC dropout prevention/credit recovery program.* Fernandina Beach, FL: Nassau County School District.

Rodeffer, J. (2008). *Evaluation of NEFEC dropout prevention/credit recovery program.* Fernandina Beach, FL: Nassau County School District.

Responding to Change

Online Education
at the College of Central Florida

Connie J. Tice

HISTORICAL PERSPECTIVE

In the mid 1950s when a group of community leaders and citizens began to envision a way to provide educational opportunities to three counties in Florida they had no idea what would happen in the decades to follow. In 1957 Central Florida Junior College was established to provide educational opportunities beyond high school to Marion, Citrus, and Levy counties. The following year Hampton Junior College opened and was one of the first Black 2-year colleges in the state. In 1966 the two colleges merged and in 1971

Connie J. Tice,
Senior Professor of Speech Communication,
College of Central Florida, 3800 S. Lecanto
Highway, Lecanto, FL 3446-9026.
Telephone: (352) 746-6721, ext. 6139.
E-mail: ticec@cf.edu

their name was changed to Central Florida Community College (CFCC). At this point in the history of the college all students attended classes on what is now known as the Ocala Campus; located in Ocala, Florida. Communication between students and the college was mostly accomplished via mail or students coming to the campus.

The college offered courses in Citrus County on a limited basis until 1984. To meet the continuing demands of the community for educational opportunities the Citrus County School Board partnered with the college and an educational complex was established in 1984, high school facilities were provided to accommodate the college classes. In 1996 a free-standing campus was opened—now called the Citrus Campus—and in 2009 a new building was opened to accommodate more classrooms and a new Learning and Conference Center.

To meet the growing needs in the Levy County area the Bronson Center was opened in 1987. In 1993 the Levy Center moved to a storefront in Chiefland, Florida where it is currently housed. In 2008 the college was able to procure a site for a permanent center in Levy County and when funds are available construction will begin (College of Central Florida, 2011).

In the fall of 2010 CFCC underwent another name change to the College of Central Florida (CCF). The name change came about because beginning in the spring of 2011 CCF began offering the community the opportunity to earn a bachelor of applied science in business and organizational management; in August 2011 a bachelor of science degree in early childhood education was also added to the curriculum.

RESPONDING TO CHANGE

According to Allen and Seaman (2008), "Over 3.9 million students were taking at least one online course during the fall 2007 term; a 12% increase over the number reported the previous year" (p. 1). Community colleges reported an increase of 11.3% in distance learning enrollment during this period; this increase accounted for the majority of the overall growth (Instructional Technology Council, 2008). As a result of this growth in distance learning on the community college campus, the institution has to look to new ways to engage both faculty and students in the learning process.

Community colleges and their faculty have been known for their ability to respond to both change and the needs of their students and the community; CCF is no exception. With the advent of the Internet and the introduction of personal technology that was more affordable the community college student began to expect and demand a different approach to education. To respond to this demand CCF not only brought more computer access in to the classroom they also developed courses that could be taught online.

EVOLUTION OF A PROGRAM

In the fall of 1997 a group of instructors, who Rogers (2003) would most likely label innovators, developed and taught the first 13 online courses for CCF. The instructors were self-taught in regard to course development for online learning and their e-learning platform was WebCT 4.1. As a response to the growing demand for online education the E-Learning Department was established in 2004; this depart-ment now provides training for faculty and technical support to both faculty and students (J. Strigle, personal communication, November 16, 2010). According to CCF's *E-Learning Handbook* (2010-2011) e-learning at the college "involves any formal delivery method in which the majority of instruction takes place via the internet or other electronic means, such as video-conferencing, pod casting, educational software, etc." (p. 11).

The target population of the e-learning courses is primarily students who live within the tricounty area; Marion, Citrus, and Levy counties. Even though these students may not be geographically distant, e-learning courses may make the difference between completing a degree and dropping out of college. Geographically distant students are also accommodated and since the fall of 2002 CCF has been able to offer an Associate of Arts degree totally online.

The E-Learning Department continues to provide technical support; however, it has taken on the additional responsibilities of faculty training and the development of specific protocols for course development. To assist in the development of courses and training, a committee comprised of faculty from multiple disciplines serves as an advisory body for e-learning. In the early development of online courses, a faculty member presented the idea to the college curriculum committee and then the course was taught. It was not until 2010 that the *E-Learning Handbook* was published with definitions of online, hybrid, telecourses, and ITV courses and a protocol concerning the development of new courses (J. Strigle, personal communication, November 16, 2010).

The protocol involves: (a) decisions regarding the need for online courses are made within each department based on both departmental and college goals; (b) the faculty member completes an application, the deadline is one month after the start of each term; (c) the application is signed by the department chair and then submitted to the dean of learning resources; (d) the dean forwards the application electronically to the e-learning advisory board for discussion and approval; (e) when the faculty member is notified of approval he or she will sign up for a series of workshops that assist in the development of the course. This training involves technical training on the ANGEL LMS as needed, instructional design training, criteria for effective online courses, assistance with converting traditional class materials and activities into online format, utilization of learning object repositories, and software designed for the development of online courses (*E-Learning Handbook*, 2010-2011).

As the program grew it was necessary to define the differences between the different online learning courses. Online courses are defined as those courses distributed through the Internet, allowing flexibility in time and/or place (*E-Learning Handbook*, 2010-2011). Hybrid courses are defined as a combination of online and traditional face-to-face courses (*E-Learning Handbook*, 2010-2011). Telecourses are defined as those courses offered in videotape/DVD formats and these are checked out from the CCF library (*E-Learning Handbook*, 2010-2011). ITV courses are defined as interactive television courses allowing distribution of live classes through video conferencing equipment (*E-Learning Handbook*, 2010-2011). The growth of the E-Learning Department, in regard to the number of sections taught for both online and hybrid courses, is reflected in Table 1.

The types of courses being offered either online or using the hybrid format include: English, Spanish, algebra, calculus, statistics, speech, art history, several psychology courses, criminal justice, micro- and macroeconomics, wellness, environmental sciences, chemistry, and world civilization. It is anticipated that several courses using the hybrid format will be used for the two new bachelor degree programs (J. Strigle, personal communication, November 16, 2010).

In the 1950s, having a computer in a classroom or office was not considered. Standard procedure was for the professor to stand in front of a class, size determined by the number of desks, location determined by where the physical college was located, write instructions on a blackboard, and sometimes provide paper handouts. Now, a professor can sit at his or her desk, communicate with any number of students located in many different geographical areas, use virtual tours, and use creative

Table 1.   E-learning Enrollment

Academic Year	Number of Online Sections	Online Enrollment	Number of Hybrid Sections	Hybrid Enrollment
1998-1999	54	712	0	0
1999-2000	71	1,065	0	0
2000-2001	65	1,094	0	0
2001-2002	78	1,373	0	0
2002-2003	82	1,724	0	0
2003-2004	103	2,460	3	54
2004-2005	135	3,120	10	213
2005-2006	173	3,812	20	251
2006-2007	206	4,451	32	509
2007-2008	240	5,288	54	841
2008-2009	299	6,886	83	1,509

programs to act as a catalyst for learning. Intermediate algebra and statistics is now being taught online using a program produced by Pearson called Course Compass; face-to-face students also use this program to practice math skills and ask questions of their professors via email.

FUTURE GOALS

The E-Learning Department has developed several goals in anticipation of an even higher demand for online education at the community college level. The E-Learning Department and the advisory committee have defined a number of goals for the next 5 years. Goals that impact the student are: increasing reliable and accessible technology support and developing courses that meet graduation requirements. Goals for faculty include: increasing reliable and accessible technology support and providing more training in regard to the development of, online, hybrid, and ITV courses. Beyond the environment of CCF the goals are to increase collaboration with other institutions, initiatives, and consortia involved with e-learning (J. Strigle, personal communication, November 16, 2010).

THE FUTURE

What will happen beyond the Internet and what is currently happening in online and face-to-face courses? According to the Horizon Report, 2009, we can expect an increase in the use of mobiles in the academic environment, the addition of cloud computing, geo-everything, the personal web, semantic-aware applications, and smart objects. This same report suggested that students are different, there is a need for both innovation and leadership in academia, institutions are pressured to prove students are learning, and higher education is expected to utilize technology.

REFERENCES

Allen, E., & Seaman, J. (2008). *Staying the course: Online education in the United States 2008.* Retrieved from http://www.sloan-c.org/publications/survey/pdf/staying_the_course.pdf

Central Florida Community College. (2010-2011). *E-learning handbook.* Retrieved from http://www.cf.edu/distance/ELhandbook.htm

College of Central Florida. (2011). Academic catalog. Retrieved from http://www.cf.edu/smartcatalog/history.htm

Instructional Technology. (2008). *Instructional technology council 2008 distance education Survey results tracking the impact of e-learning at community colleges.* Retrieved from http://www.itcnetwork.org/file.php?=2FITCAnnualSurveyMarch2009Final.pdf

Johnson, L., Levine, A., & Smith R. (2009). *The 2009 horizon report.* Austin TX: The New Media Consortium.

Rogers, E. (2003). *Diffusion of innovations* (5th ed.). New York, NY: Free Press.

COMMUNITY COLLEGES AND THEIR FACULTY HAVE BEEN KNOWN FOR THEIR ABILITY TO RESPOND TO BOTH CHANGE AND THE NEEDS OF THEIR STUDENTS AND COMMUNITY.

An Overview of the U.S. Navy Sustaining Distance Training

Derek Takara and Zane L. Berge

The U.S. Navy has been conducting a major reorganization using plans and strategies collectively called Sea Power 21 (Clark, 2002) that are heavily dependant on a high-technology environment. Admiral Vern Clark recently completed his assignment as the chief of naval operations (CNO), the Navy's top military leadership position. He was the first CNO to have an MBA degree (Clark, 2004a) and his business process knowledge, along with the transformational initiatives of the Secretary of Defense, set in motion revolu-tionary efforts that are transforming or replacing traditional Navy systems, using successful business philosophies and methodologies.

Driven by top leadership, the development of personnel capabilities is recognized as crucial for "mission accomplishment," and so individual training in the U.S. Navy has significantly increased in importance and become a significant consideration in the planning, development, and operation of the "workplace." E-learning, along with related concepts of

Derek A. Takara is a career U.S. Navy officer, specializing in logistics. He is enrolled in a Master of Distance Education program at the University of Maryland.

Zane L. Berge, Associate Professor, Instructional Systems Development Graduate Program at the University of Maryland Baltimore County, 1000 Hilltop Circle, Baltimore, MD 21250. E-mail: berge@umbc.edu

knowledge management and distance training, has been wholly embraced by senior leadership and is becoming an integral part of the workspace, along with technological capability, at a phenomenal pace.

COMMUNICATING THE VISION

The U.S. Navy has over 350,000 active duty personnel and 130,000 Ready Reserve. There are regularly over 30,000 personnel deployed (away from their home base or station) at any given time. The Navy also has over 175,000 civilian employees. All of these personnel are an essential part of the Navy's mission, and accomplish their tasks from over 280 ships and a great many bases and stations throughout the continental United States and numerous foreign countries, (U.S. Navy, *Status of the Navy*, n.d.). Communication and coordination can appear to be a phenomenal feat, but it is achieved regularly and more and more effectively as capabilities, processes and procedures improve, following guidance promulgated from the top.

The Navy's long-term vision is encapsulated in Sea Power 21, the Navy's transformational strategy used to develop operational and organizational processes, policies, and related strategies. It is "global in scope, fully joint in execution, and dedicated to transformation" (Clark, 2002). It communicates the vision on how the Navy will "organize, integrate, and transform," and consists of three fundamental concepts that will ensure the Navy continues as the supreme military seapower force in the future: Sea Strike, Sea Shield, and Sea Basing. Sea Strike enables projection of offensive power from the sea, Sea Shield extends defensive assurance throughout the world, and *Sea Basing* enhances operational independence and support for the joint force. Sea Power 21 also provides the critical concept of FORCEnet, which will enable information management (through technological capability) among the three

fundamental concepts, and empower all Navy personnel.

FROM THE TOP

Given the size and geographical dispersion of the Navy, a distance learning program capability is critical, and recognized in top leadership guidance. Each year, the chief of naval operations publishes an annual document, titled *CNO Guidance for [year]* which provides an overview on the Navy vision and mission, and assigns critical tasks or milestones to specific organization elements. This year's multipage guidance includes: Develop a postgraduate education strategy centered around the Naval Postgraduate School's resident *and distance learning programs* (italics added) that fully leverages Joint service, inter-agency, and international curricula (Mullen, 2005).

But that is just a small part of the initiative to match skills (and education, and provide training and "just in time" information) to the position. The CNO's 8 Tenets (*What I believe: Eight Tenets That Guide My Vision for the 21st Century Navy*) are further guidance intended for use by Navy leadership. Admiral Mullen (2006), current CNO, stated

> New opportunities and security challenges require new skills.... They must also be supported by the right information at the right time.... In a world of growing global connectivity, the volume of information we are able to collect matters less than our ability to identify and understand what is important. Sailors must learn to recognize what matters, to comprehend the implications of the information they gather, and then act on it instantly, with the right capabilities.

This broader concept on personnel skills is supported through a number of initiatives, including FORCEnet (for the technological capability) and what has been termed the Human Capital Strategy or "Strategy for our People" (Clark, 2004b).

STRATEGIC SCOPE

The Navy's Strategy for our People has several stated objectives, which may be paraphrased as:

- Develop a competency-focused workforce to link individual knowledge and abilities to demands.
- Align organizations, strategies, policies, and processes to effectively manage the total workforce.
- Attract, retain, and incentivize an optimal workforce (active, reserve, civilian). Set performance expectations against measurable organizational goals.
- Maximize the contribution of every individual. Create opportunities for growth and development while fostering work-life balance.
- Achieve greater diversity throughout the total force workforce.

The strategy, discussed by the Assistant Secretary of the Navy, Manpower and Reserve Affairs in 2004 (Navas, 2004) is to modernize manpower and personnel systems, integrate active and reserve military and civilian systems and coordinate separate manpower initiatives into a single strategically managed plan. It will provide the guidance and tools to assess, train, distribute, and develop the Navy's work force and will also provide use of temporary help (i.e., contractor), which can provide skill sets not available in the permanent work force. The strategy will also provide an expanded opportunity for professional and personal growth, while attempting to maximize technology development and implementation to reduce workload, with all efforts aimed at supporting current and future mission accomplishment.

INCLUDE THE INDIVIDUAL

A coordinating program called Sea Warrior connects the individual sailor with the parts of the organization responsible for training, education, and career-management systems. The primary interface is Navy Knowledge Online (NKO), a well developed Web-based resource that is available to all Navy personnel. It provides the ability to create Individual Development Plans, provides the opportunity to take many different e-learning courses (a combination of off-the-shelf and Navy-developed), and creates areas for "communities of practice" to share relevant information. It also provides links to certain personnel supporting services (such as admin and pay).

Approximately 4,000 e-learning courses are accessible by 1.2 million Navy, Marine, Department of the Navy (DoN) civilian employees, and dependents. Provided at no cost to the registered user, of which there were 450,000 as of November 2004, are courses in project management, business, desktop, simulation exercises, and foreign languages. In the active duty Navy, NKO creates the conduit between training and uninterrupted operational capability (Persons, 2004)

The Sea Warrior's organizational goal is to provide the Navy the capability to assess, train, and assign (all) personnel to ensure their best contribution to the mission. Sea Warrior's key objectives are summarized (U.S. Navy, 2006) as:

- Make career information and tools readily available to personnel for career-development.
- Combine the strengths of the current manpower, personnel, training, and education responsibilities into one aligned and centrally managed and resourced organization.
- Enable the Navy to create an agile market-like approach to career management, where sailors "compete" in a dynamic marketplace and provide the right skills to the right place.

DEDICATED INFRASTRUCTURE

Berge (2001) wrote: "Along with a strategic planning process, there are management processes such as budgeting, infrastructure development and maintenance, communication, workforce development, and policy making that are used to change the fabric of the organization in desired ways" (p. 22). To enable Sea Warrior, the Navy is undergoing an enormous organizational change to integrate its manpower, personnel, training, and education systems (referred to as MPT&E) into a single "enterprise" (meaning one funding resource) with coordinated "business" processes (Hoewing, 2005).

The Navy's MPT&E enterprise has several key supporting suborganizations. The Naval Education and Training Command (NETC) was established in mid-March 2003 in Pensacola, Florida, to oversee Naval education and training. This activity was created using relevant portions of existing organizations. It will provide strategy, policy, and resource guidance, and allow intermediate activities to manage the execution of relevant training. Most importantly, it reports directly to the CNO (top leadership), which demonstrates its relative importance to the whole organization. NETC activities are staffed by approximately 22,000 military and civilian personnel at more than 190 facilities worldwide. Each day, an average of nearly 40,000 officer, enlisted, and civilian government employees train in more than 3,600 different courses offered through NETC (Goodwin, 2003).

Another training command that has recognized and embraced e-learning as a means to train and enrich without sacrificing time and capability is the Naval Network Warfare Command (NETWARCOM). Their vision is to integrate warfighting and business operations—to fight and win in the information age. It will

  act as the Navy's central operational authority for space, information technol-

ogy requirements, network and information operations in support of Naval forces afloat and ashore; to operate a secure and interoperable Naval Network that will enable effects-based operations and innovation; to coordinate and assess the Navy operational requirements for and use of network/command and control/information technology/information operations and space; to serve as the operational forces' advocate in the development and fielding of information technology, information operations and space and to perform such other functions and tasks as may be directed by higher authority. (U.S. Navy, 2006)

In pursuing its objectives, NETWARCOM impacts the technological capability required for distant learning.

SUPPORTING SYSTEMS

The most critical implement for the availability and delivery of individual training is the Navy Marine Corps Intranet (NMCI), which is considered the largest corporate intranet in the world (U.S. Navy, DON CIO, 2006). It provides the Department of the Navy and all its (shore) personnel with a full range of network-based information services on a single, enterprisewide intranet. Eventually, the massive network will link more than 350,000 workstations and laptops for Navy and Marine Corps users in the United States and permanent sites in foreign countries. A summary from the limited access NMCI *Homeport* Web site (www.homeport.navy.mil [limited access]):

  NMCI applies the speed and might of world-class Internet technology to everything from performing routine administrative tasks to facilitating global communications and logistics during wartime. This program of unprecedented scale ensures the secure and reliable transmission of voice, video and data information worldwide, helping the Navy and Marine Corps meet the following critical objectives:

- Enhancing network security
- Ensuring interoperability across commands and with other services
- Facilitating knowledge-sharing around the globe
- Increasing productivity
- Improving systems reliability and quality of services
- Reducing the cost of voice, video and data services.

NMCI is a key component of FORCEnet, the DoN's strategy for implementing network-centric warfare, and it supports the DoD's goals for information technology superiority. In addition to moving the DoN to an e-business model, with common corporate applications and databases, NMCI supports new processes and technologies, such as knowledge management, distance learning and telemedicine to improve the quality of life for sailors, Marines and the DoN's civilian employees and support personnel.

SUPPORTING WORKFORCE

The technology, both hardware and software, and the personnel trained in the application of technology that are needed to achieve the Navy's information management (and personnel development, FORCEnet, and MNCI, etc.) requirements are coordinated through the office of the Department of the Navy's Chief Information Officer, or the "DON CIO" (U.S. Navy, DON CIO, 2006). The DON includes the office of the Secretary of the Navy, who is senior to the CNO. As the Navy advocate for IM/IT initiatives to the Department of Defense, the DON CIO has become one of the integral authorities for Navy requirements. From this office, the increased training opportunities through e-learning were conceived.

The DON CIO produces an annual publication that provides the DON's Information Management (IM) and Information Technology Strategic Plan, and provides the vision and addresses the change

needed to achieve it (U.S. Navy, DON CIO, 2006). Summarizing from the DON CIO Web site (U.S. Navy, DON CIO, n.d.), the DON CIO is devoted to IM/IT Workforce Competency Management (competencies are defined as knowledge, skills, abilities, and behaviors). Using an enterprise approach to managing the IM/IT workforce, it provides a strategy for leveraging human (IM/IT) capital by considering four key issues:

- recruit, retain, and train the IM/IT/KM workforce needed to fulfill core capabilities,
- establish IM/IT/KM competency guidelines for the non-IM/IT/KM workforce,
- develop IM cognitive skills through integrative competencies, and
- *ensure the IT infrastructure will support eLearning* (italics added), document best practices, and expand the use of eLearning technologies.

The DON CIO has created several teams to work focus areas. It is the sole responsibility of one of these teams, the Knowledge Management Team, to author, monitor, and safeguard DoN policy on portals, content management, information management, and related areas (U.S. Navy, DON CIO, n.d., Knowledge Management). Additional portal development undertakings are also the purview of the team: Task Force Web, an early initiative designed to Web-enable all essential Navy applications and databases; Navy Knowledge Online; and the Navy Marine Corps portal, which forms the basis of the Navy, have been established to encourage collaboration and knowledge sharing within the DoN and with other agencies and activities. Supported and promoted at the topmost levels of the Navy and Defense departments, the growth and expansion of these undertakings are integral to increased distance learning capabilities within the Navy.

SUPPORTING CULTURE: LOCAL IM FLEXIBILITY

The strategy and policy provided by the DON CIO and CNO are also used by other Navy suborganizations to create IM capabilities tailored for their mission needs, adding only those resources required (or allowed).

For example: the Navy Supply Systems Command (NSSC) with headquarters in Mechanicsburg, PA

> is responsible to provide U.S. Naval forces with quality supplies and services. Employing a worldwide workforce of more than 24,000 military and civilian personnel, NAVSUP oversees logistics programs in the areas of supply operations, conventional ordnance, contracting, resale, fuel, transportation and security assistance. In addition, NAVSUP is responsible for quality of life issues for our naval forces, including food service, postal services, Navy Exchanges and movement of household goods. (Source: http://www.navsup.navy.mil/portal/page?_pageid=477,261535&_dad=p5star&_schema=P5STAR)

NSSC has a Command Information Office, which is an intermediary with the DON CIO that interprets policy for NSSC senior leadership and provides their input to DON initiatives. It develops, coordinates, and disseminates a shared strategic vision among the NSSC's top-level management and information activities to champion the organization's information initiatives to effectively manage information and provide for information systems that add value to the organization. It also provides technical advice to ensure information technology is acquired and information resources are managed in a manner that best supports the organization and meets any associated legislative requirements, such as specific information reporting requirements (Source: http://www.navsup.navy.mil/portal/

page?_pageid=477,267309,477_267592&_dad=p5star&_schema=P5STAR).

Using the technology and IT professionals trained by the DON's IM/IT initiatives, NSSC has created its own intranet for local information and training relevant to its business needs, and has provided what it calls the *NAVSUP Collaboration* site which allows NSSC employees the ability to easily communicate and share information in a secure, Web-based environment. "It can be accessed by any device—desktop, laptop, or PDA—that uses an HTML-based browser. Users can host online discussions, share and revise documents and files online, conduct virtual meetings, and so forth. NAVSUP Collaboration facilitates business processes such as: Knowledge Management, Project Management Communities of Practice, and elearning" (source). This technology and foresight goes well beyond the once-worshipped, yet still essential video teleconference for transmitting information and training.

CONCLUSION: IMPORTANCE OF STRATEGIC POLICY

After reviewing numerous e-learning related case studies, Berge (2001) noted that cases focused on using sustained distance training to achieve organizational goals concentrated on workforce development, infrastructure, and budget as success tools, but they appeared to neglect the aspect of company policy.

> One key to the success of initiatives in the integration and implementation [of] technology-enhanced learning and distance education is the support of the organization's top leaders.... The most important function of organizational leadership may be to create a shared vision that includes widespread input and support ... articulates a clear training or educational purpose, had validity for all stakeholders, and reflects the broader mission of the organization. Both top-down and bottom-up support is needed for success-

ful, sustained distance training and education at the higher stages of organizational capability. In addition to the establishment of a vision, leaders link strategic planning and specific program implementation and monitoring using such tools as budgeting, infrastructure development, communication, workforce development, and policy revision. (p. 351)

Navy leadership is clearly achieving those activities on a recurring basis. The Navy's ability to manage information, including the NSSC intranet capability and others like it, is made possible and successful through top-down support and clear, well communicated strategies and effective policies that are enabled through coordinated resource requests. A necessity for a large, dispersed organization to share effectively and efficiently share a common capability.

The precepts that have guided the evolution of Navy e-learning are sound. The development of the Navy's distance learning program has been uphill, but remarkably, lessons learned have been lessons heeded. The most important strategic step into providing enterprise-wide e-learning via IM/IT has been the development of the Navy Marine Corps Intranet, which has allowed a single system to provide whatever had been made available to whoever needs it when it is needed. Without this advancement, each individual command throughout the system would have been on its own to plan and develop training models. Distance learning would clearly have taken a back seat and the subsequent successes would not exist.

A continuous effort is called for, to link project management, program management, change management and strategic planning (Berge & Smith, 2000). This has been undertaken within the Navy and the enterprise has continued to sustain change and restructuring, following guidance from top leadership, and is building e-learning capabilities into the fabric of the organization.

REFERENCES

Berge, Z. (2001). *Sustaining distance training.* San Francisco: Jossey-Bass.

Berge, Z. L., & Smith, D. (2000). Implementing corporate distance training using change management, strategic planning, and project management. In L. Lau (Ed.), *Distance learning technologies: Issues, trends and opportunities* (pp. 39-51). Hershey, PA: Idea Group.

Clark, V. (2002, October). *Sea Power 21 series— Part I, Projecting decisive joint capabilities.* Retrieved September 19, 2006, from http://www.usni.org/Proceedings/Articles02/proCNO10.htm

Clark, V. (2004a). *Edited remarks by ADM Vern Clark to defense writers group.* Retrieved September 19, 2006, from http://www.chinfo.navy.mil/navpalib/cno/speeches/clark-dwg040302.txt

Clark, V. (2004b). *CNO to NNOA: 21st century human capitall system needed now.* Retrieved September 19, 2006, from http://www.navy.mil/search/display.asp?story_id=14714

Goodwin, D. (2003, April 8). *NETC up and running; CNET disestablished.* Retrieved September 19, 2006, from http://www.news.navy.mil/search/display.asp?story_id=6635

Hoewing, G. L. (2005, April 5). *Statement of Vice Admiral Gerald L. Hoewing, U.S. Navy chief of naval personnel and deputy chief of naval operations (manpower & personnel) before the Military Personnel Subcommittee of the Senate Armed Services Committee on FY06 defense personnel programs.* Retrieved September 19, 2006, from http://www.chinfo.navy.mil/navpalib/testimony/personnel/hoewing050405.pdf

Mullen, M. G. (2005, October). *CNO guidance for 2006, Meeting the challenge of a new era.* Retrieved September 19, 2006, from http://www.navy.mil/features/2006CNOG.pdf

Mullen, M. G. (2006, January. *What I believe: Eight tenets that guide my vision for the 21st century Navy.* Retrieved September 19, 2006, from http://72.14.209.104/search?q=cache:oNUeKUOCy4cJ:www.navy.mil/palib/cno/proceedingsjan06.html+mullen+%22What+I+believe:+Eight+tenets+that+guide+my+vision+for+the+21st+

century+Navy%22&hl=en&gl=us&ct= clnk&cd=1

Navas, W. (2004, March 2). *Statement of the Honorable William A. Navas, Jr., assistant secretary of the Navy (manpower and reserve affairs) before the personnel subcommittee of the Senate Armed Services Committee on active/reserve military & civilian personnel programs March 2, 2004.* Retrieved September 19, 2006, from http:// www.navy.mil/navydata/testimony/ personnel/navas040302.txt

Persons, D. (2004, November 6). *Navy elearning migrates to Navy knowledge online.* Retrieved September 19, 2006, from http://www.navy .mil/search/display.asp?story_id=15816

U.S. Navy. (n.d.). *Status of the Navy.* Retrieved July 28, 2006, from http://www.navy.mil

U.S. Navy. (2006). *The Navy strategic communication guide playbook 2006.* Retrieved September 19, 2006, from http://www.cnrc.navy.mil/ PAO/Playbook2006.pdf#search=%22The% 20Navy%20strategic%20communication%20 guide%20Navy%20playbook%22

U.S. Navy, DON CIO. (n.d.). *IM/IT workforce management.* Retrieved from http://www .doncio.navy.mil/ (2a31nf55m0i3sp45y0ahf2yx)/ FolderDetail.aspx?ID=85&Rank=1

U.S. Navey, DON CIO. (n.d.). Knowledge management. Retrieved from http://www .doncio.navy.mil/ (thslhob333hkfuv5i2p0gonc)/ FolderDetail.aspx?ID=89

U.S. Navy, DON CIO. (2006), *Department of the Navy Information Management and Information Technology Strategic Plan 2006.* Retrieved September 19, 2006, from http://www .doncio.navy.mil/FY06StratPlan/DON_IM_ and_IT_Strat_Plan_FY06.pdf

Broward Community College's e-Learning Strategic Plan

Donna L. Merolle

A good plan is like a road map; it shows the final destination and usually the best way to get there.

—H. Stanley Judd

INTRODUCTION

Establishing an organization's direction will help in selecting the right road and assist the organization in increasing its growth and effectiveness. Periodic evaluations by institutional leaders are required to determine if the needs and expectations of its members and constituents are being met. According to Wilbur, Kudla Finn, and Freeland (1994),

Donna L. Merolle, Associate Professor, Broward Community College, and Director of Education, Memorial Hospital West, 703 N. Flamingo Road, Pembroke Pines, FL 33028. Telephone: (954) 844-7501.

"There should be a well-defined and understood strategic plan which the organization's staff, as well as its board or governing body, uses to guide program activities, allocate resources, and assess the organization's achievements (p. 1).

Strategic planning is not a laundry list of changes and programs that contributors desire. Instead, it is a realistic look at the changes that are taking place, both inside and outside the organization that are and will influence the ability of the institution to carry out its mission. A strategic plan does not provide the who, what, and when; these are the function of an operational plan. Instead, it broadly maps out the strategies the organization should pursue to maintain its desired character and identity within a prescribed timeframe (Wilbur et al., 1994, p. 2).

EDUCATION MASTER PLAN— BROWARD COMMUNITY COLLEGE

Broward Community College (BCC) has three main campuses and six educational centers. Each campus, in addition to offering a comprehensive curriculum of university transfer programs, offers career and technical programs that prepare students for careers in health science, aviation, automotive, and public safety, to name a few.

In August 2004, Broward Community College contracted with the Voorhees Group LLC to assist in the development of an educational master plan (EMP). The purpose of the plan was to address BCC's ability to respond to the projected growth in Broward County and to make strategic choices about the future of the college. The process used by the Voorhees group to establish the EMP consisted of 11 county-wide strategy sessions as well as interviews with college administrators, faculty leadership, and students. In addition, business leaders, economic development specialist, and personal from the public school system along with administrators from universities located in close proximity to BCC were interviewed. The final plan consists of 26 strategies to meet nine major goals.

The EMP called for the institution to "reach out in new ways to new and existing students thorough a range of new activities (Voorhees Group, 2006b, p. 3). Specifically, goal seven called for the re-examination of format and delivery options for all courses. Recognition of e-learning's strategic importance by BCC leadership cumulated in a task force composed of 25 faculty, staff, and administrators that went on to develop a blueprint to guide the growth and impact of e-learning at Broward Community College. The EMP elevated e-learning as a means of addressing some of the challenges BCC is facing and as a result a 3-year e-learning plan was developed that defined the scope, goals, and outcomes for e-learning along with strategies and initiatives for implementation.

E-LEARNING AT BCC

BCC has a track record of successful e-learning initiative over the past seven years. Driven by operational strategies such as "developing the 21st century professor," enrollments in fully online, blended e-learning and WebCT based course sections exceeded 47,000 in 2008. In the 2008-09 academic year, students will be able to earn an AA degree in the several programs as well as a number of AAS and AS degrees totally online.

According to Russ Adkins, associate vice president of instructional technology at Broward Community College, "What began as a faculty development initiative in the late 90s is now a strategic initiative impacting all campuses, nearly 50% of the full-time faculty, and thousands of students" (personal communication, December 13, 2006). Roundtable discussions produced the following working objectives:

- to increase strategic awareness of current flexible learning alternatives at BCC as well as how flexible learning growth is accelerating nationally and globally;
- to demonstrate how flexible learning can provide new choices for BCC especially as a tool to manage enrollment growth and classroom capacity.
- to provide twenty-first century learning options that provide flexibility for "digital natives" (students) who find commuting, employment, and family responsibilities inhibit their access to BCC;
- to use the education master plan as a tool to engage BCC's administrative leadership and faculty in planning to position flexible learning as a key strategy for student access to course and degrees;
- to create a 3-year plan to strategically increase the use of flexible learning at BCC, and secure the internal resources through BCC's budgeting cycle to effectively operate BCC's plan;
- to evaluate contemporary content, course development, and delivery models that support increasing the scale of BCC's e-learning activities while ensuring quality learning;
- to prepare BCC for a Southern Association of Colleges and Schools substantive change review of its e-learning initiatives (Voorhees Group, 2006a).

IMPETUS FOR CHANGE

Since more than 95% of courses offered at BCC are delivered face-to-face in a traditional classroom setting, what are the forces behind the increasing commitment to distance education? Several factors have been identified that address this question.

According to Oblinger, Barone, and Hawkins (2001), the force driving e-learning initiatives at most institutions falls into one of four categories. They either wish to expand access, generate new revenue, serve as a catalyst for institutional transformation or alleviate capacity constraints. Capacity constraint is one of the issues at BCC. The infrastructure cannot accommodate the growing college-aged population and enrollments, making more distance education programs necessary. It is hoped that by leveraging scalability of e-learning, existing place-bound capacity constraints can be avoided.

The timing for BCC to plan for expansion of e-learning is especially good, as e-learning throughout the United States is experiencing rapid growth. According to the Sloan Consortium (2006) "Nearly 3.2 million students were taking at least one online course during the fall 2005 term, a substantial increase over the 2.3 million reported the previous year" (p. 1). Institutional transformation is also a motivating factor. Planning for e-learning can provide a powerful catalyst for transforming a wide range of current practices at BCC as it seeks ways to best to serve current and emerging learners.

A second reason for institutional support of e-learning is that students are shopping for courses that meet their schedules and circumstances. Adult learners need flexibility, choice, and convenience. Adult focus groups conducted at BCC in 2004 found that participants agreed that flexible class schedules and learning options were major motivators in persuading them to select a school. Many stated they would be drawn to a college that understood the need to maintain full-time jobs and responsibilities associated with families. Online courses were consistently mentioned as a desired alternative or supplement to traditional course hours. Learners, including adults who commute to work in ever more congested conditions, are increasingly cautious about how they allocate their time. Development of alternative formats (compressed, 5-week, 8-week, Saturday) for courses as well as accelerated alternative online delivery strategies (Internet, hybrid, technology-enabled) will help BCC meet learner needs (Broward Community College, 2006). This was affirmed by older students who view online as a reasonable alternative to battling traffic to attend traditional classes.

Technology expectations are another driving force behind BCC's commitment to e-learning. Students are increasingly savvy when it comes to technology. Today's teenagers are unlike any previous generation in their exposure to multimedia and the Web. A recent survey by Lenhart, Madden, and Hitline (2005) found that 87%, or 21 million, teens use the Internet; 51% go online on a daily basis; 81% play games online; 76% get news online; 43% have made purchases online; 45% have cell phones, and 33% are texting; 75% use instant messaging to communicate but also share links, photos, music and video; 51% report broadband access.

Millennial students (born between 1982 and 2002) consider technology a natural part of their environment and want to learn collaboratively, online, in their time, and working on solving problems that matter (Apple Computer, 2003). The simultaneous use of multimedia (i.e., instant messaging while playing a computer game) adds up to 8½ hours of recreational media exposure daily (Kaiser Family Foundation, 2005). These traditional age students (18 to 24) are making up a large and growing segment of community college enrollments. As of 2001, students under the age of 22 constitute 42% of all credit-seeking students at community colleges (Adelman, 2005). In general, students expect faculty to incorporate technology into their teaching and be proficient at it. At the very least, communication via e-mail, access to online resources, PowerPoint presentations, Internet activities, discussion boards, and electronic classrooms are expected.

According to the Sloan Consortium (2005), online education has become part of the mainstream of American higher education. They report that the majority of academic leaders feel that online education "is critical to the long-term strategy" of their institutions (p. 7). BCC believes the development of e-learning programs and degrees is a service to their students and a marketing/positioning strategy for the college. The goal is to ensure that students in BCC's service area can find the courses, programs, and degrees they need, in the delivery format most suitable for them, without having to look elsewhere.

BCC is, however, seeing competition not only from public community college in Florida, but also private institutions who offer online associate of arts degrees. Almost 5 million of the 20 million student enrolled in degree-granting institutions attend for-profit colleges (National Center for Education Statistics, 2005). Abolishment of the 1992 federal 50% rule which in the past had prevented any college that enrolls more than 50% of its students at a distance or provides more than half of its courses via distance education from participating in federal student-aid programs, will spur on a new wave of for-profit schools offering online education (Carnevale, n.d.). Public institutions are also a big part of the growth of e-learning. In Florida, 13 of the 28 community colleges offer complete online degrees (Florida Distance Learning Consortium, n.d.).

STRATEGIC E-LEARNING PLAN

The E-learning Task force adopted seven strategies to expand e-learning options at Broward Community College.

- Strategy 1: Select programs/certificates/degrees for priority e-learning development and delivery.
- Strategy 2: Improve and accelerate the course redesign/e-learning course development process.
- Strategy 3: Develop master e-learning courses that can be readily adopted for delivery by full- and part-time faculty, collegewide.
- Strategy 4: Seek approval from the Southern Association of Colleges and Schools to offer online degrees. Satisfy all qualitative criteria associated with this "substantive change."
- Strategy 5: Align collegewide procedures, policies, and collective bargaining agreements procedures with e-learning initiatives.
- Strategy 6: Develop internal and external awareness of e-learning's role at BCC.
- Strategy 7: Ensure that e-learning delivers return on investment and is sustainable (Voorhees Group, 2006b, p. 2).

A graphical representation (Figure 1) of the strategic plan denotes a linear process that progresses through a logical sequence of events. The first step is to identify those programs/certificates/degrees that should receive priority for e-learning development and delivery. These programs will be both new and those that are nearly complete but have gaps that can quickly and easily be completed. Alignment of these programs to the mission and goals of the college will need to occur on several levels. Approval from the Southern Association of College and Schools to offer online degrees is paramount to the success of online education at BCC. Preparation for a substantive change visit will require compliance with issues related to academic and student services, course quality, congruency with the college mission statement and student readiness and success. Collegewide policies/procedures, along with faculty collective bargaining, will also have to

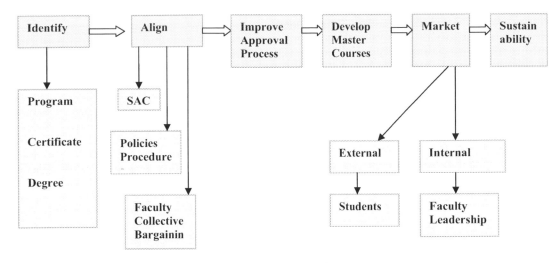

Figure 1.   Graphical representation of e-learning strategic plan.

be considered. Current contractual requirements related to work load, student contact, and office hours are not congruent with actual roles and responsibilities of online faculty. Resolution of these types of issues must be part of the strategic plan if e-learning is to move forward and diffusion of technology is to occur.

The third step will be to improve and accelerate the course development process. This will affect how courses are designed, developed, and updated. With the approval process smooth, timely, and efficient, the focus can shift to course design and development. Master course is a strategy for adding additional sections of an existing e-learning course. Full-time and part-time faculty can be utilized to teach courses they themselves have not developed. This allows flexibility and opportunities to meet scheduling needs that was not possible when a single faculty member was responsible for teaching a course.

The final two strategies are an integral part of the strategic plan. Marketing e-learning to various stakeholders at BCC is tied directly into the sustainability of the programs and department. Positioning e-learning among existing and potential students ensures that e-learning classes are full and student learning needs are being met. Consumer satisfaction goes a long way in retaining old and recruiting new students. Internal awareness by faculty and college leadership regarding the importance of e-learning is also important. The goal is to make e-learning a thread in the very fabric of BCC. Aligning strategic initiatives between the college and instructional technology is one way of doing this.

SUMMARY

There are many reasons why institutions of higher education do not develop strategic plans for e-learning. Broward Community College's work in this area is unique and will pave the way for ongoing planning, implementation, and evaluation of future e-learning initiatives. This plan will need to be modified on the short-term and definitely will undergo revision over the long-term. It does, however, provide a venue for recognizing the progress made by BCC while detailing the steps needed to continue that progress. The ultimate outcome for this plan is to increase e-learning opportunities for students. According to the Voorhees Group LLC (2006b), the accomplishment of this has been initiated by incorporating the following elements of strategy into the e-learning strategic plan:

- the foundation, direction, and outcomes for expanding flexible learning opportunities for students;
- quality assurance for e-learning, relying on assessment of learning and student feedback;
- the development and use of learning objects as an efficient vehicle for promoting quality and access to courses;
- data collection, analysis, and synthesis to guide future choice in e-learning;
- seeking wide support of the college community including periodic reporting on progress in providing flexible learning opportunities for students, whether by e-learning techniques or otherwise throughout the college's courses and programs;
- a collaborative model that ensure efficient scheduling of classes and other learning experiences for the benefit of current and future students;
- a stance that does not create dependencies on external vendors, rather a set of strategies that provides for BCC to control and refine its own curricular destiny;
- accountability for units and individuals to specific actions over specified time frames; and
- standards, criteria, and evaluation to ensure that accountability (p. 26).

REFERENCES

Adelman, C. (2005). *Moving into town—and moving on: The community college in the lives of traditional-age students*. Retrieved December 15, 2006, from http://www.ed.gov/rschstat/research/pubs/comcollege/index.html

Apple Computer. (2003). *Achievement for all children: An apple perspective*. Retrieved December 15, 2006, from http://images.apple.com/de/education/digitalkids/pdf/041503Achievement.pdf

Broward Community College. (2006). *Educational masterplan: E-learning*. Retrieved December 11, 2006, from http://www.broward.edu/confluence/pages/viewpage.action?pageId=1786

Carnevale, D. (n.d.). Rule change may spark online boom for colleges. *Chronicle of Higher Education*. Retrieved December 15, 2006, from http://chronicle.com/errors.dir/noauthorization.php3?page=/weekly/v52/i22/22a00101.htm

Florida Distance Learning Consortium. (n.d.). *Degree options*. Retrieved December 15, 2006, from http://www.distancelearn.org/degreeOptions.cfm

Kaiser Family Foundation. (2005). *Generation m: Media in the liver of 8-18 year olds*. Retrieved December 15, 2006, from http://www.kff.org/entmedia/7251.cfm

Lenhart, A., Madden, M., & Hitlin, P. (2005). *Teens and technology: Youth are leading the transition to a fully wired and mobile nation*. Retrieved December 14, 2006, from http://www.pewinternet.org/pdfs/PIP_Teens_Tech_July2005web.pdf

National Center for Education Statistics. (2005). *Digest of education statistics: 2005*. Retrieved December 15, 2006, from http://nces.ed.gov/programs/digest/d05/tables/dt05_001.asp

Oblinger, D., Barone, C., & Hawkins, B. (2001). *Distributed education and its challenges: An overview*. Retrieved December 15, 2006, from http://www.acenet.edu/bookstore/pdf/distributed-learning/distributed-learning-01.pdf

Sloan Consortium. (2005). *Growing by degrees: Online education in the United States, 2005*. Retrieved December 15, 2006, from http://www.sloan-c.org/publications/survey/pdf/growing_by_degrees.pdf

Sloan Consortium. (2006). *Making the grade: Online education in the United States, 2006*. Retrieved December 14, 2006, from http://www.sloan-c.org/publications/survey/index.asp

Wilbur, R. H., Kudla Finn, S., & Freeland, C. M. (Eds.). (1994). *The complete guide to nonprofit management*. New York: Smith, Bucklin & Associates and Wiley.

Voorhees Group. (2006a). *Planning for flexible learning alternatives: Broward Community College*. Littleton, CO: Author.

Voorhees Group. (2006b, September). *E-learning strategic plan: Broward Community College*. Littleton, CO: Author.

The Virtual College of Texas
United We Stand

Jeff Getchell

INTRODUCTION

Distance education collaborations are common among institutions of higher education. Collaborations allow institutions such as community college districts and university systems to take advantage of a pool of resources that would otherwise be unavailable due to cost restrictions. This pooling of resources has a number of cost advantages for budget-strapped institutions that include the sharing of common resources, allocation of costs over a broader base, and a wider knowledge base of faculty and administrators. One such collaborative effort within the state of Texas is the University of Texas TeleCampus. The UT TeleCampus is a collaborative effort of the University of Texas System that brings together the 15 UT campuses to offer complete Web-based degree programs (UT TeleCampus, 2007). The UT TeleCampus has been quite successful in bringing degree programs to students who would be unable to complete a campus-based degree program due to work and lifestyle schedules.

There is another lesser known yet no less successful higher education collaboration within the state of Texas that provides access to Web-based courses where otherwise there would be none. The consortium is called the Virtual College of Texas, or VCT. The VCT is a collaboration of Texas-based community college districts and technical colleges that provides access to college courses that are normally offered at a student's local institution but are unavailable during the semester needed. All VCT courses are Web-based, opening up higher education opportunities to everyone regardless of geographic or time constraints.

The purpose of this article is to provide an overview of the VCT and the unique service that it provides Texas-based community college students. The article will examine the history of the VCT, provide an explanation of the unique host-provider service model, describe the organizational structure, and discuss some of the challenges that the VCT has had over its 8 and a half-year life span. The article will conclude with possible future directions for the VCT.

Jeff Getchell, Del Mar College, Department of Distance Learning, 101 Baldwin Blvd., Library 414, Corpus Christi, TX 78414.
Telephone: 361-698-1980.
E-mail: jgetchell@delmar.edu

CONCEPT

It is simply not possible for institutions to offer every course in their catalog during every academic semester within every academic year. There are not enough resources, particularly instructors and classrooms, to provide such an all-inclusive level of service. Rather, institutions will offer credit-based courses on a regularly scheduled basis that is based on a number of factors. For example, lower-division courses will be offered more often than upper-division courses to accommodate the greater number of lower-level students; courses that are required for degree plans will be offered more frequently than elective courses; capstone courses will usually be offered once each academic year to accommodate students completing program requirements.

However, there will always be a certain number of students who somehow fall out of the normal sequencing of course offerings. These students may need to register for a course that is necessary for completion of their degree but which is not available during the academic term needed. Normally, the student would have no other option but to wait for the next academic term when the course would be offered. This is incredibly frustrating for the student who must place graduation and occupational plans on hold until the course is offered.

Colleges decide for themselves whether or not to participate in the VCT. Participating colleges also determine to what extent to participate. For example, some colleges may only provide courses to host institutions due to the large number of locally provided distance learning courses. Other institutions that have fewer numbers of distance courses may simply serve as host to institutions that are providing courses to VCT. And there are some institutions that both host courses and provide courses.

VCT HOST-PROVIDER MODEL

The host-provider model was originally developed by the community college presidents in 1996 (VCT, n.d.). The model divides the resources of the student's home institution, or host, with the institution that is providing the course content and instruction, or provider. This combining of resources allows multiple institutions to provide Web-based courses to students when needed without sacrificing critical services such as library, counseling/advising, computer access, testing services, tutoring, and others.

With the host-provider model, the host institution initiates the process of registering the student. The student contacts the host institution's VCT coordinator to begin the registration process. The host VCT coordinator verifies that the course is offered in the local course catalog. If so, the coordinator then determines whether the same course is being made available at a VCT provider institution for that term. If so, and the course has been approved by the appropriate academic chair of the host school, then the student is enrolled in that course.

The host-provider model is based on two factors. The first is that Texas community colleges are mandated by state law to use a common course numbering system. This system, known as the Lower Division Academic Course Guide Manual, or ACGM, ensures that courses using the same number have similar course outcomes and are therefore transferable to any other Texas community college. This transferability of courses allows Host institutions to record course grades directly on to student transcripts for courses taken from a provider institution.

Second, all Texas community colleges fall under the Southern Association of Colleges and Schools, meaning that each VCT member institution abides by and has been accredited by the same accrediting agency. Each VCT member institution also falls under the policies and procedures of the

Texas Higher Education Coordinating Board (THECB). The THECB requires that all Texas institutions of higher education submit a distance learning plan every 5 years.

THE HOST INSTITUTION

Once enrolled, the student is supported by the host institution in a number of ways. First, the host institution collects all tuition and fees associated with the course. The student pays in-district fees if located within the community college district of the host. The host also provides all student services to support the student that include but are not limited to access to all library materials and services, tutoring services, testing center services, special needs assistance, counseling and advising, administration of course evaluations, awarding of course credit transcript updates, and generally looks after the academic welfare of the student as if enrolled in a locally provided course. The host institution also pays the provider institution a per-student instructional fee to cover the costs of instructor and instruction.

THE PROVIDER INSTITUTION

The provider institution offers a similar set of services. The provider is responsible for defining the course content and the instructional methods for the course, for the provision of all class activities such as projects, assignments, testing, and awarding of final grades, and generally treats the student as if the student were enrolled in a locally provided course.

The provider institution is paid a per-student fee for the provision of these services by the host institution. The amount paid to the provider will vary, but is typically no more than what the host receives from the state based on contact hour reimbursement. This per-student instructional fee is always paid by the host and never directly from the student.

The host-provider model provides a number of benefits to students. First, students will have access to a robust schedule of courses incorporating all participating VCT institutions. The likelihood of not finding a course when needed is greatly diminished. Second, the student has available a full complement of student services that are provided locally by their home institution. The student will also pay in-district tuition and fees if a legal resident of the college district of the host institution, regardless of where the course provider is located. Next, all VCT courses will appear on the student's local college transcript as if taken at the student's local institution.

The VCT, along with the host-provider model that provides the foundation of the delivery model, as been approved by the Southern Association of Colleges and Schools, the accrediting agency for institutions of higher education in the state of Texas.

VCT BACKGROUND

The Virtual College of Texas began in 1997 as an initiative of the Texas Association of Community Colleges (VCT, 2004). The presidents of Texas state community colleges gathered together and established the host-provider model which created the foundation on which VCT initiative now operates. A 3-year pilot of the VCT began in the fall of 1998. Formal operations began in 2001 after the completion of a successful pilot program.

VCT ADMINISTRATION

The administration of the VCT organization is done by a number of individuals and groups. At the top is the Texas Association of Community Colleges (TACC) which oversees all aspects of the VCT. Within the TACC resides the Distance Learning Advisory Committee (DLAC), which provides general oversight, guidance, and direction for future initiatives. The TACC executive director provides immediate oversight to the VCT, while the TACC assesses the overall performance of the VCT and determines the future expansion.

The DLAC provides the VCT with general counsel and direction. The DLAC is made up of a variety of instructional, technical, and distance learning administrators from a mixture of community college districts within the state. The TACC appoints the members of the DLAC, which is comprised of two representatives from each of the six TACC-defined regions in the state. DLAC representatives serve on the DLAC for 3-year terms, with the terms from two regions expiring each year. The TACC appoints new DLAC members based on nominations received from the colleges within each of the regions. It is the responsibility of the DLAC to recommend new projects, to review and comment on current and proposed policies and procedures, and to provide general guidance on VCT plans and activities. It was the DLAC that played a key role in the initial establishment of VCT policies and interinstitutional collaborations that helped form the VCT organization.

INSTITUTIONAL ADMINISTRATION

The daily operations of the VCT are provided for by personnel at each of the member institutions, as well as a small staff at the state level. At the college level, each VCT institution appoints one individual to serve as the VCT coordinator. The VCT coordinator oversees the overall VCT program activities, which include course verification, student registration, grades, transcripts, payments, and other activities. The coordinator also provides formative evaluation about the VCT policies and procedures and provides feedback to the state VCT director.

The coordinator also plays a key role throughout the semester. Prior to the start of classes, the coordinator responds to student requests for information as well as

serving as a problem solver as issues come into play. During the semester, the coordinator assists the provider instructor with course orientation, course testing, technical assistance, assistance with student services, updating of course rosters, the tracking and processing of course withdrawals, invoicing and payment processing, and the completion of mandatory reports. The end-of-course processes for coordinators includes submission of grade reports to the host registrar, and ensuring that all provider invoices are promptly paid.

Each institution also has one or more course contacts. The course contacts are responsible for the hands-on activities of course enrollments and ancillary duties. Depending on the size of the institution and the number of students involved, the duties of VCT coordinator and course contact may be done the same person. The benefit of having locally provided VCT coordinators and course contacts is the personal service that can be provided to students when enrolling and taking courses through the VCT.

STATE-LEVEL ADMINISTRATION

At the state level, the VCT is supported by a staff that includes the VCT director, a Web manager, and supplemental contract services as needed. The state-level VCT staff coordinate the activities of all member institutions, including communications, policy and procedure questions, maintain the VCT Web site and applications, create and distribute reports and informational newsletters, create proposals, carries out the recommendations of the TACC and DLAC, and organizes statewide meetings and retreats. In addition, the VCT director represents the VCT at all TACC functions.

Administrative guidance for VCT operations comes from a set of three documents: the memo of understanding, the VCT Host and Provider College Practices and Responsibilities, and the VCT Operations Manual. The MOU, as pointed out earlier, confirms the participation of member colleges in the VCT. The MOU also confirms that the school will apply the same standards for VCT-related courses as is applied toward local courses. Lastly, the MOU confirms that the institution will follow the duties and responsibilities detailed in the operations manual and that the institution complies with all requirements set forth by regional accrediting agencies and professional associations.

The VCT Operations Manual details the various processes and procedures to be followed by host and provider colleges. This manual specifies the duties, responsibilities, and actions that are to be followed. The operations manual also specifies the critical practices that must be followed for compliance with the Southern Association of Colleges and Schools, the VCT regional accrediting agency. The operations manual also provides specific instructions on operations of the VCT Web site, particularly the online course scheduling and student reservation systems.

ELECTRONIC OPERATIONS

VCT support operations are almost entirely Web-based and supported by a number of applications. First, the VCT Web site contains access to a statewide listing of courses and schedules available to students. The Web site contains a reservation system that is used by VCT Coordinators or Course Contacts to place students into courses. The Web site contains a roster database that indicates each student and the course or courses they are enrolled in.

A function of critical importance to host institutions is the faculty rosters database containing the credentials of instructors from Provider institutions. Using this application, department chairs from host institutions can log in and verify that provider instructors have the appropriate credentials for the courses they teach.

The Web site also contains the final grade reports and the day of record, or DOR rosters. The DOR rosters determine the number of students enrolled in VCT courses as of the day of record, usually the 12th class day.

Other electronic functions available at the site include documentation of all administrative procedures, the contact information for statewide VCT staff and administrators, VCT committee members from the TACC, other significant institutional personnel, news and reports related to VCT activities, along with information on professional development activities, projects and program initiatives. Of particular note is that all transactions and information of a confidential nature are password-protected.

VCT BENEFITS TO STUDENTS

The benefits that the VCT provides to Texas students are significant. Among the most significant is the statewide schedule of courses to which students have access. This virtually assures students that the courses they will need will be available at the appropriate time in their educational plan. In addition, all VCT course are provided over the Internet. Web-based courses allow students from all walks of life and with varied work schedules to complete college courses on their schedule rather than the schedule of their local institution. The VCT model makes it much less likely that a student will be unable to register for a course at the point in time needed. VCT students are also supported with locally-delivered academic support and student services. VCT students pay in-district tuition and fees if residing within a community college district, irrespective of which college provides the course taken through VCT. Lastly, any course provided through the VCT is maintained on a single college transcript at the student's local school.

VCT BENEFITS TO PARTICIPATING COLLEGES

Each community college decides for itself whether or not to participate in the VCT, and if they choose to participate, it is up to each college to what degree they will participate. Some colleges only provide courses because they locally offer large numbers of distance learning courses that usually meet their students' needs. Other colleges, with fewer locally offered distance learning courses, may serve mostly as host colleges, meaning they enroll students in courses provided by other colleges. Still other colleges both host and provide courses.

ISSUES

Even though the VCT has created a well-functioning and meticulously planned administrative structure, the operation of the VCT is not without its organizational annoyances. For one, students from one school that are enrolled at a course from a provider school do not appear on the provider roster. Instructors must obtain a listing of VCT students from their local VCT coordinator for each course being offered through VCT. The logistics of testing at multiple locations can also cause headaches for both instructors and VCT coordinators. Obtaining test proctors or coordinating with testing centers at host institutions can be a source of frustration, particularly if student schedules change. The paperwork flow can also be burdensome. Census rosters must be obtained from each institution. Grade reports create a special set of frustrations, as multiple grading systems must be learned so that grade reports can be entered and returned.

ACCOMPLISHMENTS

The VCT was awarded the Star Award in 2000 by the Texas Higher Education Coordinating Board (VCT, 2006). The award was presented by Governor Rick Perry to the governing body of the VCT, the Texas Association of Community Colleges, which also represents all community colleges in the state of Texas. The Star Award is presented to educational programs that demonstrate excellence and that contribute significantly toward the goals of the state's Closing the Gaps higher education plan. The VCT was honored for contributing toward those goals by increasing access to and participation in higher education.

The VCT has also enrolled close to 41,000 students during the past 8 and one half years. According to Ron Thomson, director of VCT operations, "Each of these enrollments represents a student who was able to get a course at a particular point in time that was not available at their local institution at the point they needed and otherwise they would have had to delay their educational plans and pick it up at another time" (personal communication, March 27, 2007).

FUTURE DIRECTIONS

One possible direction the VCT might take is with collaborative degrees and certificates. In 2003, the TACC had the VCT examine the idea of collaboration degrees among community colleges much like what 4-year colleges and universities are now doing. Students would begin coursework at one institution and then transfer to another institution for program completion. The degree or certificate-offering institution would open up some of their courses to host institutions, with the provision that students would later transfer to the provider institution to complete the program.

SUMMARY

The VCT is providing an important service to Texas community college students. The ability to enroll in a needed course when it isn't available locally has had a significant impact on students wanting to complete educational programs but unable to do so due to scheduling issues with their home institution. Based on the number of students having enrolled in courses through the VCT, as well as the number of community and technical colleges that are current VCT members, it is obvious that the VCT service model is working, and working well. It is the united efforts among the TACC, VCT, host and provider institutions, and all other involved entities that make the system work. Massive collaboration is the hallmark of the VCT, and it will undoubtedly continue to serve the community college students of Texas well into the future.

REFERENCES

UT TeleCampus. (2007). *About UTTC*. Retrieved April 22, 2007, from http://www.telecampus .utsystem.edu/index.cfm/4,0,85,html

Virtual College of Texas. (2004). *More about VCT*. Retrieved April 17, 2007, from http://www.vct.org/howwork.htm

Virtual College of Texas. (2006). *Texas Higher Education Coordinating Board star award*. Retrieved from http://www.vct.org/star-award.htm

Virtual College of Texas. (n.d.). *Summary of VCT host-provider model*. Retrieved April 19, 2007, from http://www.vct.org/sacs/review/summaryHPmodel.htm

THE UT TELECAMPUS IS A COLLABORATIVE EFFORT OF THE UNIVERSITY OF TEXAS SYSTEM THAT BRINGS TOGETHER THE 15 UT CAMPUSES TO OFFER COMPLETE WEB-BASED DEGREE PROGRAMS.

A Closer Look at Distance Learning in the Kansas City, Missouri School District

Shelley Brown Cooper

INTRODUCTION

How, in a failing school district, does an administrative leadership team implement a district-wide distance learning program? Which district level management decisions were made? In short, how and why did Phase II of a transformation plan become a reality?

BACKGROUND OF KCMSD SCHOOL DISTRICT

It is necessary to gather a historical perspective of the large, urban, majority-

Shelley Brown Cooper,
Doctoral Student, Nova Southeastern
University, 4526 Francis Street,
Kansas City, Kansas 66103.
Telephone: (913) 710-3818.
E-mail: SC1317@nova.edu

minority Kansas City, Missouri School District (KCMSD) in order to understand the recent transformations that have taken place. Very few school districts have experienced as much turmoil, controversy, and bad press as this district. It has "shrunken from 22,000 students in 2008 to 17,000 students in 2011, and has had more than two dozen superintendents in the past four decades" (Sulzberger, 2011). It has held provisional accreditation since 2008 and lost state accreditation January 1, 2012 (About KCMSD website, 2011).

According to the *About KCMSD* website, the racial composition is now 63.3 African American, 25.4% Hispanic, and 8.6% Caucasian. It is considered a Title 1 district due to its 80.3% free and reduced lunch population (http://www.kcpublicschools.org). Discipline reports are reported to be above the state average. Discipline incident reports state wide are 2 incidents per 100 students. In the KCMSD, the rate is 8 incidents per 100 students. The dropout rate is 16. 9% for the district compared to 3% statewide. Composite ACT scores are 21 for Missouri students and 16.5 for students in the KCMSD (Missouri Comprehensive Data System, 2011).

The Missouri Comprehensive Data System (2011) reports discouraging statistics for the KCMSD because it failed to meet Missouri State Improvement Plan levels in both mathematics and communication arts for Grades 3-12 during the 2010-2011 school year (Missouri Department of Elementary and Secondary Education, 2011b). In addition, acceptable attendance levels and graduation rates were not attained in 2011. While most school districts' scores improved, the 2011 scores were lower than those reported in 2010 (Missouri Department of Elementary School Education, 2011b). Escalating Adequate Yearly Progress targets that are required under the federal No Child Left Behind law for student achievement will increase by 8 percentage points annually, on a pace to reach the federal goal of 100% proficiency by the year 2014 (Missouri Department of elementary and Secondary Education, 2011).

TRANSFORMATION PLAN

However, despite its numerous shortcomings and hardships, there was a plan. As a result of the district's drastic situation, John Covington, former superintendent of the KCMSD, has implemented a two-step transformation plan that has infused extensive technological advances into the school system during the 2009 through 2013 school years. Beginning with the 2011-2012 school year, virtual, online, and distance learning opportunities were created on the high school level. Digital portfolio assessment practices for all grade levels were to be used to promote student-centered learning. In addition, Covington incorporated student-centered and project-based learning in newly developed technology rich classroom environments (2009, p. 7).

KCMSD's mission and focus toward ensuring student readiness for the workforce has increased the district's emphasis on infusing technology in student learning, teacher preparation, administration and data management, resource distribution and technical support. The strategic planning leadership team was charged with implementing this new technology initiative throughout the district operating under demanding demographic constraints.

Covington's team developed the plan in an effort to revive a failing district and improve its chances of regaining its state accreditation. The plan is entitled The Transformation Plan: Phase I and Phase II. The transformation plan consists of five key initiatives to be executed from 2009 through 2013. It plans to create a system of student-centered learning; preparing college, career and workforce ready graduates; revolutionizing the district workforce, transforming the environment and cultivating communication (Covington, 2009).

Phase I of the transformation plan took place from 2009 through 2010 and focused on operational issues. Phase II, slotted to begin during the 2011 and 2012 school years, involves right-sizing the buildings and staff by cutting costs and unnecessary or antiquated programming. Covington uses the term "right-sizing the school district" instead of "down-sizing" to describe cutting the budget by more than $50 million to provide a balanced budget and saving the KCMSD from bankruptcy (p. 4). Over half of the district's 64 schools were closed and nearly 1,000 employees were eliminated. During Phase II of Covington's transformation plan, the district plans to "right-size" the school district and "implement a rigorous and relevant prekindergarten–12th grade system of student-centered teaching and learning" (Covington, 2009). One important tenet of this phase of the transformation plan involves building "technology rich classroom environments." As part of this technology initiative, massive changes were implemented during the 2011-2012 school year including a 3-year initiative:

> Equipping classrooms with interactive white boards, video projectors, classroom computers, audio systems, DVD players, and document cameras. Distance learning labs will be installed in each of the seven high schools and the Foreign Language Academy. In addition, a second lab will be added to each high school and

Carver Elementary School (Covington, 2009, p. 4).

Transformation Plan Phase II's five key initiatives are focused on producing more college, career and workforce ready graduates by providing additional technological learning opportunities. The plan specified implementing "virtual, online and distance learning" activities in order to provide KCMSD's students "access to a wide range of courses from advanced placement to fine arts to foreign language courses that they can access anytime, anywhere." Distance learning labs were specifically identified due to their ability to allow for virtual learning experiences, expand students' abilities to take college and dual-credit courses, and provide educational experiences not available in traditional classroom settings (Covington, 2009).

DISTANCE EDUCATION

The distance learning goals provided by the Missouri Department of Elementary and Secondary Education (2011a) dictate that "distance learning should enable students to achieve their educational goals by delivering academically sound courses and educational support services that are flexible, responsive and innovative. In addition, the distance learning courses should provide the same academic standards, criteria, quality, and content as traditional on-site programs" (p. 2). Also, the recent loss of accreditation by the KCMSD might possibly impact the implementation of the distance learning program within the district. Further study is needed to examine the implications resulting from the loss of accreditation on new curriculum efforts within a school district. In light of a possible state takeover, procedures are needed on how future planning will be conducted to proceed with the distance learning initiative within the KCMSD.

Distance education has a history spanning over 160 years. Simonson, Smaldino,

Albright, and Zvacek (2012), Moore (2007) and Rice (2006) trace the innovations in this educational method from correspondence, radio, television through present day video conferencing and Internet techniques.

Simonson et al. (2012), Moore (2007) and Smith (2009) describe the benefits of distance learning as the instructor and learner can be separated by time and space; instructor expertise can be utilized by many more students worldwide, regardless of either participant's location; collaborative activities can be explored via distance education and learning environments are no longer dictated by logistics. Simonson et al. (2012) also notes that distance education can "supplement existing curricula, promote course sharing among schools, and reach students who cannot (for physical reasons or incarceration) or do not (by choice) attend school in person" (p. 138). Harrison (2005) reports several reasons for the pursuit of distance learning in the K-12 school system, namely: the course is not available locally; to resolve timetable conflicts; to meet diploma requirements; for program enrichment; course required, and to improve grades (p. 15).

While it is difficult to estimate the scope of K-12 distance education, virtual schools have had a national impact for many years (Moore & Anderson, 2003). Virtual schools are present in Florida, Arkansas, Mississippi, Iowa, South Dakota, Kansas and many more (Simonson et al., 2012). Participation in K-12 distance education is more prevalent in rural areas due to lack of qualified instructors and potential low enrollment in more sparsely populated school districts.

The strategic planning conducted by the leadership team included a multitude of details: funding acquisition, facility design, construction, equipment purchases, staff training and development to curriculum design and evaluation. Leadership teams must seek funding for distance education programs. Increased use of the federally funded Star Schools Program has been cited as an example of supplemental distance learning with urban K-12 learners. However, some researchers claim that rural schools are more likely to achieve equity objectives through distance learning than high-minority and low-income schools (Tushnet & Fleming-McCormick, as cited in Moore & Anderson, 2003). Leadership teams in Iowa, Mississippi and Alabama sought Star Schools funding to assist in their distance education programs (Three Statewide Approaches to Distance Education, 2000).

Moore and Anderson (2003) reported that the federal government has seen educational technology and distance learning utilized as tools for use in education reform and school improvement efforts, such as group-based videoconference courses. These funds are geared more toward high-need school districts and low-income populations (p. 685). The KCMSD recounted unacceptable results in math, communication arts, and attendance and graduation rates. Its population consists of more than 80% eligible for free and/or reduced lunches. While distance learning technologies are far more commonly used for student enrichment in K-12 schools than for direct K-12 instruction, the superintendent's decision to implement distance learning opportunities throughout the district would provide additional avenues to address low test scores and declining graduation rates (Clark, 2003, as cited in Moore & Anderson, 2003).

After studying the literature, the KCMSD's strategic planning leadership team collaboratively suggested offering Advanced Placement courses within the distance learning labs at the six high schools (McBeth, 2011). The majority of courses taught via distance education in most high schools are Advanced Placement courses. The respective state boards of education mandate the requirements for Advanced Placement courses. English, U.S.

history, biology, chemistry, physics, calculus, and selected foreign languages were offered via distance learning at the majority of the high school's distance learning labs (Bral, 2007; Henly, 2009; McBeth, 2011; Sabatino, 2008; Smith, 2009; SREB, 2006).

Many of the decisions made by these areas with statewide distance learning programs provided guidance to the KCMSD's strategic planning leadership team. Specifically, South Dakota, Oklahoma, and Iowa began offering distance education in their schools. In 1996, South Dakota initiated the "Wiring the Schools Project" by wiring of all K-12 schools within the state allowing for high speed Internet and videoconferencing (p. 5). This initiative resulted in the Digital Dakota Network that linked every school building to a compressed video network. Oklahoma participated in the Star Schools Assistance program in 1988. It was selected to participate based on its status of being underfunded and disadvantaged (Martin, 2009). This early initiative equipped 35 schools with equipment necessary to participate in satellite-based programming: TVRO satellite C/Ku band antenna and receiver, television/monitor, videocassette recorder, TV/VCR cabinet and cordless telephone (Martin, 2009, p. 53). The purpose of this telecommunications project is to improve instruction at the elementary and secondary school levels, primarily in the areas of mathematics, science, and foreign languages (Martin, 2009, p. 51).

Berg (2002) posits five elements of distance education: physical separation; administration by an educational organization; frequent use of various media, including print, video, film, computer and audio; communication between student and teacher, synchronous or asynchronous; and administrative focus on the nontraditional learner (p. xvi).

Boschmann (1995) insisted that two fundamental steps take place when designing and building a distance learning lab: establish a design team and listen closely to the faculty and students. In addition, permanent and portable technologies need to be determined, along with distribution of electronics (p. 34). Designing a distance learning laboratory consists of three categories of design decision making.

> Environmental design is related to the project's architect. Technology design focuses on integrating audio, optical, video and computer technologies into one system. The third category, interface design, deals with ergonomics and human-technology systems. (p. 39)

When the distance learning labs were being built, the leadership team needed to utilize the expertise of the Facilities Management Department as the numerous design and construction issues were considered. Boschmann (1995) advise that four categories need to be considered when contemplating designing an electronic classroom: (1) when, where, and how people learn; (2) what and why they learn; (3) the evolving role of faculty; and (4) the future of the institution itself. The classroom must allow for interactive discussion, flexible model of student-teacher interaction. Access to information is an integral part of the design therefore, it must encourage learning that must be allowed to continue across time and place by expanding information resources and communication outside the classroom. The distance learning labs will allow for individuals to continue the learning process at different times, at different paces, and at different places, even when they happen to gather in the same place at the same time.

Three additional major categories of design must be considered when creating a distance learning facility: environment, technology, and interface. The environmental design project architect considers comfort factors, projection screens, lighting, writing boards, acoustics and audio systems, ergonomics, and ADA compliance (Americans with Disabilities Act). Technol-

ogy design focuses on integration of multimedia, audio, video, optical, and computer technologies into one workable system. The design team should also consider whether the equipment is user-operated, expandable, reliable, upgradable, capable of handling multiple platforms, maintenance-friendly, and secure. Interface design issues deal with ergonomics and human technology systems. In other words, can the equipment interact with humans and operate with other forms of technology. The human technology interface should be simple to operate and accessible to tech support 24/7 (Boschmann, 1995).

PLAYERS

The key players involved in the KCMSD's Strategic Planning Leadership Team are the superintendent, the executive director of instructional technology (technical), the director of secondary schools (curriculum), the manager of instructional technology (academic), the director of guidance and counseling (scheduling), and the director of facilities management (construction).

DEFINITION OF TERMS

Definitions of major concepts: distance learning, synchronous education, distance learning lab, distance learning facilitator, codecs, student-centered learning.

- Distance learning: Institution-based, formal education where the learning group is separated, and where interactive telecommunications systems are used to connect learners, resources, and instructors" (Simonson et al., 2012, p. 7).
- Synchronous education: live, two-way interaction in the educational process; occurring simultaneously and in real time. Teachers lecture, ask questions, and lead discussions. Learners listen, answer, and participate (Simonson et al., 2012).

- Distance learning lab: classroom providing instruction utilizing two-way, full motion video and two way live audio broadcasts to and from a remote location with a certified teacher acting as a facilitator (Moore & Anderson, 2003).
- Distance learning facilitator: certified teacher, trained as a distance learning instructor in a technology-enhanced, distance learning classroom
- CODECs: "A coder-decoder ... is used to convert analog signals, such as television, to digital form for for transmission and back again to the original analog form for viewing" (Schlosser & Simonson, 2010, p. 110).
- Student-centered learning: Students take ownership of their learning and show mastery through hands-on, project-based education (Covington, 2009).

BUILDING THE DLLs (COSTS/ EQUIPMENT + FACILITIES)

Each of the six KCMSD high schools located within the KCMSD contain distance learning labs with the following equipment: theater seating, CODEC, two interactive whiteboards, multiple monitors and microphones, document cameras, COWS (carts on wheels) with 33 laptops loaded with Microsoft Office, Rosetta Stone Spanish, and Rosetta Stone French. These schools are: East, Northeast, Southwest Early College Campus, Paseo Academy of Fine and Performing Arts, Lincoln College Preparatory Academy, and Central High Schools.

The Implementation Team's planning begins six months prior to the beginning of the next school year. Microsoft Project software that performs computerized Gantt charts assists the implementation team in designing, construction, ordering supplies and installation of equipment. The approximate cost of each distance learning lab is $160,000-$190,000 (Anstaett & Brenneman, 2011).

POLICIES AND PROCEDURES

Sabatino (2008) offers suggestions for classroom management techniques to be utilized when teaching K-12 students at a distance. Since videoconferencing and virtual environments offer the greatest potential for interactivity, classroom management is critical to optimum learning (Sabatino, 2008; Urban, 2006).

TRAINING FACILITATORS

New facilitators should be brought in and taught the Tandberg (videoconferencing) format. However, when facilitators are temporary, or if the Tandberg system needs to be revised, adjustments will be made accordingly. It is necessary that the full installation of the new system and the control boards are supervised to ensure they are installed correctly (Anstaett, 2011).

SCHEDULING

Six to 8 weeks prior to the beginning of school, the implementation team begins reevaluating and revising the distance learning lab facilitator training classes. Facilitators must be hired and trained on the job skills necessary to fulfill the facilitator's responsibilities. The teachers are assigned to labs and will complete training in ample time before schools. If necessary, training on the previous system might be necessary until the new system can be completely installed. Training documents should be developed to instruct teachers in running the document cameras, microphones, CODECS, computers, ENO interactive white boards and other equipment utilized in the distance learning labs (Anstaett, 2011; Brenneman, 2011).

Information technology trainers and the distance learning lab managers should work together in classrooms with facilitators and teachers to assist as they entered this new method of delivering education. Teacher reassignments and scheduling changes were made to accommodate the changes in curriculum and staffing. Additional construction and installation requests were made and are in the process of being completed. The labs are expected to be completely operational and identical in most design details. At that time, all teachers and facilitators will be provided additional and extensive training. The teachers have been the stable foundation for most of this (Anstaett, 2011; South Dakota Department of Distance Education, 2003).

TEACHERS

Several teachers are participating in the distance learning lab program by teaching the following subjects: Advanced Placement literature, Advanced Placement biology/chemistry/physics, French I and II, Spanish 3 and 4, calculus, and accounting.

SUCCESSES

All of the distance learning labs were open on time, according to the transformation plan. Students are able to take courses not offered by their local schools. Budget constraints were adhered to. Students can enjoy a state-of-the-art facility. Students can receive extrinsic motivation by learning in a separate setting from their peers.

CHALLENGES AND CONCERNS

Various distance learning lab hardware and equipment installation are not fully operational. Bell and assembly schedules periodically experience conflicts. There is concern that Advanced Placement courses will be discontinued and replaced with International Baccalaureate courses that are more holistic and very expensive. The state of Missouri pays for students to take the Advanced Placement examination to earn college credit. Some teachers would like to see a dual credit opportunity for students to get high school and college credit simultaneously. Communication between

facilities needs to be better defined. More teacher and facilitator training is needed for troubleshooting equipment and software.

STATE TECHNOLOGY PLAN

The KCMSD's Technology Plan includes the installation of one additional distance learning lab in each of the district's six high schools by August 2012. One-to-one mobile/tablet devices are also planned to increase technical expertise within the student population.

FUTURE PLANS AND EXPECTATIONS

The distance learning labs will be used to initiate relationships with students in New York, England, France, and Spain. Neighborhood connections will commence as afternoon and evening programming is started in the distance learning labs. It is hoped that the increase in academic rigor will aid the KCMSD in raising its standardized test scores.

EVALUATION

An evaluation of the results of the combined efforts of the strategic planning leadership team and other departments will determine the success of the distance learning labs. Simonson et al. (2012) discussed the importance of evaluation as "part of the plans to move from traditional face-to-face instruction to distance education" (p. 348). In this work, Simonson (2012) describes an evaluation of distance education programs using five steps: reactions (Did they like it?); learning (Did they learn it?); transfer (Will they use it?); results (Will it matter?); and return on investment (p. 349). These evaluation steps will provide insight into the success of the new technological initiative.

The AEIOU Evaluation approach by Fortune and Keith (1992, as cited in Simonson et al., 2012), provided program evaluation specifically for distance education implementation projects. The five components of the AEIOU approach provide "formative information to the staff about the implementation their project and summative information about the value of the project and its activities (p. 353). Accountability (A) asks "Did the project planners do what they said they were going to do?" Effectiveness (E) asks "How well done was the project?" Impact queries "Did the project, course, or program make a difference?" Organizational Context (O) poses "What structures, policies, or events in the organization or environment helped or hindered the project in accomplishing its goals?" Unanticipated consequences (U) inquires "What changes or consequences of importance happened as a result of the projects that were not expected?" (p. 353).

These questions will provide insight into the processes, methods and decision-making activities utilized by the strategic planning leadership team while developing a distance learning program within the KCMSD.

REFERENCES

About KCMSD. (2011, January). Retrieved from http://www.kcpublicschools.org

Anstaett, D. (2011, September). Kansas City, Missouri School District Distance Learning meeting.

Berg, G. A. (2002). *Why distance learning? Higher education administrative practice.* Westport, CT: Greenwood.

Boschmann, E. (1995). *The electronic classroom: A handbook for education in the electronic environment.* Medford, NJ: Learned Information.

Bral, C. S. (2007). *An investigation of incorporating online courses in public high school curricula.* Available from ProQuest Dissertations and Theses database. Retrieved from http://ezproxylocal.library.nova.edu/login?url=http://search.proquest.com/docview/304844162?accountid=6579

Brenneman, T. (2011, September). Kansas City, Missouri School District Distance Learning meeting.

Clark, M. S. (2003). *Student support for academic success in a blended, video and web-based, distance education program: The distance learner's perspective.* Available from ProQuest Dissertations and Theses database. Retrieved from http://ezproxylocal.library.nova.edu/login?url=http://search.proquest.com/docview/305330802?accountid=6579

Covington, J. (2009). *Transformation phase II.* Retrieved from http://www2.kcmsd.net/pages/AboutKCMSD.aspx

Harrison, M. K., (2005). *Developing a model and evaluation tool for the laboratory component of K-12 senior science courses delivered by distributed learning methods.* Royal Roads University (Canada), AAT MR10813

Henley, B. F. (2009). *Developing eLearning: A case study of Tennessee High School.* Available from ProQuest Dissertations and Theses database. Retrieved from http://ezproxylocal.library.nova.edu/login?url=http://search.proquest.com/docview/304874653?accountid=6579

Martin, C. M. (2009). Oklahoma's Star Schools: Equipment use and benefits two years after grant's end. *The American Journal of Distance Education, 7*(3), 51-60.

McBeth, M. (2011, September). Kansas City, Missouri School District Distance Learning meeting.

Missouri Comprehensive Data System. (2011). Retrieved from http://mcds.dcse.mo.gov

Missouri Department of Elementary and Secondary Education. (2011a). *Distance learning policies and procedures.* Retrieved from www.dese.mo.gov

Missouri Department of Elementary and Secondary Education. (2011b). *Student MAP Scores Continue Slow Climb, 45*(58).

Moore, M. G. (Ed.). (2007). *Handbook of distance education* (2nd ed.). Mahwah, NJ: Erlbaum.

Moore, M. G., & Anderson, W. G. (2003). *Handbook of distance education.* Mahwah, NJ: Erlbaum.

Rice, K. (2006). A comprehensive look at distance education in the K-12 context. *Journal of Research on Technology in Education, 38,* 425-448.

Sabatino, C. (2008). *Videoconferencing? Assessing its effectiveness as a teaching tool in the high school.* Available from ProQuest Dissertations and Theses database. Retrieved from http://ezproxylocal.library.nova.edu/login?url

=http://search.proquest.com/docview/304478924?accountid=6579

Schlosser, L. A., & Simonson, M. (2010). *Distance education: Definition and glossary of terms* (3rd ed.). Charlotte, NC: Information Age.

Simonson, M., Smaldino, S., Albright, M., & Zvacek, S. (2012).*Teaching and learning at a distance: Foundations of distance education* (5th ed.). Boston, MA: Allyn & Bacon.

Smith, S. G. (2009). *High school students' perceptions of distance learning.* Available from ProQuest Dissertations and Theses database. Retrieved from http://ezproxylocal.library .nova.edu/login?url=http://search.proquest .com/docview/305080539?accountid=6579

South Dakota Department of Distance Education. (2003). *Final report of the evaluation team of the South Dakota Alliance for Distance Education: South Dakota's Star Schools project (SDADE).* Retrieved from http://www2 .plymouth.ac.uk/distancelearning /finalreport.pdf

Star Schools Project (Producer). (2000). *Three statewide approaches to distance education.* [Video case study]. Available from www.schoolofed.nova.edu/cms/itde

Thomas, W. R. (2006). *Electronic delivery of high school courses: Status, trends and issues.* Atlanta, GA: Southern Regional Education Board Publications.

Tushnet, N. C., & Brzoska, K. (1994). Research in distance education. In B. Willis (Ed.), *Distance education: Strategies and tools* (pp. 41-66). Englewood Cliffs, NJ: Educational Technology.

Urban, L. L. (2006). *Developing a strategic plan for distance education at a multi-campus two-year technical college.* Available from ProQuest Dissertations and Theses database, Retrieved from http://ezproxylocal.library.nova.edu/ login?url=http://search.proquest.com/ docview/304909085?accountid=6579

Reaching Beyond the Conventional Classroom
NASA's Digital Learning Network

Damon Talley and Gamaliel "Dan" Cherry

THE DIGITAL LEARNING NETWORK

The National Aeronautics and Space Administration's (NASA) Digital Learning Network (DLN) connects K-16 students, educators, and families to NASA scientists, engineers, and education specialists through videoconferencing and webcasts. The DLN consists of all 10 NASA Centers across the country: Ames Research Center, Dryden Flight Research Center, Glenn Research Center, Goddard Space Flight Center, Jet Propulsion Laboratory, Johnson Space Center, Langley Research Center, Marshall Spaceflight Center, and Stennis Space Center. Each center has a unique and important role in NASA's mission.

Luckily one does not have to search across 10 different centers to find content of interest. The content catalog and webcast schedule can be found at: http://dln.nasa.gov/dln. Registration and scheduling of "events" or modules is free. Events in the catalog range from asteroids to robotics and users determine the date and time of the connection. Event descriptions include pre-/postactivities, a teacher lesson plan,

Damon Talley,
Digital Learning Network Coordinator,
Mail Code: OSU, NASA Kennedy Space
Center, FL 32899.
Telephone: (321) 867-1748.
E-mail: damon.b.talley@nasa.gov

Gamaliel "Dan" Cherry,
Human Resources Development Specialist,
NASA Langley Research Center, Mail Stop:
309, Hampton, VA 23668.
Telephone: (757) 864-6113.
E-mail: gamaliel.r.cherry@nasa.gov

and the corresponding national standards. DLN coordinators at each center facilitate scheduling, test connections, and presentation of events. DLN coordinators are highly trained in NASA content and bring diverse teaching backgrounds to the DLN.

The DLiNfo Channel section of the DLN website serves as a calendar of upcoming webcasts and provides the webcast stream. DLiNfo Channel webcasts can reach large audiences but still maintain interactivity through a chat room or questions submitted via e-mail. Webcasts include guest speakers, educational product showcases, and special events such as NASA launches.

AMERICA'S SPACEPORT: JOHN F. KENNEDY SPACE CENTER

NASA's John F. Kennedy Space Center is the launch site for all U.S. human spaceflight and many of NASA's unpiloted vehi-

cles. One of the most popular events on the DLN is an award-winning interactive virtual field trip to America's Spaceport. This author (Talley) grew up near Kennedy Space Center and is happy to share my excitement for it every single time I connect with students. Stunning aerospace imagery and enthusiasm is important in videoconferencing because "ultimately it is the photogenic nature of these displays, together with the affability and open-endedness of the student presenter dialog, which determines the level of meaningful engagement" (Sumption, 2006, p. 931).

Participants in America's Spaceport explore the Vehicle Assembly Building (VAB), which was the largest building by volume at the time it was constructed. Originally designed to stack the Saturn V Moon Rocket in the vertical position, the VAB's high bay doors could accommodate the Statue of Liberty. The journey continues aboard the largest tracked vehicle in the

Figure 1.   VAB.

Figure 2.   Crawler.

entire world, the Crawler-Transporter. Capable of moving 12 million pounds worth of rocket and launcher, the Crawler gets 42 fpg (that's feet per gallon) and traverses the 4-mile journey to the launch pad in only 8 hours. Finally, students experience a Space Shuttle launch—sometimes live!

DLN "launchcasts" countdown launches live via a webstream on the DLiNfo Channel. Launchcasts usually begin streaming live at T-minus 60 minutes to launch and include content on: vehicle, payload, crew, and the mission. Participants can submit questions and get answers during the program live via e-mail. The prelaunch program includes special guests such as NASA engineers, scientists, program managers, and celebrity guests. Our biggest "get" was Neil deGrasse Tyson, director of the Hayden Planetarium in New York and host of *Nova scienceNOW*. Tyson braved a very hot day in May to help countdown the STS-125 Space Shuttle mission to service the Hubble Space Telescope.

INTEREST IN SCIENCE

NASA (2006) Category 2.4 regarding student involvement K-12, is to Engage: Provide K-12 students with authentic first-

Figure 3.   STS-125 launch.

Figure 4.   Talley with Neil deGrasse Tyson.

hand opportunities to participate in NASA mission activities, thus inspiring interest in STEM (Science, Technology, Engineering and Mathematics) disciplines. America's Spaceport transports students to NASA's Kennedy Space Center, providing just such an opportunity. Jarvis and Pell (2002) noted that after a visit to UK Challenger Learning Center "it is remarkable that a 2-to-3 hour experience should have been such a lasting positive experience for nearly a quarter of the children with regard to raising their career aspirations to become scientists" (p. 997).

Student feedback and teacher testimonials submitted via the online evaluation system evidence positive results in student interest in STEM after participating in NASA DLN sessions.

This author sees the evidence first hand every time I connect with a group of students on the DLN by watching the looks on their faces.

INTERPRETATIONS OF INQUIRY-BASED INSTRUCTION

Educators frequently have various interpretations of what inquiry learning is along with how they should practice inquiry-based instruction (Camins, 2001). The U.S. Department of Education has noted attention to inquiry-based science curricula since the late 1950s. Discussions of inquiry generally fall into two broad classes of inquiry: describing what scientists do professionally, and as a teaching and learning process. Evaluators from the National Research Council (1996) expressed this dichotomy in the following way:

> A scientific inquiry refers to the diverse ways in which scientists study the natural world and propose explanations based on the evidence derived from their work. Inquiry also refers to the activities of students in which they develop knowledge and understanding of scientific ideas, as well as an understanding of how scientists study the natural world. (p. 23)

Inquiry also refers to the actions of students in the classroom. Students should view themselves as scientists by recognizing science as a process, engaging in activities that reflect the work of scientists, designing investigations, revising knowledge, and understanding how scientists examine and make explanations about natural phenomena (NRC, 2000). Students are often encouraged to use prior knowledge to raise questions about the world around them and predict or formulate hypotheses about explanations and solutions to their questions. They are also asked to design and complete simple investigations, use observations to collect data, develop explanations based on collected data, consider alternative explanations, and communicate findings to other classmates (Biological Sciences Curriculum Study [BSCS], 1994; Layman, 1996; NRC, 1996). Applying an inquiry-based approach can pose challenges when presented with the constraints of a videoconferencing environment. However, using a learning cycle approach to instruction allows teachers to have flexibility when teaching science.

THE LEARNING CYCLE

The learning cycle approach to inquiry-based instruction is a widely used inquiry-based format for science instruction providing a structured way to implement inquiry in the classroom (Marek, 2008). This type of inquiry-based instructional methodology engages users in hands-on and minds-on activities throughout instruction providing learners with several opportunities to explore new concepts. Nuthall (1999) supported this approach, suggesting that elementary students need three or four experiences with a topic before they commit the information to long-term memory. These findings indicate that students should have the opportunity to use their prior knowledge and their experiences in an attempt to create new knowledge and understanding. Fur-

Table 1. Summary of the BSCS 5E Instructional Model and Teacher Roles

Phase	Summary
Engagement	Prior learning is assessed and accessed to encourage problem solving, engagement, or the exploration of a new concept. Teacher role: facilitator, lecturer
Exploration	Activities in current topics are provided to encourage and facilitate conceptual change. Teacher role: facilitator
Explanation	Students' attention is focused on explaining their conceptual understanding of the new concept, process, or skill. Teacher role: facilitator, lecturer
Elaboration	Teachers challenge opinions and explanations to encourage a deeper understanding and cognitive engagement of the students. Teacher role: facilitator
Evaluation	Students evaluate their own understanding of their new abilities. Teacher role: facilitator

Note: Adapted from Bybee et al. (2006).

ther research suggested that student achievement, retention, and comprehension improve as a result of using the learning-cycle approach to instruction (Cavallo, 2005). One example of the learning cycle, the 5E model of instruction, draws from prior research in student learning.

5E-INSTRUCTIONAL MODEL

A more widely adopted learning cycle is the 5-E instructional model: engage, explore, explain, elaborate, evaluate (Bybee, 1997). This model was developed in the mid-1980s in part from the previous success of the Science Curriculum Improvement Study model by the Biological Science Curriculum Study and International Business Machines (1989). This model incorporates the three core learning-cycle phases of the Science Curriculum Improvement Study model as its core, but adds engagement and evaluation components to facilitate change.

PULLING IT ALL TOGETHER

Adjusting both content and presentation style to incorporate a 5E approach in a regular videoconferencing setting presents a few challenges. The instructor at the far end site is faced with the dilemma of how to adjust the 5E model on the fly. Originally, the 5E model was rooted in the science classrooms that depended on labs for instructional purposes, so some customization of the model is needed in order to achieve learning outcomes. The cyclical nature of the 5E instructional model allows instructors to build on what they have in a classroom, as opposed to trying to shoehorn an approach. For instance, Digital Learning Network presentations are developed to cover approximately 60 min of instructional time. The propensity for not completing a full learning cycle approach in a 50-60 minute block of instruction is very high. Thus, DLN presenters rely on teachers for pre- and post-activities that will make the experience more meaningful for the students when using a 5E approach. Despite evidence that points to using an inquiry-based approach to teach science, the amount of research examining instructional strategies used via videoconferencing suggests room for a closer look.

REFERENCES

Biological Sciences Curriculum Study. (1994). *Middle school science & technology.* Dubuque, IA: Kendall/Hunt.

Biological Sciences Curriculum Study & IBM (1989). *New designs for elementary science and health: A cooperative project between Biological Sciences Curriculum Study (BSCS) and International Business Machines (IBM)*. Dubuque, IA: Kendall/Hunt.

Bybee, R. W. (1997). *Achieving scientific literacy*. Portsmouth, NH: Heinemann.

Bybee, R. W., et al., (2006) *The BSCS 5E Instructional Model: Origins, Effectiveness, and Application*. Colorado Springs, CO: Biological Sciences Curriculum Study and National Institutes of Health.

Camins, A. (2001) Dimensions of inquiry. *Full Option Science System Newsletter, 18*, 8–13.

Cavallo, A. 2005. Cycling through plants. Science *and Children, 42*(7), 22-27.

Jarvis, T., & Pell, A. (2005). Factors influencing elementary school children's attitudes toward science before, during, and after a visit to the UK National Space Centre. *Journal of Research in Science Teaching, 42* (1), 53-83.

National Aeronautics and Space Administration. *NASA Education Strategic Documents* Retrieved from http://insidenasa.nasa.gov/ portal/site/insidenasa/menu-item.448b8e4ce1c84d12b649cc1036793ea0/

National Research Council. (1996). *National science education standards*. Washington, DC: National Academy Press.

National Research Council. (2000). *How people learn: Brain, mind, experience, and school* (expanded ed.). Washington, DC: National Academy Press.

Layman, J. (1996). *Inquiry and learning: Realizing the science standards in the classroom*. New York, NY: College Entrance Examination Board.

Marek, A. E. (2008). Why the learning cycle? *Journal of Elementary Education, 20*(3), 63-69.

Nuthall, G. (1999). The way students learn: Acquiring knowledge from an integrated science and social studies unit. *Elementary School Journal, 99*, 303–341.

Sumption, K. (2006). Beyond museum walls: An Exploration of the origins and features of web-based, museum education outreach. In J. Weiss et al. (Eds.), *International handbook of virtual learning environments* (pp. 915-937). The Netherlands: Springer.

"DESPITE EVIDENCE THAT POINT TO USING AN INQUIRY-BASED APPROACH TO TEACH SCIENCE, THE AMOUNT OF RESEARCH EXAMINING INSTRUCTIONAL STRATEGIES USED VIA VIDEO-CONFERENCING SUGGESTS ROOM FOR A CLOSER LOOK."

The Virtual Campus at the International Academy of Design and Technology-Online

Andrea Vassar

INTRODUCTION

The International Academy of Design and Technology (IADT) is a for-profit, 4-year art and design career college. It has traditional "brick and mortar" campuses in 10 cities in the United States. IADT is owned and operated by its parent company, the Career Education Corporation (CEC). In 2005, CEC began to discuss the initiative to expand IADT into the field of distance education with the addition of a new branch campus—the International Academy of Design and Technology-Online (IADT-Online). Leaders at both CEC and IADT envisioned a virtual college that could serve as a self-contained branch campus, as well as offer distance education opportunities to the current traditional IADT students in a hybrid format. IADT-Online offers prospective students a way to earn a career-focused, creatively driven degree.

> IADT Online offers the opportunity to earn a degree tailored to your dreams, imaginative ideas and creatively motivated professional goals. When innovative technology hooks up with the power of a broadband Internet connection, amazing things become possible for motivated students who have the talent to think visually and communicate graphically. (IADT, 2009b)

The cornerstone of the IADT-Online virtual college is the proprietary learning management system (LMS), the Virtual Campus (VC). The VC was developed by a team of information technology specialists, instructional designers, and software developers at CEC. After conducting research of currently available LMSs, the team determined that an entirely new LMS, rather than an existing proprietary

Andrea Vassar,
International Academy of Design & Technology, 5104 Eisenhower Blvd.,
Tampa, FL 33634.
Telephone: (813) 889-3406.
E-mail: avassar@academy.edu

system, was the best solution for IADT-Online for two reasons: the ability to have control over the look and feel of the interface so that it could match the existing IADT brand identity; and to integrate with the college database system, CampusVue, already in use by all of the IADT branch campuses.

The Virtual Campus was launched along with newly developed online general education and graphic design courses in July of 2007. This has since been expanded and students can now pursue degree programs in the following areas: graphic design, web design, web development, fashion merchandising, advertising and design, game production, and digital media production (IADT, 2009a). In the last two years the VC has grown and evolved with these new programs into a very successful LMS; upgrades and new features are continually being added to improve the quality of interaction for both students and instructors.

Today, the IADT-Online VC provides quality educational experiences to over 1,400 online college students and approximately 900 hybrid students at the traditional campuses (Carlson, 2009). It is a vibrant learning community. As frequently debated in the field of distance education regarding virtual learning environments, it is a place that is far from "virtual," where actual interactive, engaging, and innovative learning in happening in real time (Simonson, Smaldino, Albright, and Zvacek, 2009).

KEY FEATURES OF THE VIRTUAL CAMPUS

The Virtual Campus is a fully functioning online college campus. It has many of the key features that students expect to have access to on a traditional campus. There are some features that are only available through the technology of the online environment and are currently unavailable to traditional students. These features include: 24/7 technical support, online student services, and instant messaging with all contacts, classmates, and instructors. An example of the VC interface can be seen in Figure 1.

The VC can be accessed by any computer platform through a standard Internet connection. Certain aspects of the VC can also be accessed through mobile technology. The VC uses MobiClass, a mobile software program that supports a long list of mobile devices. MobiClass allows students to stay current with their courses by allowing them to download course podcasts, download course videos, view class assignments, access school e-mail, check their grades, and access faculty contact information (IADT, 2009c).

Many best distance education practices are an integral part of the VC. Both synchronous and asynchronous learning are supported and encouraged through its design and technological features. The VC is divided into five distinct areas, each one designed to assist the students in their learning: the classroom, online library, learning center, virtual commons, and technical support.

THE CLASSROOM

The virtual classroom is the place where all essential learning activities occur both in real-time and on-demand. Online students can access important information that they need in order to successfully complete each course. Figure 2 shows an example of an online course in the VC. The students can access the course overview which includes the syllabus and the list of assignments for the course. The course work section of the virtual classroom includes the discussion board feature. The discussion board assignments are mandatory for all online students for every course to ensure quality interaction with the course content. The course work feature includes a course gallery where the art and design students can post their class proj-

Figure 1.   IADT-Online Virtual Campus.

Figure 2.   IADT-Online classroom.

ects for critique by both instructors and peers. This is also the section where students submit assignments and receive communication from their instructors regarding their grades.

The most dynamic feature of the virtual classroom is the interactive learning section. This section has three main areas: course materials, small group discussions, and live chat. The course materials are Flash-based, animated, and interactive materials and provide additional course content that supports the reading assignments, individual and group projects, and discussion boards. An example of interactive material is seen in Figure 3. The small group discussion feature is a vehicle for instructors to organize students into groups for the purposes of collaborative learning assignments and projects.

The live chat feature is the cornerstone of the virtual classroom. All courses are required to provide two live chat sessions per week on pertinent course topics such as software demonstrations, lectures, and project critiques. Live chats are primarily delivered synchronously, but are recorded for students to use asynchronously. Figure 4 shows a recorded live chat session that can be viewed by students at their convenience. The live chat feature is also used for all additional synchronous academic events including tutoring, academic advising, meetings, and seminars.

Adobe Acrobat Connect Pro is the software that is used to support the live chat feature. It is an effective, robust tool that can be used for eLearning due to its design and capabilities. Adobe promotes Adobe Acrobat Connect Pro for specific online classroom use:

> Technology should make eLearning a rich, interactive experience—not a slow, cumbersome ordeal. That's why Acrobat Connect Pro offers a captivating interface and interactive tools to help participants learn and retain the material that you teach in virtual classes and self-paced

Figure 3. Flash-based interactive learning material.

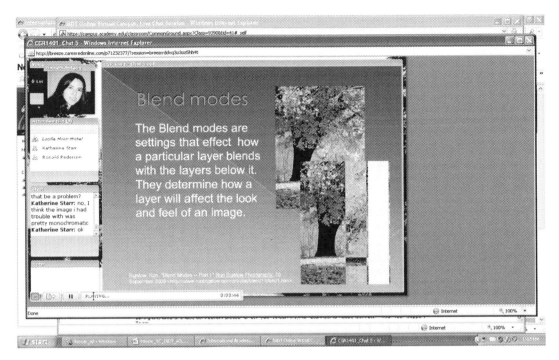

Figure 4. Live chat session.

courses—and enjoy doing it. You can quickly design compelling courses with templates and a library of content, teach more effectively with instructor management tools, and track learner progress to make sure your eLearning is actually achieving its goals. (Adobe, 2008, p. 2)

The flexibility and interactivity are the elements that make the IADT-Online VC classroom a successful learning environment. Students are able to learn at convenient times and to collaborate with their instructors and classmates to complete career-focused, problem-based learning tasks.

ONLINE LIBRARY

The VC online library, or eBrary, is a full-service online media center as seen in Figure 5. The IADT-Online VC library is linked to the CEC-owned company-wide online library the CECbrary. The CECbrary is used by all colleges and universities in

the CEC system of school and therefore can provide extensive media resources to all its schools. Online students have instant access to these electronic library resources.

The eBrary provides student access to eBooks through NetLibrary, PsycBOOKS, and Safari Tech Books. The eBrary also subscribes to an extensive list of online library databases featuring journals and periodicals including the new resource, EBSCO-host Mobile, for learners who access course content via mobile technology. Additionally, the eBrary has web learning resources that are listed by subject. This is a list of about 2000 webpages selected by librarians, students and instructors as being high quality information sources on the topics discussed in the IADT-Online general education and design courses (IADT, 2009b).

There is always a qualified, professional online librarian available to assist students with research questions at flexible times. This assistance is provided either through specific live chat times, the instant messag-

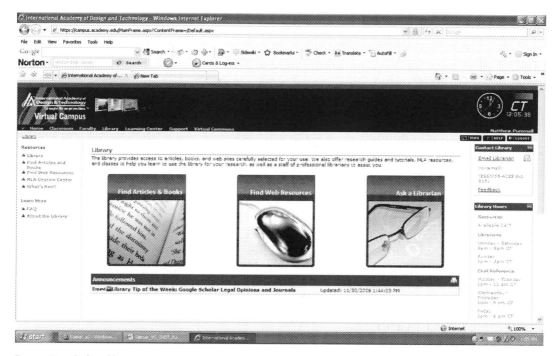

Figure 5. Online library.

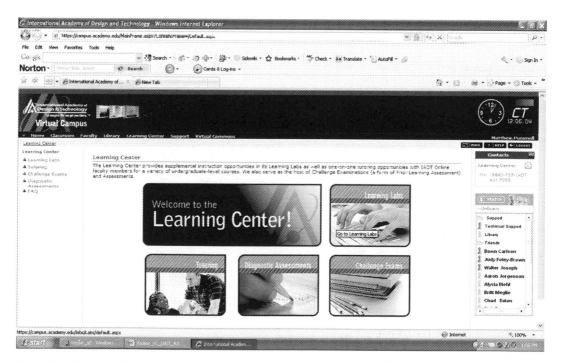

Figure 6. Learning Center.

ing feature, e-mail, or phone. There is also the MLA Citation Center to assist with the formatting and citation of sources in research-based papers and assignments.

LEARNING CENTER

The Learning Center (LC) feature of the VC provides an additional level of in-depth educational support to online students. The LC is shown in Figure 6 and encompasses learning labs, tutoring, diagnostic assessments, and challenge exams. Learning labs are a unique student-centered feature of the VC. Learning labs are geared toward students' areas of interest. Learning labs are available in two forms—generic interactive Flash-based tutorials (as seen in Figure 7) or specially recorded Adobe Acrobat Connect Pro live chats conducted by instructor on pertinent and/or specialized design topics.

Students attend live tutoring sessions in the LC in a variety of subject areas including college-level mathematics and English

composition. Tutoring sessions are also offered in core concentration subject areas. Tutoring sessions are scheduled by individual instructors and conducted through the live chat feature.

The diagnostic assessments and challenge exams in the LC are designed to assist students in the preparation for life-credit test-out examinations. Students who possess certain prerequisite skills, educational experience, or life experience can qualify to take an examination and earn college equivalency credit for those skills and experience. The LC gives them a way to prepare themselves for the test-out process.

VIRTUAL COMMONS

The Virtual Commons is an online community that allows IADT-Online students to participate in social networking opportunities with other students and instructors. The Virtual Commons also has the instant messaging feature that is integrated

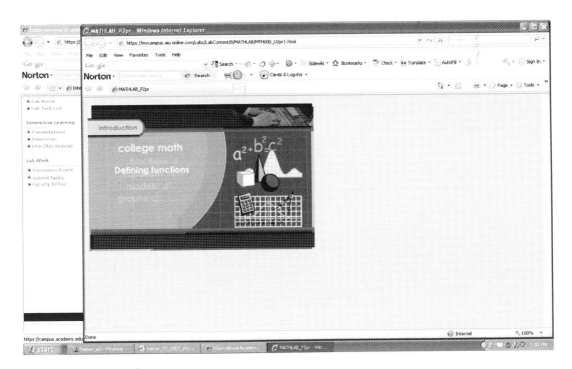

Figure 7.   Interactive learning presentation.

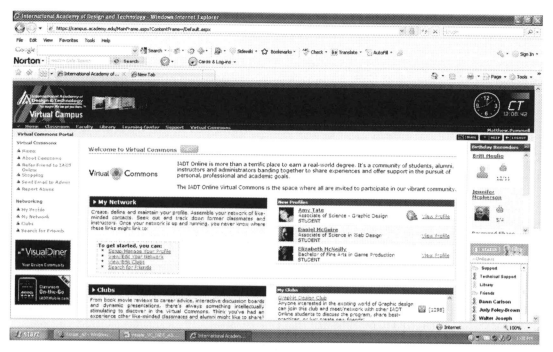

Figure 8.   Virtual Commons.

Figure 9.   Profile listing in the Virtual Commons.

into every "place" a student visits in the VC. This feature can be seen in Figure 8. Like all social networking websites, the Virtual Commons allows its users to create profiles (Figure 9) and become "friends" with other members of the university community. These friends become part of a student's social network.

Like traditional students, online students want to get involved in campus life. This can be challenging in a virtual learning environment. The Virtual Commons in the IADT-Online VC provides students with student club opportunities. Virtual student clubs have faculty moderators, members, and hold virtual club meetings using the same live chat feature that is used in course delivery. These clubs are academic in nature and give the students a chance to participate in book and movie reviews, get career advice, join interactive discussion boards, and attend dynamic presentations (IADT, 2009b). A sample of these clubs is listed here: Graphic Design Club, Military Students Club, Study-Buddy Club, The Fashion Forward Club, and The Freelancer's Society.

During each term, the student clubs in the Virtual Commons host an event. An event is a live chat session in which guest speakers discuss topics related to the subject area of the club. The guest speakers have a wide knowledge base of the club's subject matter and provide valuable information to students on this topic. Topics for events originate from club members and the faculty moderator. Events typically last one hour and provide time for a question and answer period.

TECHNICAL SUPPORT

A feature that is always present but very much working in the background is the 24/7 technical support feature. This is where students go to get technical assistance, important software downloads, and the ability to check a computer for the required Internet browser plug-ins. The technical support area also includes contact information for important functional departments of the online university such as financial aid, student accounts, student services, and the registrar.

Technical support runs on a ticket system as shown in Figure 10. If a student has a technical issue, he or she submits a ticket and a professional information technology specialists work on its resolution, contacting the student when the ticket is closed. Students can also contact technical support from the instant messaging screen, by e-mail, or by phone. Because technology is a part of every experience in the VC, technical support keeps things running smoothly so that students can focus on the important task at hand—learning.

ADVANTAGES AND LIMITATIONS OF THE VIRTUAL CAMPUS

According to Simonson et al. (2009), there are many advantages, as well as limitations, of online learning as compared to conventional teaching. Some of these advantages are: the fact that students can participate from a variety of locations; access asynchronous course components 24 hours a day at their convenience; work at an independent pace; learning materials are available across the Internet and work on multiple platforms; the Internet can provide a student-centered learning environment; and online courses provide a variety of active learning experiences that allow for different learning styles.

There are also limitations of online course delivery models, including: potential students do not have the access to the technology; well-designed online courses require many labor-intensive resources; courses that were teacher-centered are not sufficiently adjusted and adapted to the learner-centered model; instructor-student communication and feedback may be significantly delayed and can affect the quality of learning; bandwidth limitations impact the use of advanced technologies;

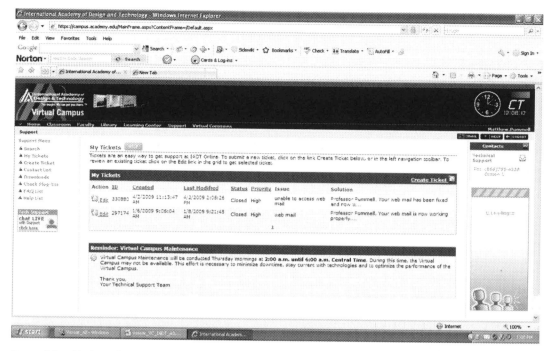

Figure 10. Technical support.

and the technical support infrastructure may be minimal.

When compared to these lists of advantages and limitations, the IADT-Online Virtual Campus measure up very well. It is a vibrant learning environment with very few limitations. The advantages of the VC are its flexible delivery model, student-centered learning, interactive experiences, and creative community. The two biggest limitations of the VC are the significant amounts of bandwidth space required to deliver the industry-current technologies and the time and resources it takes to produce the quality interactive learning experiences (Pummel, 2009).

FLEXIBLE DELIVERY MODEL

The VC emphasizes the flexible delivery model by providing many types of learning in multiple formats. Students can participate in both synchronous and asynchronous learning. They can access course materials from anywhere, at any-

time via the Internet, as well as through advanced mobile technology applications and devices. Students learn independently and have control over when, where, and how they learn course content.

STUDENT-CENTERED LEARNING

The primary focus of the VC is on the student. This is evidenced by the many in-depth support services available to students, from the extensive online library resources and customized web resources to the personal tutorials, interactive learning labs, and student-centered extracurricular clubs. The VC at IADT-Online is all about the student and the students' learning experiences are designed to provide them with quality career-focused education.

INTERACTIVE EXPERIENCES

Every "place" in the VC is interactive—from the classrooms to the technical support center. Instant messaging is a feature throughout the campus. Each classroom has a library of course-related interactive materials. The Learning Center and the Virtual Commons also provide students with interactive experiences. The live chat, the foundation of the VC, is completely interactive allowing the students and instructors to communicate in real-time.

INDUSTRY-CURRENT TECHNOLOGY

CEC and the IADT family of schools have invested many resources on the technology behind the Virtual Campus. The VC is industry-current and provides many applications of advanced technologies including multimedia, graphic, and mobile delivery options. The students participate in the classrooms using the latest Internet meeting software, Adobe Acrobat Connect Pro. Additionally, the students at IADT-Online pursue art and design degrees that require them to use the newest graphic, web, and production software—Adobe Creative Suite 4 Master Collection. Every student and instructor is provided with this software so that they can effectively learn and use these tools in the virtual classroom.

CREATIVE COMMUNITY

The Virtual Commons is a unique feature of the VC allowing students to collaborate with mentors and peers through a common social networking community. This experience greatly enhances every online student's learning experience through the networking opportunities associated with the student-centered clubs and events. This creative community effectively mirrors and simulates the networking that occurs so often in the professional design community. This gives students a real-world experience that transfers to their potential careers in design and technology.

BANDWIDTH LIMITATIONS

The greatest limitation for the VC is the advanced technology that it utilizes and relies on for course delivery. Bandwidth limitations are a serious concern for the CEC and IADT instructional designers and developers. They are tasked with the creation of interactive multimedia and video content that must be effective when delivered via the Internet. Similarly, the same bandwidth issues that affect content development also have an impact on the live chat feature and content delivery. Although video is enabled in the live chat application, many instructors choose not to use this option because it "bogs down" and "lags" during the class causing the flow of course content delivery to be interrupted. In response to this issue, many instructors choose to deliver the chats only using the audio features.

COURSE DEVELOPMENT

An additional limitation to the VC is the amount of time, funding, resources, and personnel involved in the creation of original content and its continual updating. IADT-Online is part of the larger corporation, CEC, and must rely on budgetary and resource limitations from this level of administration. This significantly slows the natural cycle of curriculum development and causes great frustration for those at the local administration level. The VC is proprietary and the program chairs and instructors have very little control over quickly changing course content to meet the ever changing students' needs (Pummel, 2009).

SUMMARY

The IADT-Online Virtual Campus is an exemplary distance education application. It is obvious that attention to best practices of distance education were considered by the CEC and IADT instructional designers and software developers during the creation of the VC. This virtual career college has a long list of advantages when compared to the relativity few limitations. The highlights of the VC are its interactive, student-centered, flexible features; the utilization of advanced instructional and web-based communication technologies; and the truly unique creative social networking community of the Virtual Commons. In the words of an IADT-Online graphic design instructor, Glen Perotte (2009), the Virtual Campus is "an exciting, interactive experience for the students."

REFERENCES

Adobe. (2008). *Adobe Acrobat Connect Pro: High-impact web conferencing and eLearning that everyone can access*. San Jose, CA: Adobe Systems Incorporated.

Carlson, D. (2009). *Current IADT-Online enrollment figures* (A. Vassar, Ed.). Tampa, FL: International Academy of Design and Technology.

International Academy of Design and Technology. (2009a). *IADT Online*. Retrieved from http://online.academy.edu/

International Academy of Design and Technology. (2009b). *IADT Online Virtual Campus*. Retrieved from https://campus.academy.edu/login.aspx?ReturnUrl=%2fdefault.aspx

International Academy of Design and Technology. (2009c). *IADTmobile.com*. Retrieved from http://online.academy.edu/iadtmobile/?url20=%2Fiadtmobile%2F

Perotte, G. (2009). *Benefits of the live chat feature* (A. Vassar, Ed.). Tampa, FL: International Academy of Design and Technology.

Pummel, M. (2009). *Advantages and limitations of the Virtual Campus* (A. Vassar, Ed.). Tampa, FL: International Academy of Design and Technology.

Simonson, M., Smaldino, S., Albright, M., and Zvacek, S. (2009). *Teaching and learning at a distance* (4th ed.). Boston, MA: Allyn & Bacon.

IN THE WORDS OF AN IADT-ONLINE GRAPHIC DESIGN INSTRUCTOR, THE VIRTUAL CAMPUS IS AN EXCITING, INTERACTIVE EXPERIENCE FOR THE STUDENTS.

U.S. Army and U.S. Navy Staff Officer Distance Education Programs

Lawrence L. Gruszecki

I n a recent copy of *Army*, the magazine of the Association of the United States Army, Lieutenant General (Retired) James M. Dubik paints a grim picture of the education needs of Army's officers. Dubik warns that, "The current leader-to-led ratio is too low for what the Army is being asked to do now and in the future" (Dubik, 2010, p. 22).

America's continual and increasing involvement in areas such as Iraq, Afghanistan, and Kuwait is creating a demand for a particular type of officer, the staff officer.

Lawrence L. Gruszecki,
Science Teacher, E. T. Booth Middle School,
Woodstock, GA 30189.
Telephone: (770) 926-5707.
E-mail: lawrence.gruszecki@cherokee.k12.ga.us

Within these areas of operation, America's military forces are molded into "joint forces" to meet combat, intelligence, logistics, and civil affairs requirements in these countries. Additionally, U.S. military forces are engaged with the forces of other countries creating multinational headquarters. Even more demand is created by reorganizing large units into numerous smaller units. These units are represented by the brigade combat team, which consists of approximately 4,000 personnel (Brigade, n.d.).

Dubik notes that the leader-to-led ratio in the Army alone has steadily risen over the past 20 years. The interaction of America's four military branches, interaction of their forces with the military of other countries, and a greater quantity of smaller units has created a need for more officers. He advises that well educated and experienced leaders are presently required. To meet these needs, Dubik further identifies the need for these officers to attend the necessary military schools to be prepared to perform as leaders and staff officers.

Staff officers plan and control military operations as well as provide administrative, intelligence, and logistic support. An historical statistic from Desert Storm suggests that the staff officers of the United States military can be quite effective. Realizing that political issues and operational concerns are not exactly parallel, the comparison is nevertheless provocative. From

1963 to 1964, the U.S. military transported only 184,000 personnel to Vietnam. As a contrast, in preparation for Desert Storm, 184,000 personnel were moved into Saudi Arabia in less than 90 days (Swain, 1994).

One may find staff officers of many different ranks ranging from lieutenant to colonel. The level of staff officer of particular concern is at the O-4 field grade rank. In the Army, the O-4 field grade officers are majors and the Navy's O-4 field grade is lieutenant commander. These officers are also referred to as middle grade officers.

The examination of the Army and Navy officer education program for these officers presents an interesting contrast based on their operations. As is seen in various media, Army operations are conducted on and above land and the Navy's operations that are principally conducted on the seas and oceans of the world. Regardless of the geographic location, the work of field grade staff officers is an integral component.

The Army's field grade staff officer education program is the Command and General Staff College and is located at Fort Leavenworth, Kansas. The Navy's field grade officer program is the College of Naval Command and Staff and is taught at the Naval War College located in Newport, Rhode Island.

The Joint Chiefs of Staff's Office of Professional Military Education Programs determines the curriculum of both colleges, as well as the Marine and Air Force colleges. The Joint Chiefs of Staff prescribe policies, guidelines, and procedures, which are followed by each service. As the college of each branch of service teaches a common curriculum, the graduates of the Joint Military Education Program Phase I are imbued with the same knowledge.

The Joint Military Professional Education curriculum is required by the Goldwater-Nichols Defense Reorganization Act of 1986 and established by the Skelton Committee on Armed Services in 1989. The Goldwater-Nichols legislation stressed the interoperability of the services. The completion of the Command and General Staff College or the College of Naval Command grants an officer a Joint Military Professional Education Phase I diploma. (Joint Professional Military Education, n.d.).

Both colleges strictly follow the Joint Military Education Program curriculum and undergo accreditation reviews by the Joint Chiefs of Staff. Additionally, each college presents the curriculum from their service's point of view. Regardless of approach, both colleges educate and train officers to be adaptive leaders, capable of critical thinking, and prepared to plan and conduct operations within their service, other services, governmental agencies, and multinational environments (J. Hickey, personal communication, July 20, 2010; T. Kallman, personal communication, July 26, 2010).

Approximately 950 active officers are chosen per year to attend the resident courses at Fort Leavenworth or the Naval War College. However, many more field grade officers compose the ranks of the Army and Navy. As Dubik indicates, officers should be afforded the education that will allow them to be effective staff officers in many different types of assignments.

To reach all field grade officers, both colleges project a demanding and vibrant non-resident distance education program to the balance of the Army and Navy personnel. Active, Reserve, and National Guard officers as well as officers of sister branches and senior Federal employees can earn the Joint Military Education Program Phase I diploma through these distance education programs. As an example, the Command and General Staff College extends their program to approximately 6,000 officers each year who are at duty locations around the world (Command and General Staff School Mission, 2010).

The Command and General Staff College organizes the Joint Military Education Program Phase I curriculum into the Intermediate Level Education Core and the

Advanced Operations and Warfighting Course. The Intermediate Level Education Core course is composed of six components, which account for approximately 300 hours of classroom instruction with a focus on the spectrum of operations which the Army currently accomplishes along with warfighting. Instruction begins with the foundations component. Topics range from creative thinking and problem solving to topics as international security environment, leader development, operational law, and civil-military relations. The strategic environment component follows and addresses topics as strategic concepts, national security, national strategies, strategic communications, and strategic logistics. The doctrine component provides instruction in Joint Operations with operational design, operational art, and battle command. Joint operations instruction continues with Joint Functions component, which studies topics as the command and control of forces from sister services when they operate together. The planning component specializes in the understanding of the joint operations planning process and its application.

The Command and General Staff Advanced Operations Course is adapted to the officer's functional area as Infantry or Communications. The instruction is divided into components over a period of four months (Command and General Staff School Mission, July 2010).

The College of Naval Command and Staff Joint Military Education Program Phase I curriculum is organized into three core courses. Instruction begins with the National Security and Decision Making course. Instruction provides an insight into command and staff decision-making. Topics include political science, leadership, psychology, management, anthropology, and other related disciplines. Strategy and War is the next course. It is an analytical study of war, which focuses on the methods to achieve global and multi-national interactions, strategic and political inter-

ests, and goals. The Joint Military Operations course addresses the Joint Operational Planning Process to plan the employment of U.S. military forces across the range of joint and combined military operations, prepare military officers to participate in joint operational planning and to advise senior commanders (Academics, n.d.).

The Army and Navy nonresident Joint Military Education Programs provide face-to-face classes, online, and compact disk instructional formats. They represent a tremendous effort to provide high quality instruction to officers across the United States as well locations around the world. The Army and Navy nonresident programs also fulfill Dubik's concern for developing and maintaining well-educated officers.

The Total Army School System is the overarching administrative organization for the Army. The Total Army School System prescribes and supports all levels of education for recruits to general officers provided by the Army (Army Regulation 350-18, 2007). The Command and General Staff College is included in the Total Army School System.

The Army projects face-to-face instruction to nonresident students in six regions of the United States. A training division serves each region. A seventh training division provides support to personnel in Germany, Japan, Korea, and Puerto Rico. The administrative personnel and instructors of the divisions include active and reserve military and Federal civilian employees.

A professional development brigade is assigned to each division. A battalion in each brigade is dedicated to the Command and General Staff College instruction. The Command and General Staff College at Fort Leavenworth is responsible for the curriculum taught by the instructors. The Command and General Staff College is also responsible for the training and certification of the instructors in the battalion who teach the Joint Military Education Program curriculum.

The face-to-face program taught by the battalions consists of three phases. The instruction may take place during active duty for training or inactive duty for training formats. Instruction is based on a ratio of one instructor to eight students. Additionally, a portion of the instruction is completed online. Students are required to comply with a strict attendance policy.

An 18-month web-based nonresident course is also offered to students. Much support is provided to the students throughout their instruction. As an example, students are assigned a counselor during their enrollment. Students interact with each other as they participate through Blackboard and SharePoint asynchronously. While students and their counselor or an instructor may meet synchronously in a chat room, instruction is asynchronous due to the many time zones in which the students reside. Weekly assignments, threaded discussions, and instruction through Blackboard are enriched with Flash files of video instruction. Notably, the distance education staff is attempting to expand this type of instruction with Adobe Flash Mobile so the instruction may be seen on Android type cell phones and soon on iPhones.

The third format is designed for officers who are assigned to remote locations and do not have access to the Internet. These officers are provided the program courseware on compact disks. The compact disks include activities and instruction of the web-based format. (CGSC Circular 350-3 dated 1 December 2005; T. Kallman, personal communication, July 26, 2010; D. Ward, personal communication, July 26, July 28, and August 2, 2010).

The Fleet Seminar Program of the Navy provides similar coverage across the United States. The program is administered by the Naval War College's College of Distance Education. The program is offered at 20 locations in and around the

United States. Norfolk, Virginia, Jacksonville, Florida, New Orleans, Louisiana, San Diego, California, and Everett, Washington represent locations along the east, south, and west coasts of the United States. Inland locations include Great Lakes, Illinois, Millington, Tennessee, and Fort Worth, Texas. The Fleet Seminar Program is also offered at Pearl Harbor, Hawaii.

Each Fleet Seminar location offers one to all three of the Navy's core courses. Students enroll each year for a particular course. Courses begin in September and meet 34 weeks for 3 hours until the following May.

One unique location offering the Fleet Seminar Program is the Naval Post Graduate School at Monterey, California. The Naval War College at Monterey offers the three core courses in a class format. To attain their Joint Military Education Program diploma, students complete four courses (Naval War College Monterey, n.d.).

The Web-Enabled Program is available to officers who have Internet connectivity. When students are enrolled they are assigned to online cohort groups. Students are also assigned a Naval War College faculty member who assists the student as a tutor.

Interaction among students and their advisors is typically asynchronous. Synchronous interaction is inhibited due to the numerous time zones in which the students reside. Academic requirements include readings, an active requirement each week, threaded discussions online, and responses.

The Web-Enabled Program is designed to be completed in about 18-24 months. The Naval War College recognizes that student success is predicated on the amount of time dedicated to coursework. As a result, when students enroll they accept a commitment to dedicate a minimum of two study periods of 3 or more hours each week.

Officers of all services may apply to the Fleet Seminar Program and Web-Enabled Program. Eligibility is extended to all senior lieutenant to captain sea service officers who are active and reserve, and defense-related civilians. Army and Air Force officers majors and above are also eligible.

The Naval War College also extends the Joint Military Education Program instruction to officers who cannot attend the Fleet Seminar Program or do not have Internet access. The CD-ROM program is composed of video lectures by Naval War College professors and audio presentations, student activities, and self-assessment exercises to broaden and emphasize the content. The program is designed for officers on sea duty or assigned to remote or isolated locations. The student is expected to complete the CD-ROM program in 18 months (Naval War College Provides JPME I to the Fleet, 2004).

The distance education staff of each college is composed of experts in instructional design and distance education. Each staff possesses the expertise to create their own courseware. Both colleges follow a similar distance education course instructional design process.

A central concern in the course design is to maintain their accreditation by the Joint Chiefs of Staff. To do so, instruction adapted for distance delivery is based on the essential content that is presented in the classroom. To ensure alignment of the classroom format and distance education format the colleges follow a rigid development process. As an example, the Command and Staff College distance education developers form a working group for each course.

A unique quality control element of course development is the inclusion of the author of the resident course in the process. The resident author is a member of the distance education course development group. To ensure equivalency of the resident and distance education courses, the resident author takes ownership of the content. With the essential content is identified, the distance education staff selects or develops appropriate media to deliver the instruction. While the Dick, Carey, and Carey (2005) model of instructional design is not specifically used, the distance education course developers in the staffs at each college speak in those terms and elements of the design process are used (D. McGill, personal communication, July 28, and August 5, 2010; D. Ward, personal communication, July 26, 28, and August 2, 2010).

Both colleges recognize that the quality of the instructors is a critical component of the nonresident education process. Distance education instructors for the web-based programs are typically retired military and are specifically trained to facilitate the online courses (J. Hickey, personal communication, July 20, 2010; T. Kallman, personal communication, July 26, 2010).

A significant indicator of the course design success is the end-of-course assessment. As an example, assessment is highly regarded by the Naval War College distance education department. Student cannot continue on to the next instruction until they have submitted their assessment of the completed course. Data from the required assessments is anonymous and reviewed by the distance education faculty (J. Hickey, personal communication, July 20, 2010).

The administration and support of online students in the Army's Web-Based course or the Navy's Web-Enabled Program is similar to online schools in the public sector. The descriptions of the Command and General Staff College and Naval War College online programs indicate a significant connection to each student as well as support. Students who enroll in these programs realize that their continued career progression is dependent on the successful completion of the Joint Military Education Program Phase I instruction. As a result, they are quite motivated (J. Hickey, personal communication, July 20, 2010).

The descriptions of the programs suggest a student-centered support paradigm. The student is surrounded by components that support their academic success. Students may converse with instructors and other students through the threaded discussions on Blackboard. Chat rooms are available for students to converse with counselors and instructors. Students may contact their instructors and counselors by telephone and e-mail. Students of both services have full online access to their college's libraries. Counselors play a key role, as students must be aware of the requirements placed upon them to graduate and that they must complete the requirements within a specific amount of time (T. Kallman, personal communication, July 26, 2010).

From an overall perspective, America's military has two general components. One component is referred to as the generating force and the other is the operating force. The active and reserve faculty members and resident students of each college are part of the generating force. As Dubik (2010) indicates, fewer military personnel are being assigned to the generating force, which suggests that each college has a reduced faculty. It appears that the web-based programs serve as an educational multiplier by being able continue high-level support and expert instruction to officers in operational duty assignments.

The online distance education program of today's military, particularly the Army and Navy, appear to be as contemporary as leading online schools. Both colleges are adapting current technology to virtually place the online line student in the resident classrooms. One example is the use of MilBook, which is the Department of Defense's combined version of Facebook, Twitter, YouTube, and Wiki (D. Ward, personal communication, July 26, 28, August 2, 2010).

Just over a decade ago, the Joint Military Education Program for the Command and General Staff College distance education program was the exchange of printed course materials between an instructor at the college and the student (T. Kallman, personal communication, July 26, 2010). This relationship is almost reminiscent of the late 1880s University of Wisconsin correspondence course for farmers (Simonson, Smaldino, Albright, & Zvacek, 2009).

Since those days, the distance education departments at both colleges have become as current as any online university. As an example, distance education experts of the Naval War College attend the University of Wisconsin's yearly Conference on Distance Teaching and Learning. This year, distance education faculty of the Naval War College presented a workshop on "Best Practices in Military Distance Learning" (D. McGill, personal communication, July 28 and August 5, 2010).

During the Sister Service College conference in January of 2010, Lieutenant General Caldwell, the commandant of the Command and General Staff College, aptly described the education mission of the all the services Joint Military Education Programs. He noted that all the colleges are composed of world-class faculties that develop, administer, and teach. The courses at the colleges are designed to create adaptive leaders with command, control, and support skills to succeed in complex missions during operations (Caldwell, 2009). The students of these colleges, resident and nonresident, receive common instruction specified by the Joints Chief Staff. They compose the core of a formidable force, as they are equally capable to be staff officers and leaders in their respective assignments.

The distance education faculties of the Command and General Staff College and of the Naval War College are answering Dubik's (2010) call for more leaders and staff officers. The nonresident programs of these colleges are a dynamic part of meeting the need for well educated officers.

REFERENCES

Ausiello, D. (2004, April). Naval War College provides JPME I to the fleet. *Navy.mil Official Website of the United States Navy.* Retrieved from http://www.navy.mil/search/display .asp?story_id=12523

Army Regulation 350-18. (2007). *The Army school system.* Retrieved from http://www.tradoc .army.mil/tpubs/regs/r350-18.htm

Brigade. (n.d). *Brigade unit of action.* Retrieved from http://www.globalsecurity.org/military/ agency/army/bua.htm

Caldwell, W. (2010, January.) *5 questions for the Command and General Staff College commandant.* Retrieved from http://www.army.mil/- news/2009/01/22/15992-5-questions-for-the- command-and-general-staff-college-com- mandant/

Command and General Staff School Mission. (2010, July). *Command and General Staff School (CGSS) mission* [PowerPoint presentation]. Fort Leavenworth, KS: Command and General Staff College.

Dick, W., Carey, L., & Carey, J. (2005). *The systematic design of instruction* (6th Ed.) New York, NY: Addison-Wesley.

Dubik, J. M. (2010, August). Studying the future security environment. *Army, 60*(8), 22-24.

Office of the Joints Chief of Staff. (n.d.). *Joint professional military education (JPME)* Retrieved from http://www.mcu.usmc.mil/ MilitaryEducation/JPMEInfo.pdf

Naval War College. (n.d.). *Academics.* Retrieved from http://www.usnwc.edu/Academics .aspx

Naval War College Monterey. (n.d.). *Naval War College at Monterey.* Retrieved from http:// www.nps.edu/Academics/Programs/NWC/

Simonson, M., Smaldino, S., Albright, M., & Zvacek. S. (2009). *Teaching and learning at a distance: Foundations of distance education* (4th ed.) Boston, MA: Pearson.

Swain, R. (1994). *"The lucky war" Third Army in Desert Storm.* Retrieved from http:// www.cgsc.edu/carl/resources/csi/swain/ swain.asp

U.S. Army Command and General Staff College. (n.d.). *CGSC Circular 350-3 dated 1 December 2005.* Retrieved from http:// www.cgsc.edu/repository/dde_ 7_catalogAppC.pdf

"THE ONLINE DISTANCE EDUCATION PROGRAM OF TODAY'S MILITARY, PARTICULARLY THE ARMY AND NAVY, APPEAR TO BE AS CONTEMPORARY AS LEADING ONLINE SCHOOLS."

Part III

International Applications of Distance Education

Challenges in Higher Education Distance Learning in the Democratic Republic of Congo

Banza Nsomwe-a-nfunkwa

INTRODUCTION

Open and distance learning has created opportunities for all sorts of people in all walks of life to access education (Badza & Chakuchichi 2009). However, distance learning in the Democratic Republic of Congo is still a field demanding a lot of research and practice to ensure successful implementation.

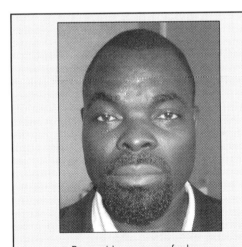

Banza Nsomwe-a-nfunkwa,
Associate Professor,
University of Kinshasa,
Democratic Republic of Congo.
E-mail: nfunkwa@hotmail.com

The use of information and communication technology (ICT) in distance learning in the higher education sector is facing a lot of problems in the Democratic Republic of Congo. This article addresses only some of the main obstacles; the complete list is very long.

The first problem is the limited technologies. The Democratic Republic of Congo depends on its ICT through imported goods; all hardware and software are made outside of Democratic Republic of Congo.

The second problem is the exorbitant costs for such technologies; because all the equipment is imported, it is subject to taxes, shipment fees, and so on.

The third problem is that many higher education institutions are located in rural areas that stable electricity—or lack electricity entirely, creating a major obstacle to the effective use of ICT for distance learning.

The fourth problem is that in some corners of my country, old technologies such as tape recorders and video are still a novelty; how can we even think to talk about new technologies in those areas?

The fifth is a lack of trained instructors. Technologies can be readily available at any place, but it will be very complicated to use it effectively because of the lack of trained people.

NEED FOR DISTANCE LEARNING

The Democratic Republic of Congo, with 49 years of independence from Belgium, has never entered such a huge problem of reconstruction and development as today. The program of reconstruction of the country is divided into five sectors: education, electricity, water, health, and infrastructure. In light of this huge program, the country is in great need of skilled people to contribute to and participate in the Congolese work market.

Because the country has a high rate of illiteracy, a new condensed and functional version of the content of learning is needed so the population can learn in their spare time. Many workers are highly interested and motivated to learn in their spare time, because they can be working and learning at convenient times, improving their skills to match the evolution of their jobs. People are working under stress created by new jobs, social need, and economic situation; self-training is needed for many people to update their skills and knowledge.

CHALLENGES TO DISTANCE LEARNING IN THE HIGHER EDUCATION SECTOR

It is easy to talk about distance learning and its needs in the Democratic Republic of Congo but is very hard to talk about the challenges because they are so numerous.

The first challenge is connected to the quality of materials. Here the big question is how much the people trying to develop these materials are qualified for this job, abiding by national requirement and policy.

The second challenge is related to a lack of financial resources. In the last few years of war, the financial area is facing many problems. It is unclear if the Democratic Republic of Congo is ready to provide adequate financial resources to distance learning.

The third challenge concerns the attitude of Congolese society to distance learning. From the colonial educational system, psychology, and the attitude of the Congolese people, they were and still are prepared to respect and accept conventional education and not really to consider distance learning. They argue that the face-to-face educational system is the best.

The fourth challenge is the lack of distance learning management skills. In the Democratic Republic of Congo, distance learning is hesitantly being accepted step-by-step by few people. However, the management of the distance learning system is still a huge challenge.

The last challenge is technophobia.

STRATEGIES

Distance learning is a very complex and complicated system. To find solutions to all challenges facing the Democratic Republic of Congo in the establishment of distance learning in the higher education sector, I put forward some suggestions:

1. Information about distance learning should be provided to the people of the Democratic Republic of Congo.
2. If distance learning in the Democratic Republic of Congo is to succeed, it is an obligation to prepare distance educators.
3. Organize conferences, seminars, discussions and reflection on the topic of distance learning and its impact on the Congolese people's well-being.
4. Organizing training on the management of distance learning by the Congolese people.
5. Organizing workshops on the design and development of distance learning courses.
6. Help new distance educators learn about methods of teaching
7. A huge campaign to encourage the people of the Democratic Republic of Congo to study at a distance.

8. Organizing training on the evaluation system before, during, and after the lesson.
9. Prepare counseling and support services for distance learners.

CONCLUSION

Effective use of distance learning in higher education in the Democratic Republic of Congo is still a long way from realization. I do believe that a huge campaign on the impact and benefit of distance learning in the Democratic Republic of Congo will contribute to development of appropriate solutions to the many challenges facing distance learning in my country. Then this developing country can enjoy the benefits of new information and communication technologies.

REFERENCE

Badza, A., & Chakuchichi, D. (2009). Women access to higher education through open and distance learning: Challenges and learner support. *International Journal of Open and Distance Learning, 2*, 45-57.

BARRIERS TO DISTANCE EDUCATION IN THE REPUBLIC OF CONGO

1. LIMITED TECHNOLOGIES
2. EXORBITANT COSTS FOR TECHNOLOGIES
3. UNSTABLE ELECTRICITY
4. NEW TECHNOLOGIES HAVE NOT REPLACED OLD TECHNOLOGIES

Distance Education and the Well-Being of the Rural Poor
Case Study of the Kabongo Region in the Democratic Republic of Congo

Banza Nsomwe-a-nfunkwa

As a result of war and the economic situation in the Democratic Republic of Congo, the people of the country are suffering extreme poverty. The population of Kabongo depends on agricultural output and the generated income, primarily from the production of cassava. At present, cassava is suffering from diseases and the consequence is a decrease in production. The decreased production leads to less food, and there-fore even higher rates of malnutrition. Also, there are fewer products to sell, resulting in less money, more children with no access to school, a higher rate of school dropout, a lack of clothing, a lack of access to medicines and a higher rate of street kids stealing or begging. As a result of the problems leading to decreased production of cassava, the rural people in the Kabongo region are seeking a solution to the problem. By solving the problem of the diseases affecting cassava there will be increased production of cassava and an increase in farmers' incomes.

To solve this problem, we suggest a functional education program for the rural people on cassava. The objective is to develop a teaching and learning curriculum designed specifically to meet the needs of rural people; this curriculum will be focused on adult learners who are illiterate, as well as not able to speak the official language, French, or even the four national languages. The people of Kabongo will frequently only speak the local dialect. These people are geographically scattered and isolated in the local area. To solve the problem of the scattered nature of the target audience, where there is an absence of electricity, telecommunication (and in short all new technologies are lacking), we have chosen to produce a distance education program using radio broadcast. To enable learners to provide

Banza Nsomwe-a-nfunkwa, Faculty of Psychology and Educational Sciences, Kinshasa University, Congo and Doctoral Candidate in Educational Technology, Nanjing Normal University, China. Telephone: +86-25-83715127. E-mail: nfunkwa@hotmail.com paralotodo@yahoo.fr

feedback and reduce the need for direct contact between the rural adult learners, our plan is to use "radio broadcasting reception centers." These centers will be staffed by trained people, who are qualified teachers, and at the end of training they will be posted to the reception centers. These facilitators will assist adult learners, answer their questions, explain complex aspects of information broadcasted, organize workshops and practical activities, as well as provide "counseling" services.

In the case of this rural distance education by radio, linear design will be predominantly used; in some cases in which the learner or learning activities need another rhythm of learning, the linear design will be combined with other instructional designs to achieve the objective.

This curriculum will be the first in the domain of rural, illiterate, adult learners. Also, it will be the first time a curriculum has been designed to meet the specific needs of the rural people in the Kabongo region.

INTRODUCTION

Kabongo is located in the province of Katanga in Democratic Republic of Congo. This region is characterized by various daily problems. Transportation in this region is a major issue, and reaching nearby major cities is problematic. The principal means of transportation to Kamina, a city only 200 kilometers away, are truck, train, and bicycles. During rainy season, this 200-kilometer trip can take up to two days by truck or slow train. This area also does not have electricity, running water, television, radio broadcasting, and Internet; essentially, there is a total absence of all new technologies.

In the Kabongo region, the vast majority of people are farmers, and they live off their agricultural produce. From the sale of their produce they gain money and participate in the standard economic cycle; there-fore, they are able to buy clothes, medicines, send children to school, and try to fight against premature school dropout, along with being able to deal with the normal daily problems.

This corner of Congo is facing a very high level of poverty. The poverty was intensified by the consequences of 5 years of war, and recently diseases present in cassava plants. Cassava is the staple food source for most people in the Kabongo region. Its importance is that the root is eaten as bread and the leaves as vegetables. Cassava is central to the rural economy. Cassava is currently suffering from diseases, and these have very negative consequences on the production rate and quality; the decrease of cassava production seriously affects the well-being of rural people.

In order to see an improvement in the well-being of the rural people, it is essential to solve the problem with cassava production. The best way to solve this is to provide information and functional education about cassava production, diseases present in cassava, and related environmental issues.

Education in the rural area of Kabongo faces many obstacles: these include a high rate of adult illiteracy, language problems because these adults are often able to speak only local dialects and not the national languages, and the scattered geographical nature of the people within the area. As a result, it is essential that there is a specific curriculum designed for adult learners to counteract the issues related to cassava.

The development of a teaching and learning curriculum for isolated rural adult learners, and the delivery of such a curriculum via radio broadcasting is the most effective means to inform and educate the people facing such circumstances. This curriculum will be divided into two sections: a compulsory (in some ways) and an elective component. The compulsory section will contain information about cassava production, cassava diseases, and some content will be focused on the environment and issues related to soil. The elective section will contain lessons about Kabongo's history, general knowledge, public awareness campaigns, and community building.

CASSAVA PROBLEMS AND SOLUTIONS

NETWORK OF CASSAVA PROBLEMS, CAUSES, AND EFFECTS

As a result of war and the economic situation in Democratic Republic of Congo, the population is suffering extreme poverty. The population of Kabongo depends on agricultural output for their income, and much of this income generated from the production of cassava. Cassava is the most important staple food and accounts for up to 70% of the population's income in the Democratic Republic of Congo (IITA, 2000). At present, cassava is suffering from diseases, and these diseases are resulting in a decrease in production. The decreased production leads to less available food, and consequently higher malnutrition. Also, there are fewer products to sell as a result of less money in the economic cycle, and therefore more children are not able to access education, there is a higher rate of premature school dropout, a lack of clothing and medicines, and an increase in the rate of stealing and begging. From the decrease of cassava production the level of poverty is increasing; and the well-being of the people of Kabongo is negatively affected.

As a result of the problems leading to decreased production of cassava, the people in the Kabongo region are seeking a solution to the problem. The result of solving the problem of the diseases affecting cassava will lead to increased cassava production and hence an increase in the incomes of the rural peoples.

From Figure 1, we can read that the central problem is the decrease in the production of cassava. Some of the causes for this reduction are diseases (mosaique du manioc, bacterie du manioc, anthracnose du manioc, structure brune du manioc, cercosporioses), magical beliefs, bad luck from ancestors, lack of knowledge of diseases, agricultural cycles, environmental issues, and problems with the soil. The consequences of the reduced production are malnutrition and under-nourishment, inability to send children to schools, higher school dropout, poor choices for lifestyle, and a lack of clothing and medicine.

NETWORK OF METHODS AND SOLUTIONS

The aforementioned information outlined how the decreased production of cassava is affecting the well-being of the rural poor of the Kabongo area. Hence, there will now be an analysis of how to solve such decreased production of cassava and suggestions presenting the methods and means used to solve the problems. The promise is that a functional education program designed for the rural people about cassava diseases, its origin, and how to fight against such diseases can alleviate the situation. Also, this program should include the new techniques of cassava cultivation and practices, along with information on soil and the environmental situation.

An increase in cassava production is central to overcoming decreased cassava production. To seek this solution, functional education regards the present diseases and their origins as critical. Also, the people need to be educated to overcome the acceptance of diseases, education including more modern farming methods, an awareness of environmental issues, cultivation of cassava, and replacement crops, all of which will result in improved conditions for the rural people.

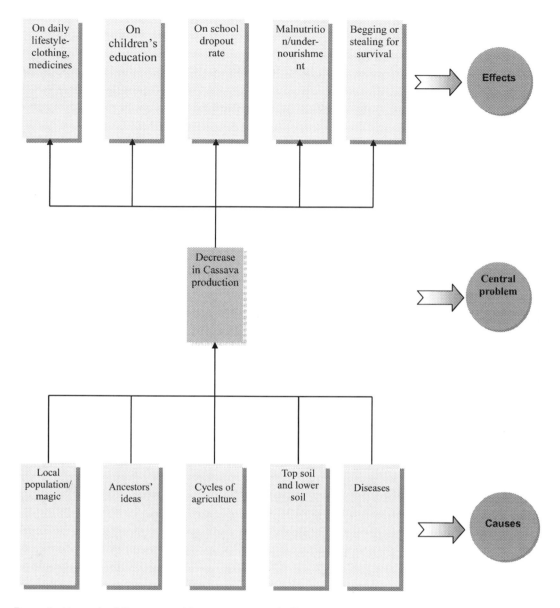

Figure 1. Network of Cassava problems, causes, and effects.

CURRICULUM FOR RURAL DISTANT LEARNERS

Our objective is to develop a teaching and learning curriculum for rural people. This program will be focused on adult learners who are illiterate, cannot read and write French or any of the four national languages but are only able to speak their local dialect. These same learners are geo-graphically very scattered in the local area; hence distance education is our chosen mode of teaching.

Furthermore, instructional objectives will assist the teacher in selecting appropriate content, teaching strategies, resources, and assessment, and can also support the teacher in educational activities (Cohen, Manion, & Morrison, 1998).

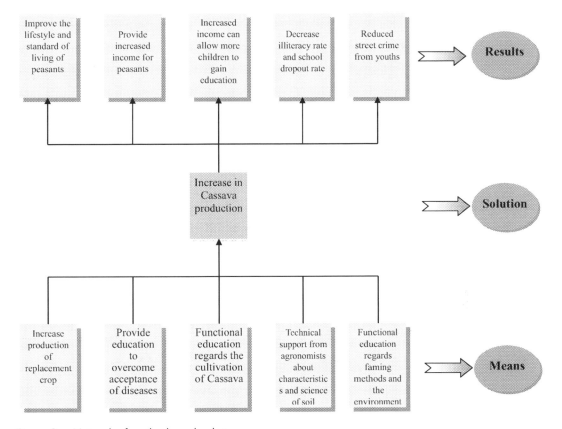

Figure 2.   Network of methods and solutions.

As stated above, this program has two parts: a compulsory and an elective. In this specific case of distance education for adult learners who are illiterate, some questions concerning planning, implementation, and evaluation will constantly present themselves when designing the curriculum.

PLAN

When planning, many questions are raised: How is the curriculum developed? How is the subject matter developed? How are curriculum objectives defined? How is curriculum content selected? How to organize the curriculum content? We start to think about the learner (target audience), teacher (and facilitator), and the instructional technology. Dunn, Beaudry, and Klavas (1989) contend that it is crucial for teachers to match their teaching styles

with students' learning styles; every person has a learning style. It is as individual as a signature. When the students' learning styles are identified, then classrooms can be organized to respond to their individual needs.

The Kabongo target audience constitutes adult learners (who are illiterate) living in scattered rural areas of the Kabongo region, and who are generally only able to speak the local dialect (Kilubakat), but not French (the official language) or the four national languages. Most of our learners are farmers, leaving the village in the morning at about 5 a.m. to go to the fields; they work all day and return home in the afternoon at about 5 p.m.

Research was conducted in the Kabongo region to ascertain the most convenient times for the local citizens to receive educational broadcasts and the reasons for this preferred time. The results showed that 79.9% responded that evening time was the most convenient and 20.1% felt that mornings were convenient. Those preferring evenings indicated that during morning time, they were busy with agricultural work and other daily activities. Their preference for evening time was because by evening time everyone is already back at home and ready to listen to the broadcast and available to meet others for discussion. As a consequence, it is important that the classroom environment provides opportunities for the adult learners to feel accepted in the classroom and have teachers/facilitators who listen to their requests and can respond to their specific questions. That is why Tomlinson (2002) contends that students seek affirmation that they are significant in the classroom.

In the planning of curriculum and delivery, a major point of consideration has been to place the learners at the center and make the program meet their needs, such as taking into account the time available for the learners, the age of the learners, and the cultural behaviors of the learners. The primary goal is the overall well-being of the learner, so we have to equip learners with skills to address and overcome daily problems. These skills will enable them to address the problem of the decreased production of cassava and help them develop the skills to solve future problems. This program will also enable these adult learners to draw on their previous experience in agricultural fields to deal with present and future problems, all of which can allow the learners to participate in the new lessons. This method will provide the adult learners, who culturally must be respected because of age and experience, to draw on their farming experience with cassava and share their methods and successes. The learning plan is to keep the adult learners motivated by involving them in all kinds of activities and practices; in this way they will cooperate and participate to the program.

Teachers need to consider the following questions when matching their learners. How is each learner's self concept being developed? How does a teaching style meet learners' individual differences of need, interest, ability, and skill? How does a teaching style develop in each learner? How does the organization of the class and school facilities foster security in each learner?

In this stage of planning, the distance educator is determining tasks to be done at the end of each module and by the end of the curriculum. They must also plan the way learners will cooperate among themselves, with the teachers, or with the facilitators. Here we think that practical activities, workshops, small seminars, and simple discussion will enable the learners to have a hands-on, interactive role in their learning. Also the teacher must plan and think about the technological tools to be used for delivering content. In the case of the Kabongo region, radio broadcasting will be the chosen form of technology, with the use of other media, such as DVD, CD-ROM, tapes, print, and booklets. Those technologies will help with the transmission, but the content should always respond to the needs of the learners and should be translated into their local language (Kilubakat). During the research survey, local citizens were asked which language they would prefer the broadcast in. The local citizens overwhelmingly requested Kilubakat (92.1%). Other languages that were offered as choices were Tshiluba (0%), Kikongo (0%), Lingala (0%), Swahili (4.9%) and French (3%) (Nsomwe-a-nfunkwa, 2005).

Geographical distance between the broadcasting center, teachers, and learners will certainly be an issue. The reality for the local citizens in the Kabongo region is that the people are scattered throughout different rural villages. To address this problem, qualified teachers will be trained in the content and they will become facilitators at the end of training sessions and will be sent to different "radio broadcasting reception centers." These facilitators will have the role of assisting adult learners by answering their questions, explaining sections of the broadcast that were not understood, and organizing workshops and practical activities. They will also provide counseling services to support students through their learning.

After introducing the situation for the learners and teachers, it is then appropriate that the instructional technology and design is discussed. The article has mentioned some of the realities of Kabongo, which can plainly be characterized by no electricity and no access to advanced technology; hence, the primary technology to be employed is radio broadcasting and other media. Considering the old machines, the target audience, and their needs and challenges, what kind of instructional design is going to be used for the Kabongo distance education adult learners?

Many authors have written about instructional design models: linear design, branched design, hyper-content design, and learner-directed design. Taking into account the differences between the learners in Kabongo, a linear design, designed by Simonson (2006), will be predominantly used.

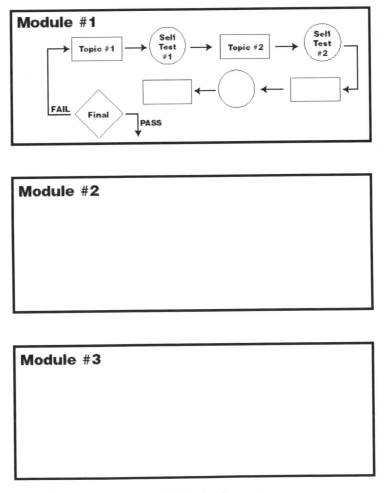

Figure 3.   Linear design model. Used with permission.

In the case that a learner or learning activities need another rhythm of learning, other instructional designs will be employed. The overall goal is to meet the objective for every module and for every adult learner.

IMPLEMENT

Scott (1999) said a curriculum, however well designed, must be implemented if it is to have any impact on students. Fullan and Panfret (1977) said that implementation is a critical phase in the cycle of planning and teaching a curriculum.

After planning, it is time to implement what has been planned. This implementation is where the adult learners start to receive lessons from radio broadcasting. Before starting the broadcast, the reception center will have already received all didactic supports such as booklets, prints, pictures, DVDs, CD, tapes, and so forth.

Students will study every day, and the facilitators must ensure that the adult learners master the daily module, pass the daily test and, after success, then pass on to the following module. In some cases, the student will have to pass a practical test held out of the reception center; the facilitator can then confer with the student if he can continue on to the next module and if necessary pass the oral or practical test. Here, all distance learners will be receiving the same content at the same time, but they will be in different locations within the region.

A common problem facing distance education programs is feedback; in the case of the Kabongo's cassava education program, the solution lies in the training of facilitators who will be located in the local area. The facilitators will report to the radio broadcasting center; these reports will encompass didactics needs, difficult questions where support is required, the evolution of learners and their participation, the quality of content broadcasted, and the attitude of adult learners towards the program. Also, the facilitators will be the connection between the radio broadcasting reception centers and the radio broadcasting center. The radio broadcasting center will try in some ways to help learners of different radio broadcasting reception centers to share their experiences by inviting some adult learners to participate in the preparation and broadcast content and engage in discussions at times. During the research survey stage local citizens were asked if they would like to participate in the preparation and broadcasting processes in a community radio on a weekly basis. There was an overwhelmingly positive response, with 86.7% asking to be involved and 10.3% who indicated they did not want to participate and only 3% who were undecided.

As this will be the first opportunity for the rural people to have a radio broadcasting center in their own area, it will be important to try to respond to the requests of the local people. If the information gained from the survey can be followed, then it is possible to meet the needs of the community. During the research survey, citizens were asked if such things as agricultural issues, health issues, educational issues and cultural issues would be good points to focus on. 89.3% of the community responded with a definite yes to the aforementioned issues and 0.1% said no with 10.6% of the responders undecided.

Following the implementation steps is the evaluation of the two precedent steps.

EVALUATION

Mager (1984) points out that if you are teaching things that cannot be evaluated, you are in the awkward position of being unable to demonstrate that you are teaching anything at all. Intangibles are often intangible because we have been lazy to think about what it is we want students to be able to do. This is another important step, from which the designer will discover if the curriculum was helpful and useful following the need of the learner.

Talking about evaluation, we think about planning and implementation. From here, it can evaluate the work of the student and discover if he has mastered what was planned for him to master. In the case of the Kabongo distance education broadcasting, the evaluation process must include an assessment to ensure the learners understand the issues related to cassava and are able to transfer this knowledge to daily life. If the result of students' evaluation is very good, this can enable the designer to understand that the plan was greatly successful; if the results are poor, this will let the designer reconsider the design, the content, the tools used to deliver the content, the environment, and the instructional design, and hence review the areas that are leading to poor performance.

Formative evaluation, and in some ways the summative evaluation, will be used to evaluate learners. The formative evaluation will allow the teacher and the learners to understand the evolution and the mastery of the present module prior to continuing on to the next module. From the formative evaluation the teacher will be able to provide some assistance and advice to learners. That is why Fehring (2005) stated that students have the right to know about their own literacy learning achievements, and that this is still the most salient reason for the assessment and reporting processes used in teaching and learning educational environments.

In terms of formative evaluation, the Kabongo distance education broadcast also faces some obstacles due to the illiteracy of the local citizen, and hence we must use oral evaluation. Questions will be asked to adult learners and, from their answers, decisions will be made concerning their mastery of the modules. Also, from practical activities, discussions, presentations and explanations, and workshops on the module, the teachers and facilitators will decide if the students can make the transition to the new module.

Concerning summative evaluation, attention should be paid to the cultural issues of local people in the Kabongo region. These cultural values include that adult answers are the correct answers. If we have to tell the adult learners, who are fathers to at least five children and considered the spirit, the chief, the decider, the person most responsible for the family, that their answers are incorrect; this will manifest itself as a frustration for those adult learners. Possible consequences could be that, step-by-step, the learners will lose motivation towards the program and, potentially, adult learners could drop out.

Summative evaluation is important in the sense of motivating learners. The Kabongo distance education broadcasting case is the first experience of teaching adults and often illiterate learners in that corner of Congo, and hence the plan is to provide a "certificate of participation" to all adults who participate in the program. This can motivate others to come and join the program in the future, for either agriculturally based curriculum or for other social/educational based curriculum.

RADIO BROADCASTING

When assessing the technology, each resource should be examined for its unique qualities and its potential benefits for rural teachers and adult learners. In the case of the Kabongo region, we should not use a tool because it is new and available. Each innovation should be suited to the needs and the realities of the environment. It has been said by many that there is a tendency to dispose of old machines. This is a good idea for some parts of the world, but a very bad decision for those who have never seen nor touched such "outdated machines." This is the case in the Kabongo region in the Democratic Republic of Congo. In Congo, 60% of people are affected by a high rate of poverty and live in rural areas, where they have never seen electricity, television, radio broadcasting or computers. The area has roads in very poor condition, slow trains, and the people are scattered throughout the region. In such a situation, if we have to deliver distance education to isolated learners, the first choice would be radio broadcast. Such a method is practical; people are able to buy a radio receiver and batteries, and not rely on electricity. They can all receive the lessons simultaneously. Given the local realities: the scattered population, the high rate of illiteracy and language diversity, we believe that radio remains the most popular, accessible, and cost-effective means of communication for rural people of the Kabongo area. Radio can overcome all of the aforementioned obstacles.

In order to achieve success, radio broadcasting combined with booklets, DVD, CD, and tapes can ensure the delivery of information. All content to be broadcasted must be contained on DVD, CD, tapes, and printed booklets. These will be used as didactic support. The content will be the same in the DVD, CD, tapes, and booklets. This means that the DVD will use local language and will contain voice, images, and content. The CD will contain voice, images, and texts; and tapes will contain voices, and the booklets will have written text and pictures. (Booklets will be useful for literate people.)

In comparison to other distance education based on radio broadcasting, our innovation is that the rural people will first be trained to become facilitators in different villages that are chosen as centers of reception for the broadcasting. Second, before the broadcasting of lessons, all materials such as booklets, DVD, CD, and tapes will be sent to the areas. Third, when broadcasting the content, the facilitators must be with the rural adult learners, organize a short explanation on location, collect and answer any questions from the learners, discuss the content with the learners, and

plan some activities as practice for the learners. Fourth, the trained group originating from different villages (centers of broadcast reception) will travel to the central broadcast place for curriculum evaluation and from this evaluation consider alterations to the curriculum.

TIME OF DELIVERY

The radio will broadcast every day from morning to evening, but the educational content will only be in the evening, following the wishes of the target audience. There will be lessons three times per week focused on agriculture, three times for lessons on values and community building, and two times for general knowledge. Sunday morning is culturally the time of religion, and at noon as for all days, the national news will be broadcast.

MANAGEMENT AND BROADCAST

The radio broadcasting will be managed by the nongovernment organization called Community and Social Development Organization (www.odcs-rdc.org) located in Kabongo. Experts who make up the broadcasting management team will be native speakers of the local language, Kilubakat. This team will include expertise in areas such as: information and communication technologies, distance education, adult education, adult psychology, journalism, agriculture, and climatology.

In terms of the broadcasting regulations, the first regulation will be that everyone hoping to become a broadcaster for this educational radio must be an educator. They must understand the principles of education; teaching and learning and the psychological principles of rural adults. The radio will be used as a tool to reach the remote target audience, so it is very important in this step to follow the qualification criterion to become a qualified teacher of distance education. The second condition is also very important, and that is mastery of the local language (Kilubakat). The target audience, as stated previously, constitutes rural adult learners who are illiterate, and often cannot speak French or other national languages, only their own local language.

It is hoped that gradually they can train the local people to become presenters to share local farming knowledge. The local people expressed in the survey that 88% would like to listen to broadcasts made by the local community and only 1.3% answered no. There was 10.7% undecided on the topic.

TIMETABLE

As noted above, every week there will be three lessons focused on agriculture, three lessons focused on values and community building, and two lessons devoted to general knowledge. Each lesson we take one hour; there will be two information delivery sessions, the first segment will be 20 minutes and then a 5-minute break (containing some music, perhaps), the second segment is 20 minutes, and 15 minutes at the end of the lesson for review and discussion.

SUGGESTION

Distance education should be regarded in the case of the Kabongo region as a vital option in continuous rural problem solving, youth empowerment, and a means to fight premature school dropout. The Democratic Republic of Congo, and in particular the region of Kabongo, has a majority of the population living in rural areas, and they are poor, illiterate, physically isolated and scattered, and facing all kinds of daily problems. The schools are characterized by late primary entrance, high grade repetition and a high rate of dropout. Distance education can be a good way to empower the rural people, youth, and women. These groups can be offered all kinds of skills and then they will be able to solve the daily problems encountered in the agricultural sector, along with other sectors such as education and training, family planning, environment and pollution, communication and transportation, and electricity and water.

CONCLUSION

This curriculum is innovative as it is the first one in the domain for rural, illiterate, adult learners. Also, it is the first time a curriculum has been designed to take into account the needs of rural people in the Kabongo region.

This distance education curriculum will be delivered by radio broadcast and it will use an experimental curriculum. After its effective implementation, evaluation will

Table 1
Broadcast Timetable

	MON	TUES	WED	THURS	FRI	SAT	SUN
AM	LI	LI	LI	LI	LI	LI	LI
	ADV	ADV	ADV	ADV	ADV	ADV	RELIG
NOON	NI	NI	NI	NI	NI	NI	NI
PM	M	M	M	M	M	M	M
	RA	RA	RA	RA	RA	RA	KB
EVENING	KH	KB	KH	K	KH	KB	K

Key: LI = local information; ADV = advertisement; NI = national information; M = messages; RA = recreation activities; KH = know how; KB = knowledge being; K = knowledge; REL = religion.

allow for development and enhancement as well as develop into other subjects.

It is believed that distance education is an appropriate means to educate rural people in different ways on all kinds of challenges they are facing in their daily life. Also in the case of the Kabongo region, where they are facing numerous social and economic issues such as a high rate of illiteracy and permanent school dropout, family-related problems, issues of environment and pollution, agricultural problems, bad roads and transportation, and a lack of telecommunication, we are sure that through distance education we will succeed to educate the population of Kabongo. This education will empower them with specific transferable skills and these skills will allow them to be able to solve the different kinds of problems they are facing and those that may be encountered in the future.

REFERENCES

Cohen, L., Manion, L, & Morrison, K. (1998). *A guide to teaching practice* (4th ed.). London: Routledge.

Dunn, R., Beaudry, J. S., & Klavas, A. (1989). Survey of research on learning styles. *Educational Leadership, 46*(6), 50-58.

Fullan, M. G., & Pomfret, A. (1977). Research on curriculum and instruction implementation. *Review of Education Research, 47*(2), 335-339.

Fehring, H. (2005). Critical analytical and reflective literacy assessment: Reconstructing practice. *Australian Journal of Language and Literacy, 28,* 335-339.

IITA. (2000). *Mission Report: In the context of war and the resulting distrurbance of trading activities, the phytosanitary situation of cassava.* Retrieved February 20, 2006, from http://www.rdfs.net/linked-docs/booklet/bookl_congo_en.pdf

Mager, R. F. (1984). *Preparing instructional objectives* (3rd ed.). Belmont, CA: Lake.

Nsomwe-a-nfunkwa, B. (2005). Survey concerning the implementation of a community radio in Kabongo's region. *PSE review, 1*(2).

Scott, G. (1999). *Change matters.* Sydney, Australia: Allen & Unwin.

Simonson, M. (2006). *Seven key concepts: Integrating instructional technology in the classroom.* Retrieved January 17, 2006, from http://www.Fgse.nova.edu/itde/faculty/Simonson/it/intro_it.ppt

Tomlinson, C. A. (2002). *The third wave.* New York: Bantam Books.

Distance Learning and Bilingual Educational CD-ROMs in Rural Areas of the Democratic Republic of Congo

Banza Nsomwe-a-nfunkwa

Nowadays, many countries, especially those that are developed, are concerned by the use of new technologies in teaching and learning in different areas of the daily life of their citizens in different societies. But this is not the case in developing countries, such as

Banza Nsomwe-a-nfunkwa,
Nanjing Normal University, China.
E-mail: nfunkwa@hotmail.com

the Democratic Republic of Congo, where even the old technologies are still a huge obstacle. In a country such as the Democratic Republic of Congo where, in the case of rural areas, everything is lacking in terms of the information and communication technology (ICT) infrastructure, add to this the lack of electricity and not even a generator nor solar power in some corners of rural areas. Addressing this situation, and our need to participate in, and improve, the well being of the scattered population in the rural areas, is the concept of development of a distance learning system. *What should be the content of this distance learning program? What kind of technology should we use in order to meet the needs of all distance learners? Which language should be used for the teaching and learning?*

In rural areas of the Democratic Republic of Congo, people are facing different kinds of problems connected to the lack of education and training on a daily level. These are adults characterized by a high level of illiteracy. In the case of the research done in the Kabongo region, the province of Katanga, in the Democratic Republic of Congo, people are facing huge problems related to Cassava diseases and its effect. The effects include a loss in their daily income and consequently a lack of food and hunger, higher child school-dropout rates because there is not enough money for schooling fees, a lack of clothing, and a lack of money to buy medicine in the case they are sick.

The rural people hope to solve the problem of cassava diseases. The best way to help them is to educate and train them about cassava diseases and the possible ways to fight against those diseases. In this case, the teaching and learning must be done in the local language of the illiterate distant learners.

In this article, the author explains the process of the design and development of the content contained in an educational CD-ROM. In this age of high technology, everyone is trying to focus on new technologies and in some way trying to bypass the old technologies. This is the case of many developed countries, but not in developing countries, such as the Democratic Republic of Congo, where the situation is catastrophic in term of the use of technologies in teaching and learning activities. In rural areas for example, there are still some people who have never seen or used a television, never seen or touched a computer, never used the old and new technologies and, in addition to this, the rural areas lack electricity and all kinds of ICT infrastructure. In these rural areas, there is a high rate of illiteracy and extremely high child school-dropout rates. At the same time, the people in the rural areas of Congo are facing all kind of problems and need to be educated or trained in the way to be able to solve their daily problems. The majority of rural dwellers are farmers living scattered across huge areas in villages. In this case, the use of distance learning is the best way to reach the people. At this point, the question is to know what technology can be used correctly, reliably, and appropriately.

Distance learning via CD-ROM is an opportunity for rural people of the Kabongo region to study wherever, and at whatever time, they choose. All content—audio, evaluation, and photographs—is provided on CD-ROM, and additional prints and tapes will also be provided to help facilitate the successful use of the CD-ROM. To help give students feedback, facilitators will be available for consultation via mail, or face to face.

Distance education uses various media to deliver learning information and to link students and teachers. Some media can be used for both purposes, but they generally fall into two categories: those that can be used to convey subject content, such as print materials, video tapes, audio tapes, television, computer-based courseware, and CD-ROM, and those that permit communication between teachers and students, such as fax, radio, teleconferencing, videoconferencing, and the Internet (The Commonwealth of Learning, 2006). With the CD-ROM, distance learners have a huge opportunity to learn or to train in their own time at their own place (Distance Learning Zone, 2006).

CD-ROM PRESENTATION

The program contained in this CD-ROM is designed to address the basic needs of the rural people in order to solve their daily problems connected to cassava disease and its impact on their daily life, on kids' education, on clothing, etc. This CD-ROM "Le Manioc et ses Maladies" is an educational CD-ROM containing several elements: Images of Cassava, summary, introduction and conclusion; including seven chapters. Chapter 1: History of Cassava, Chapter 2: Importance of Cassava, Chapter 3: Cassava Diseases and Insects, Chapter 4: Importance of Cassava Diseases, Chapter 5: Moment of Decreased Production, Chapter 6: Fight Against Cassava Diseases, Chapter 7: Cassava Dangers and Solutions.

LEARNING DESIGN

This CD-Rom is adheres to all steps of instructional design. Another advantage with this CD-ROM is that the self-directed learner has flexibility to opt for linear, branched, hypercontent, or learner directed design. The chapters are connected in terms of numbers, but in terms of the content, the learners are free to decide from which chapter to start. But to complete the program, the learner must learn all modules and pass the test for each chapter. For the self-directed learner, the CD-ROM also contains questions for evaluation. But for adult learners who are illiterate, the evaluation will be oral and practical.

In terms of learning design, the specificity of this CD-ROM is that the learners have multiple choices of daily content; they can start from any chapter and head to the evaluation of the chapter (see Figures 1 and 2).

CHOICE OF LANGUAGE

Here we have to say that this CD-ROM allows the learner to make a language preference following his skills in one language or another. As noted above, our target audience constitutes a huge percentage of illiterates learners; to help them to have a chance to study something on the cassava matter, we decided to design the same content in two languages. This has the advantage of giving each learner the choice of language in which he prefers to learn.

To make a choice between languages is very easy for everyone even for the illiterate learners. It only requires you to move the mouse on the top of the name of the language and click once, and the result is that you have the content in that language (Figures 3, 4, and 5).

FLEXIBILITY OF USING VOICE

An advantage of this educational CD-ROM is that it has voice in both French and Kilubakat language. The voice can be used following the pattern of the learner. It can be stopped in order to make a comment or assess if the learner understood the teacher, or just for a small pause. Also it

Figure 1.   Learning design giving multiple choice of study (French version of CD-ROM).

Figure 2. Learning Design giving multiple choice of study (Kilubakat version of CD-ROM).

Figure 3. French language.

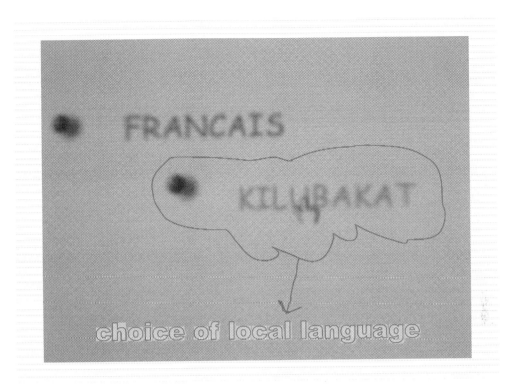

Figure 3.   Kilubakat language.

Figure 4.   Choice of language.

gives the possibility to preview or to forward through the content.

DIFFICULTIES AND OBSTACLES

When designing this CD-ROM, we faced many kinds of difficulties and obstacles connected to time and financial matters. This CD-ROM was designed to meet the needs of the rural people living in the rural areas of Kabongo, in province of Katanga in the Democratic Republic of Congo. The economic situation of this country has a negative impact on all sectors of the people's lives. From the major city (Lubumbashi) to the rural area where I collected data, the distance is approximately 800 kilometers. It took me 3 to 4 days to reach this area because of bad roads and the lack of good transportation.

The survey I conducted with the local people in order to identify their problems was in French, it took me time to translate it into the local language so as to be understood by the local illiterate people (the people who have not had an education and do not speak French).

From their answers to the survey, I discovered that their problems were connected to the agricultural sector, the economic foundation of their well-being. After discussions with them, I discovered that the main issue of focus was cassava diseases and its impact on their life, their children's education, their clothing problem and so on.

Not being an expert in the agricultural sector, I contacted experts and they informed me that there are many kinds of research completed on cassava disease, and the research results were available in the library. After visiting different libraries, I discovered that all research was completed and published in the French language (the official language of the Democratic Republic of Congo), but French is used by few rural illiterate peo-

ple. The language problem was the first obstacle for the rural people in accessing this information. The second obstacle was the lack of trust in the diseases, the third obstacle was also the resistance to the new agricultural practice, and the lack of appropriate educational strategies for educating rural adult people, and another obstacle was the scattered nature of the population.

From this situation, I developed a program suitable for adult learners living in the rural areas of Kabongo, Katanga Province, in the Democratic Republic of Congo. This program would make efforts to find a resolution to the aforementioned obstacles.

Because of the poor technological infrastructure present in Congo, the choice was made for the use of radio broadcasting to reach the scattered adult learners. The radio will be used in combination with print, audio and video. From this I decided to also design an educational CD-ROM to be used both by teachers, facilitators and self-directed distant learners.

SUGGESTIONS

In the case of developing countries such as the Democratic Republic of Congo, the use of educational CD-ROM plays a huge importance in urban and rural areas. Attention should be paid to all obstacles enumerated such as language problem, location of target audience, the nature of the audience, needs of learners, etc.

I do believe that given the lack of new technologies, radio broadcasting, print, CD-ROM, audio, video are all still needed in developing countries, and especially in local regions, where almost all forms of technologies are currently lacking. The realities of the absence of technologies in these areas mean that the use of new technologies is not viable. But in some cases the use of older technologies can meet some of the needs of the population in the terms of education and training.

CONCLUSION

From this experience from the rural area of Kabongo, Katanga Province, Democratic Republic of Congo, I do believe that the use of radio, CD-ROM, audio, video, print, etc can facilitate distance learning (distance education) for the rural people, and they can benefit from this.

The main goal of distance education should be firstly, and most importantly, focussed on the educational objectives, and not firstly on the technological equipment. This is not to say that new technologies are not welcome in the rural areas of developing countries, such as Congo.

The meaning is that at this level where the economical situation of developing countries, such as Congo, is still delayed, the countries cannot afford all new technologies for rural areas; therefore it is better at present to think of new technologies, but in the meantime use the old technologies.

REFERENCES

The Commonwealth of Learning. (2006). *The use of multimedia in distance education*. Retrieved June 15, 2006, from http://www.col.org/knowldges/ks_multimedia.htm

Distance Learning Zone. (2006). *QM&T'S distance learning products*. Retrieved June 2, 2006, from http://www.qmt.co.uk/distl.htm

---

IN RURAL AREAS OF THE DEMOCRATIC REPUBLIC OF CONGO, PEOPLE ARE FACING DIFFERENT KINDS OF PROBLEMS CONNECTED TO THE LACK OF EDUCATION AND TRAINING ON A DAILY LEVEL.

The Activities and Educational Model of CARID of the University of Ferrara

Giulia Calvani and Silvia Micarelli

"If the industrial era nourished our physical being, the Age of Access feeds our mental, emotional, and spiritual being."

—Jeremy Rifkin

INTRODUCTION

The age of information, as ours has been defined, has knocked down space and time distance in all human activities: from politics to religion, from business to personal relations. And education, understandably, couldn't be left out. That is why, today like never before, the world of education is at a turning point, and, especially at an academic level, it needs to relate to the technologies of its age.

A new and diffused demand for instruction is forcing universities to rethink their organizational model. In order to do this, they have to elaborate and combine new

Giulia Calvani,
Via Val di Chienti, 10 – 00159, Rome, Italy.
Telephone: 0039-3334947702.
E-mail: giulia.calvani@gmail.com

Silvia Micarelli,
Via Nocelli, 2 – 67018, L'Aquila, Italy.
Telephone: 0039-3281492627.
E-mail: silvia.micarelli@gmail.com

languages, concepts, methodologies, and learning strategies.

Taking this into account, the University of Ferrara was one of the first in Italy to create new learning models and start distance education activities through CARID.

CARID

CARID, Research Centre Athenaeum for Innovation and Distance Education, is a multidisciplinary research and education structure that promotes innovation and the practice of teaching/learning through multimedia technologies on the Web. It is one of the most important realities in the development and delivery of distance education in Italy. The center offers courses at a distance for all graduate and postgraduate academic titles: degrees, postgraduate master's, specialization courses, updating, and professional training courses.

In order to better understand CARID, its activities and its future, we have interviewed Paolo Frignani, director of CARID since 1997 and Professor Giorgio Poletti, head of the educational design team of the structure. The main strength of CARID, according to Frignani, is

the fact that it deals with distance learning but mostly with teaching innovation. And distance learning is part of this innovation. Innovation which means the use of technologies in post-secondary education, in particular in the creation of courses, learning paths completely at a distance or the use of technologies as an added value to traditional teaching.

HISTORY AND PERSPECTIVES

Because in Italy CARID is one of the centers which has been operating in e-learning the longest, it has dealt with the profound changes that this educational model has undergone in the last 10 years. Professor Poletti explains how CARID has adapted to these changes:

I'd say that it followed the evolution of the interactions in the Web. We can't deny that the Internet has given the rhythm to the evolution of the interaction models and therefore of the educational models. The evolution can be summarized in the fact that it started as one-way and it became two-way, so when education used a one-way network you could send a fax, then a book, then a Web site with little interaction but the idea was "I send you something, you're the final recipient." E-learning was a tool but not a new educational model.

As it always happens, when computer science walks in, it ends up modifying the process which had evoked it and improving it.

By increasing the level of interactivity the e-learning model changes as the web does. E-learning tries to create education in the Web and not using the Web as a mere communication medium.

CARID is an extremely dynamic structure that, in the past, was able to adapt to constant changes. That is why we asked Frignani about CARID's future perspectives. He told us that it is right now

evolving into two separate structures which will work together: an "e-learning school," an athenaeum for distance learning which will manage distance and blended education, and "CARID lab," which will essentially have a research purpose on the diffusion of new technology in a postsecondary context.

MISSION AND ORGANIZATION

The mission of CARID is to promote innovation in the practice of teaching/learning models. In particular, CARID has two main objectives: first, "to analyze the methodological and technological aspects of distance education through research and publishing" and, second, "to manage university courses experimentally in a distance modality (integrated with full time traditional activities such as seminars and labs) in collaboration with education, technology and content experts" according to Poletti.

In CARID, the staff is divided into two units, each composed of two team members:

Research Unit

- Team A: communication experts involved in training and supporting coordinators and tutors and in analyzing the methodological aspects in research activities.
- Team B: instructional designers and programmers in charge of developing the technological platform which supports the learning activities and of developing new models of personal learning environment (PLE)

Operative Unit

- Team C: coordinators and tutors who manage the learning activities.
- Team D: system analysts and multimedia content producers involved in the management and archive of contents on the platform.

E-learning courses are therefore the result of different professionals who cooperate in order to create efficient and effective learning environments.

THE OPERATIVE MODEL

The operative model of CARID is based on the distance management of five essential elements: design, production, delivery, tutoring, and assessment

DESIGN

The design phase of the courses involves many people who work in team. The group is made up of education experts specialized in different subjects and experts in communication systems and data elaboration. In general, during the design phase the objectives and target learners are defined; the learning strate-

gies and the technical solutions to be adopted follow together with the time to be reserved to individual support.

We asked Poletti how he structures an online module:

It depends on the students and on the level of elaboration it requires. There is usually a first part in which we organize all the paper documents and consulting material, a second phase related to the interaction through a video-lesson, or chat or other synchronous tools and a forum phase which maintains the attention and leads the students.

PRODUCTION

Content experts coordinated by a scientific area manager are in charge of defining the cognitive fields of the learning units and deciding on the tools (printed text, audiovisual support, digital documents) necessary to content delivery.

The development phase consists in preparing the materials needed to carry out the courses. This task is carried out by teachers and researchers who have skills in both distance education and their subject matters.

The objectives, the content, and the procedures are selected and defined in detail together with the timing. The materials are then gathered through tools of exploration and learning of cognitive fields, tools of content delivery, multimedia tools, and assessment tools.

Poletti describes the main difficulties in preparing a learning model destined to online delivery: "It is a problem of adequate time availability for the learning production because if a 1-hour lesson means an hour and a half preparation, to prepare a learning object I need 5, 6, 8, 10 hours of preparation."

DELIVERY

Learning activities managed at a distance are based on the use of a technologi-

Figure 1. Online platform CARID homepage.

cal platform that the students access through a Web site. The model of distance education applied in CARID and implemented in the online platform is characterized by asynchronous communication among those involved in the learning process: users, tutors, and content experts. The platform is only accessible to them through an identification form: the online user is presented with a general page on the course organization, containing the links to general documents (initial quiz, general forum, news, general info) and the links to the pages of the single subjects; these contain the links to the contents, the exam organization, and to the structured forum.

Printed units are used to lead in the exploration of the cognitive context of the subjects and are integrated with other resources organized in Web pages, interactive hypertexts and hypermedia, and bibliographies.

Assessment and self-assessment is based on a number of questions (generally 25) which match four short answers: each online quiz is immediately followed by the communication of the result on a Web page that includes feedback on why each answer is or isn't correct.

The structured forum is a fundamental tool of asynchronous interaction on the Web among students, tutors, and teachers: it allows users to not only define the title and text of the question, but also to monitor contributors and their exact moment of participation by selecting a topic from the course menu. Because of this organization, each contribution is placed in the correct position within the course context, and because it easily traceable, it optimizes the

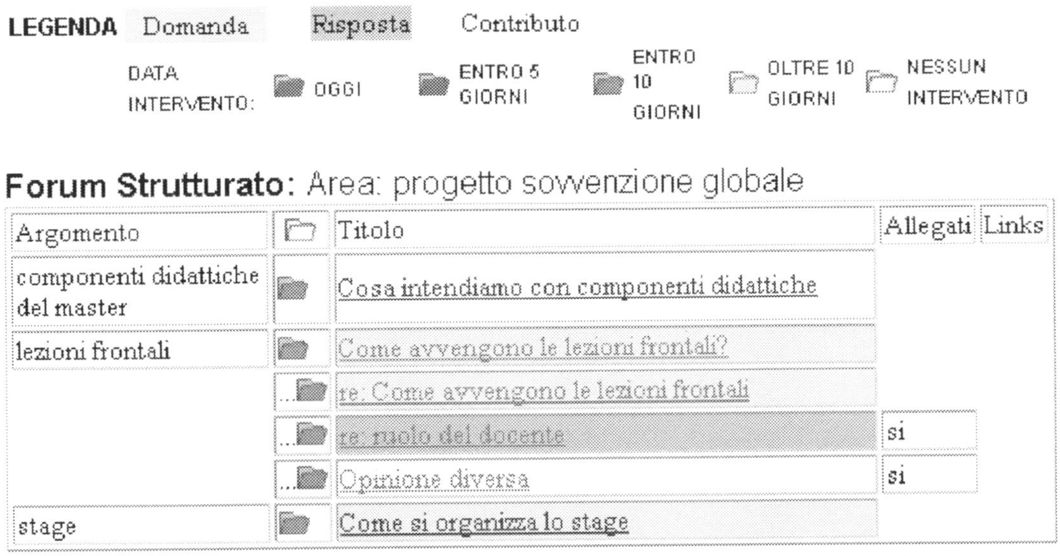
LEGENDA Domanda Risposta Contributo
DATA INTERVENTO:
OGGI
ENTRO 5 GIORNI
ENTRO 10 GIORNI
OLTRE 10 GIORNI
NESSUN INTERVENTO
Forum Strutturato: Area: progetto sovvenzione globale
Argomento
Titolo
Allegati
Links
componenti didattiche del master
Cosa intendiamo con componenti didattiche
lezioni frontali
Come avvengono le lezioni frontali?
re: Come avvengono le lezioni frontali
re: ruolo del docente
si
Opinione diversa
si
stage
Come si organizza lo stage

Figure 2. CARID online structured forum.

organization of knowledge gathered through the use of the Web.

We asked Professor Poletti to further deepen the aspects related to the use of the platform by the teachers.

> We have a double plan because we have a convention which links the University of Ferrara to the technological pole of Argenta for distance courses and the use of a proprietary platform naturally means that some activities need to be adapted to what this offers, a sort of compromise. On the other hand for both traditional and distance courses we manage and test a series of LMS systems and open source modules mainly toward personal learning environment with the possibility of learning environments in which teachers and learners access to those modules they're interested in.

The use of e-learning technologies tends to elevate the level of structure of the cognitive contexts through cognitive maps related to the different courses, which have the double function of communicating the main relations of the subject and of supporting them through forums and quizzes. In other words, the current pattern of navigation inside the single courses is characterized by the presence of option menus, destined to evolve toward a cognitive map in which assessment, contributions, and forum participation can be linked and be visited, at the level of single topic in the learning context; this development entails higher quality in the organization of knowledge and in the definition of the internal logical connections in the cognitive field, providing flexibility, thanks to the possibility, exclusive to the dynamic systems of information such as that adopted by CARID, to easily modify the structure of connections.

In this direction the distance learning platform follows these guidelines supported by innovation in hardware and software:

1. Knowledge is organized in cognitive maps in which the contributions are constantly updated, whether produced by teachers, experts, tutors, or users, in the form of resources, links, and forums.
2. Documents are written through digital tools that require the progressive defi-

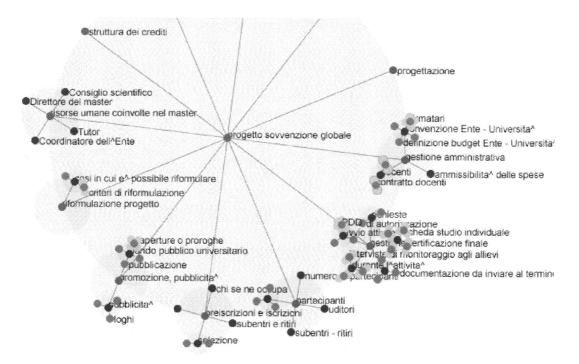

Figure 3.   CARID course structure cognitive map.

Figure 4.   CARID e-learning platform.

Figure 5. CARID introductory seminar.

nition and differentiation of a new interactive and multimedia language, characterized by certain grammar and symbols.

3. Learning is customized and registered by structuring and transmitting the contents within structured maps. Tools, modules, and personal contributions are registered in the data warehouse of distance education, allowing tutors to deeply analyze the educational process.

These three lines come together in CARID in the design of an e-learning platform that answers to the diffusion of a structured communication culture, in relation to the potentialities offered by the current technologies.

TUTORING

Each student can rely on adequate services of support and educational assistance that builds the interaction process by eliminating the condition of physical distance. Learning assistance is provided during the entire learning path through appropriate communication media and face-to-face conversations. Qualified and competent staff carry out the function of "tutor" who not only provide general technical information, but also detailed information on the contents of a specific course.

To better understand the function of such an important figure, we have interviewed tutor Alessio Pellegrini, who answered in this way to the question on his activities toward the learners:

> It depends on the academic year. At first we do orienteering, we answer e-mails and phone calls to provide information on the courses. Then we organize the initial seminars. Then just before the beginning of the lessons we give learners access to the platform and allow them to familiarize with it in order to solve the

main problems and show how the course works. During the year we organize internships, labs and seminars, providing answers to possible doubts.

Pellegrini adds that on these occasions the relation with students becomes informal, and

> it gets easy to understand problems especially when at the beginning it's difficult for them to understand how courses are managed and the university system in general. As they go on they solve this problem connected with distance. We try to help by organizing seminars and labs where study groups are created and sharing occurs. This kind of relationship is encouraged in appropriate spaces in the platform.

ASSESSMENT

In distance education, maybe more than in other learning situations, it is necessary to constantly assess learning activities and the participation of students. The evaluation system implemented in CARID provides constant information through an initial analysis of the characteristics of the students, a constant monitoring of the mandatory and spontaneous interactions in the forums, intermediate tests, and final verifications.

In order to fully understand the evaluation model used in CARID we have asked Poletti, who tells us:

> Until now we have had two separate evaluation methods according to whether they were for graduate or postgraduate courses. For degrees there are formally three evaluation moments: interaction through a forum during the entire length of the course; a self-assessment stage through structured tests with an immediate feedback; a final written or oral face-to-face examination.
>
> In master's there is a triple evaluation: one on the interaction on the web, (forum participation, language use, interest in the topic) which carries about 20, 25% of

the final score, one on a series of timed tests on the web, and the third phase of a more traditional final exam in presence which carries about 50% of the result.

CARID has progressively acquired and consolidated the necessary technological and methodological skills and tools for the management of e-learning courses for each of the phases described.

ONLINE STUDENTS

At the end of this analysis the question is how the students of CARID deal with online learning, on how they use the interactive tools made available by the structure and what kind of relationship they have with the other actors of the e-learning courses.

An interesting consideration on the relation between online teachers and students is offered by Poletti, according to whom:

> distant learners are the most present ones. The relationship with them assumes a continuity which is rare with students in presence. Traditional students know that the lesson is the topical moment and if there's a reception room they come to ask for explanations but they see these moments as the direct support to their learning and they have books at home. Distant students have instead the idea that they should be somehow supported so usually we use continuative relationship devices such as emails.

In order to better understand the point of view of the students, we spoke with Enrico Margotta, enrolled in the second year of the degree course "Technologist in Audio-visual and Multimedia Communication," who told us about his learning experience. First, we dealt with the relation between students and teachers:

> The relationship with students is a little particular because you don't see them every day. When it happens that you

Figure 6.   The online student.

meet someone who you've seen at other exams, then you chat, you get to know them. Otherwise it's hard to have a strong relationship. With teachers, it depends; generally they're very helpful.

The next point was on the tools that are used daily. Margotta told us that most of the activities are carried out on the platform but that he also finds the site www.tecnologo.net very useful to share information and materials on the degree course with other students.

Tecnologo.net is a virtual community created by and completely managed by students and doesn't have an administrative link to the University of Ferrara. Students exchange information and material to easily deal with the learning activities. They also organize face-to-face moments out of learning obligations.

THE INNOVATIONS OF **CARID**

A fundamental part of the activities of CARID is research and educational innovation. An example of such activities is the latest success of CARID: CaridTV. The idea of this new application is explained to us by Frignani: "We tried to put together and use not only computer science but also video in the management of distance courses for students in order to create a television format which is highly interactive."

In order to comprehend how this application will be used within the teaching model of CARID, Professor Poletti tells us about how he is working to implement this tool within his courses and which are the main difficulties:

At this moment we are still designing CaridTV, we haven't used it within a course,

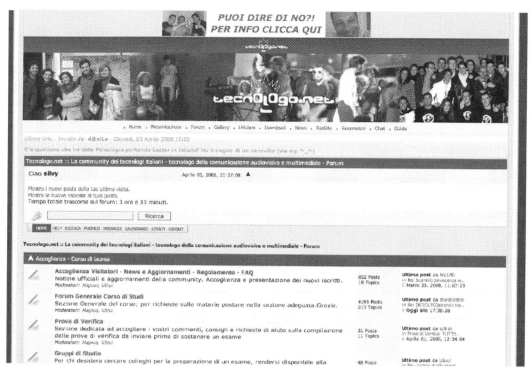

Figure 7.   Tecnologo.net.

Figure 8.   CARID television.

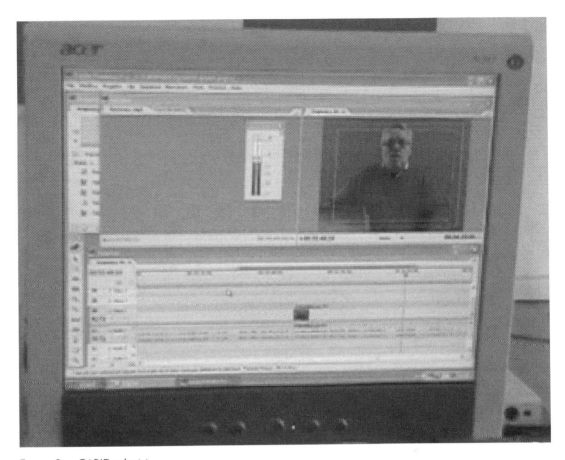

Figure 9. CARID television.

except for spot interventions, to introduce some seminars but we haven't integrated in our course yet. I'm thinking of using it synchronously for documents, that is giving the chance to provide handouts in the moment I'm discussing them, sort of like what happens in class.

Thanks to the project CaridTV, CARID has recently won the prize Aldo Fabris with the following notation: "The project allowed CARID to develop a university web-tv 'Carid-tv' able to implement and deliver multimedia learning materials, enabling the audience to access a variety of personalized learning paths." [Note: At its sixth edition, the Prize "Aldo Fabris" intends to point out universities, schools, companies, public administrations and

people who have created and developed learning projects which are marked by impressive results in learning obtained at an individual, team and organizational level through the promotion of the growth and development of the people and working communities.]

CONCLUSIONS

The origins of the success of CARID, says Frignani, are in "having believed in e-learning" and in "having created a degree course which has a double objective, that of being innovative and it is still today the only one in the National area, and that of being completely delivered at a distance."

CARID understood the importance of some fundamental concepts in e-learning, but today the world view of e-learning is changing: the enormous interest in interoperability of platforms for content exchange, the development of new technologies of document management opens the way to a modular classification of the cognitive supports, which is a true base of sharing and integration. Research in CARID is aimed at giving value to its great assets of contents in relation to their structure and interchange with other organizations in the field.

Perspectives on e-Learning
Case Studies From Cyprus

Charalambos Vrasidas, Lucy Avraamidou, and Symeon Retalis

INTRODUCTION

During the past decade there has been tremendous progress in the advancement of educational technology, making innovative learning solutions such as e-learning and online education increasingly more feasible in many educational settings. In several countries, the use of e-learning has now begun to noticeably contribute to economic growth. In Cyprus, an island in the Mediterranean Sea located at the crossroads of Europe, Asia, and Africa, many large-scale e-learning initiatives are cur-rently being undertaken by both public and private organizations, establishing the country as a center for education in the region.

Between the 1960s and 1990s, educational technology efforts in Cyprus schools were limited to the use of traditional audiovisual equipment and a few educational radio and television programs produced by the government. In recent years, however, considerable efforts have been devoted to promoting lifelong learning and integrating information and commu-

Charalambos Vrasidas,
CARDET - University of Nicosia,
Metochiou 66, Engomi 2407, Cyprus.
Telephone: +357-22461566 ext. 227.
E-mail: pambos@cardet.org

Lucy Avraamidou,
CARDET - University of Nicosia,
Metochiou 66, Engomi 2407, Cyprus.
Telephone: +357-22461566 ext. 223.
E-mail: lucy@cardet.org

nication technologies (ICTs) in all levels of education. These efforts have been supported in large part by significant investments in the island's telecommunications infrastructure, which is one of the most developed in the region.

THE CYPRUS EDUCATION SYSTEM

Cyprus has a centralized educational administration system, with the Council of Ministers as the highest authority for educational policy, and the Ministry of Education and Culture (MOEC) responsible for delivery of education in Cyprus. Specifically, the MOEC is entrusted with the administration of education, the enforcement of education laws and, in cooperation with the Office of the Attorney General, the preparation of education bills. Education is compulsory up to the age of 15 and elementary and secondary education is free. The education system in Cyprus consists of the following levels:

Symeon Retalis, University of Piraeus, Karaoli & Dimitriou 80, Piraeus 18534, Greece.
Telephone: +30-2104142765.
E-mail: retal@unipi.gr

- *Preprimary Education.* One-year preprimary education that has recently become compulsory for children over the age of 3.
- *Primary Education.* Primary education is compulsory and has duration of 6 years.
- *Secondary Education.* Secondary education consists of two 3-year cycles of education—Gymnasio (lower secondary education) and Lyceum or Secondary Technical and Vocational Education (upper secondary education).
- *Higher Education.* There are currently three public universities (Cyprus University of Technology, Open University of Cyprus, University of Cyprus) and three private universities (University of Nicosia, Frederick University, European University Cyprus).

After several private higher education colleges had been operating on the island for decades, Cyprus established the first public university, the University of Cyprus, in 1992. With the additional expansion of operations by the renowned Cyprus Institute of Neurology and Genetics, government spending on research and development increased substantially and efforts began to promote Cyprus as a center for services, business, and education in the region. These efforts also included a plan to improve higher education provided by both public and private institutions and a recent law now allows the establishment and operation of private universities in Cyprus. The positions that are allocated to Cypriot high school graduates for studies in higher education institutions are distributed among the candidates based on the results of the competitive entrance examinations that are held every year by the Department of Higher and Tertiary Education.

Cyprus' accession to the European Union (EU) on May 1, 2004 also had a strong impact on the country's education, economy, and culture. Cyprus had been a member of the Council of Europe since 1960 and followed policies similar to those of the EU member-states in the field of education. With accession to the EU, Cyprus has been more actively participating in EU-funded projects in the areas of education, e-learning, and vocational education.

E-LEARNING IN CYPRUS

All European nations have established policies for using e-learning and incorporating ICT in education. Their objectives have focused on the categories of equipment, the acquisition and development of software, the skills of teachers, the skills of students, and the use of the Internet. After the special evaluation report of the Cyprus education system, conducted in 1997 by the International Institute for Education Planning (1997), a number of reforms were implemented on the island in an effort to raise the quality of education, such as the integration of computers and Internet connectivity into all levels of classroom teaching.

In a recent study (Empirica, 2006) about the use of computers and the Internet in schools in Europe, it was found that almost all schools in Cyprus now use computers for teaching and have Internet access, with the highest percentage being achieved in primary schools (95%). Only 31% use the Internet via a broadband connection, ranking Cyprus 25th among the 27 countries participating in the survey. However, the survey did not make clear how many computers are used per class, and the study was based on limited observations.

While schools in Cyprus appear to be well-equipped with technology and an ICT in education plan exists for formal education, what has generally been lacking is a holistic e-learning strategy encompassing education, business, and industry. To that end, the recent International Council for Educational Media 2007 conference, hosted in Cyprus by CARDET (Centre for

the Advancement of Research and Development in Educational Technology), invited key national experts in the area of e-learning to present their views and engage in a public dialogue on e-learning. Participants included representatives from the MOEC, the Pedagogical Institute, the University of Cyprus, the Open University of Cyprus, the European University Cyprus, and the University of Nicosia. The findings of the symposium revealed that several initiatives are currently under way which use a wide variety of technologies to offer education opportunities to learners of all ages. Some of these projects are presented and discussed in the following section.

E-LEARNING CASE STUDIES

Cyprus and the European Union have signed several protocols on financial and technical cooperation providing substantial financial aid to the island. In addition, Cypriot public and private organizations are increasingly participating in various EU-funded educational initiatives. Recently, the European Commission integrated its various educational and training initiatives under a single umbrella, the Lifelong Learning Program. With a significant budget of nearly 7 billion euro for 2007 to 2013, the new program replaces the existing education, vocational training, and e-learning programs, which ended in 2006. The new Lifelong Learning Program consists of several subprograms, including Comenius (for schools), Erasmus (for higher education), Leonardo da Vinci (for vocational education and training), and Grundtvig (for adult education).

Among the critical factors impacting the development and implementation of e-learning initiatives, are the skills and competencies of online tutors. One recent example of an e-learning project, funded under the Leonardo da Vinci subprogram, is *METER* (Monitoring, Evaluating and improving e-trainers competences in a lifelong learning environment). The project lead partner is the Institute for Adult and Vocational Education, under the Greek Ministry of Education. CARDET is the partner organization from Cyprus focusing on needs analysis, curriculum development, and quality assurance. The aim of the project is twofold: (1) to provide the means for training organizations to monitor, evaluate, and improve the competences of trainers regarding skills required for efficient and effective use of ICT, and (2) to develop training curricula for e-trainers of vocational education organizations to be offered throughout Europe. The projects aims to build the competencies of individuals and organizations involved in e-learning in Europe and at the same time raises the quality of education and training offered across sectors with the use of online technologies.

Another EU-funded project in which Cyprus participates is called *Multiple Intelligences Instructional Design Framework for Virtual Classes*. The program is in collaboration with the Waterford Institute of Technology and five other EU partners. This project uses the theory of multiple intelligences as a conceptual tool for the design of e-learning programs, and has developed and validated an instructional design framework for virtual classes. Pilot courses are being developed in the area of construction safety, and will be offered and evaluated in the participant countries.

One of the key challenges of European collaborations has to do with the multicultural nature of the organizations participating in the projects across borders. A project funded by the European Commission and which focuses on cultural diversity is called ADAPT (Adapting e-learning to Small Medium Enterprises Cultural Diversity). The project leader is Henley College of Management in the United Kingdom, with partners from Cyprus, Italy, Sweden, and Lithuania. This project aims to analyze and compare the findings from five previous EU-supported projects

and to consult with national and regional businesses, trainers, and e-learning developers to explore how e-learning needs can be adapted for different cultures and regions. The project will produce and disseminate an expert report to wider education and training communities in each country, which will inform future e-learning training providers about the specific e-learning needs of various sectors.

In addition to the e-learning offerings by the recently established Open University of Cyprus, there are several e-learning initiatives being implemented by both private and public organizations. Research centers, universities, and colleges have established agreements and collaborations with institutions from abroad. For example, the University of Nicosia has signed agreements with several EU- and U.S.-based universities to offer joint degrees using distance learning technologies. Also, the Mediterranean Virtual University allows students from leading universities in the Mediterranean region and Europe to enroll in various online courses developed and offered by the 11 partner universities. Since September 2006, 40 online courses in computer science and engineering and four courses in development studies have been offered (http://ls-ewdssps.ces.strath .ac.uk/MVU/).

A further EU-supported e-learning initiative is UNITE (Unified eLearning Environment for the School). This is an Information Society Technologies project under Framework Program 6 of the European Commission, and the local partner in this project is the University of Cyprus. The UNITE consortium has developed and established a technical platform enhanced with pedagogical guidance for the creation of high-quality e-learning content for secondary school. UNITE's technology has the flexibility to adapt to the learner's cultural environment and to his or her personal learning style. The UNITE portal-like platform supports the reuse of content material, the exchange of best practices, and the improvement of pedagogic models (http://www.unite-ist.org). Based on a socioconstructivist approach, UNITE developed a "best-practice" pedagogical framework that harnesses the potential of mobile technologies to foster enquiry/discovery learning and autonomous learning.

A large-scale open and distance learning initiative is the *Virtual University of the Small States of the Commonwealth* (VUSSC) launched in 2001 by the Commonwealth of Learning. The VUSSC is a consortium of institutions from small states of the Commonwealth (populations < 4 million), enabled by appropriate ICT applications, collaborating in practical ways to plan programs, develop the required content and ensure the delivery of those programs and support services to learners. Through the VUSSC, learners from island nations in the Caribbean, Pacific, Mediterranean (including Cyprus), Indian Ocean, as well as small countries in Africa, can gain online access to open educational resources designed to meet the development needs of participating countries. These non-proprietary course materials are integrated into accredited programs at postsecondary institutions in the participating countries, strengthening their educational capacity and outreach (http://www.wikieducator.org/VUSSC).

Finally, recent developments in mobile learning technologies have allowed the implementation of projects that use mobile devices and handheld computers in educational settings. Two ongoing research projects integrating mobile learning are *Handlearn* and *Technoskepsi* (http://mlearn.cardet.org), both supported by the Cyprus Research Promotion Foundation. These projects investigate the use of handheld technologies within nonformal science learning settings as a means to support scientific inquiry and reasoning at the elementary school. Specifically, these two projects aim to: develop and implement curriculum material informed by perspectives on the nature of science

issues, and the use of mobile technologies to support learning; investigate the role of handhelds in outdoors science investigations, and; produce material for both teacher education and teacher professional development. The learning context of the two projects combine formal (i.e., classroom), nonformal (i.e., Web-based), and informal (e.g., park) learning environments and engage students in data collection and analysis of authentic data regarding local environmental problems. Furthermore, the two projects try to address current gaps in the literature of mobile learning by exemplifying the theoretical aspects and the characteristics of design frameworks associated with mobile learning, demonstrating rich and complex pedagogical practices that use mobile devices and, characterizing the processes by which students come to understand science through the use of mobile wireless devices.

Successful e-learning initiatives often rely on solid partnerships among organizations that bring together a set of complimentary knowledge and expertise. An example of a partnership among information technology companies, e-content developers, academic institutions, and research centers, is a recent project that is being developed for the Cyprus Ministry of Education and Culture. The project goal is to prepare learning objects for 13 subjects of upper secondary schools and technical education including mathematics, physics, carpentry, English language, and culinary arts. The partnership is led by HS DATA and SIVECO, with supporting partners the University of Nicosia and CARDET. This project is cofunded by the European Social Fund and the Cyprus government, and it builds on a project that has been running for a year now, which is also led by HS DATA and SIVECO and which aims to establish a pilot implementation of an e-learning solution (Learning Management System—LMS) at seven schools in the public education system.

The two projects are related in the sense that all learning objects and e-content that will be developed, will be disseminated and made available to schools through the LMS. It is in the immediate plans of the MOEC to have the whole public education system connected with the LMS solution, which consists of a set of services that are designed to support the education process within a lifelong learning environment. This system is designed to support teachers in their everyday activities, the students in accessing educational content, and the parents in monitoring school activities.

CHALLENGES AND POSSIBILITIES

There are several challenges faced by organizations trying to promote e-learning initiatives in Cyprus and the European Union. Most notably, these include the lack of solid strategic plans and the issue of accreditation of online programs. The projects discussed earlier are a small sample of the types of e-learning initiatives currently under way in Cyprus in collaboration with EU countries and the eastern Mediterranean region. Although individual organizations engage in the development of e-learning programs, there is no comprehensive strategic plan that coordinates these initiatives and provides ways to leverage the rich expertise being developed in both public and private organizations on a broader scale. Such coordination is essential and can help establish Cyprus as a truly competitive regional knowledge center.

As in many other countries, e-learning degrees offered at a distance in Cyprus are not always held in the same regard as face-to-face degrees. However, technology is blurring the boundaries between traditional face-to-face and distance education, and educators should revisit their fundamental assumptions about teaching and learning (Vrasidas & Glass, 2002). Educational institutions need to be flexible and open to adjustments brought by technological developments and changes in social needs and the education environment. This is particularly urgent, since higher education institutions are increasingly being criticized for not being able to accommodate the increasing number of students seeking education, and for using ineffective teaching methods such as lectures to large numbers of students (Daniel, 1996; Vrasidas, 2002). Commercial developers and providers of educational content are also rapidly emerging in Cyprus to capitalize on these issues. Private companies that offer training and diplomas in both face-to-face and online are flourishing. A similar trend is evident in higher education.

To bring about the necessary changes and encourage the increased adoption and acceptance of online education, all education stakeholders in Cyprus need to emphasize both the content and process required to develop successful e-learning strategies. All parties impacted by these strategies need to have an input. Personnel from private and public higher education institutions including faculty, heads of departments, technology coordinators, business and industry representatives, as well as government officials and K-12 educators, should participate in the planning, implementation, and evaluation stages of e-learning initiatives.

In developing e-learning strategies, one should begin with the skills and resources that are already available. In higher education institutions and at the MOEC there are often faculty and staff involved in research and development, yet their efforts are not widely known by most of their colleagues. There is a need to establish better communication channels for developers, organizations, faculty, and scholars to share ideas and collaborate on projects. Sharing one's work and discussing projects can help build the collegiality needed to bring faculty and officials together in planning the strategies.

Also, investments are an important component for the success of e-learning and the general expertise needed to develop and offer distance learning courses. If Cyprus wants to engage in serious research and development to improve education and the quality of life of its people, all stakeholders have to take research more seriously and put in place the mechanisms for providing the necessary funds, in particular for e-learning initiatives. For e-learning to grow and to continue to offer Cyprus a competitive advantage, the government needs to establish policies and procedures that will facilitate the growth and accreditation of e-learning courses, certificates, and degree programs. Higher education institutions should collaborate more closely with all other levels of educational organizations and pursue research grants from corporations and the European Union. It is only through close partnerships that a clear vision for a better education will be realized.

Accreditation is often associated with quality assurance. Without well-defined quality management of online programs, it is difficult to build a good reputation. A quality assurance system should consist of the policies, attitudes, actions, and procedures necessary to ensure that quality is being maintained and enhanced (Kefalas, Retalis, Stamatis, & Kargidis, 2003). Unfortunately, there haven't been any commonly accepted approaches. Therefore, many obstacles to implement and achieve quality can be found in practice. However, the new quality standard ISO/IEC 19796-1 was developed to overcome problems of choosing and implementing the appropriate quality assurance system. Yet, ensuring quality in an educational organization is a complex task requiring competencies, commitment, and resources (Pawlowski, 2007). Content providers and institutions in Cyprus need to have a well-defined quality assurance policy based on clearly articulated frameworks and methods for review. Institutional review addresses the

ultimate responsibility for the management of quality and standards that rests with the institution as a whole. Moreover, the missing quality assurance management for online learning is one of the reasons why the Cyprus government is reluctant to take appropriate legislative action for online learning.

CONCLUSION

With the help of e-learning, Cyprus has already made great strides toward becoming a regional center for education and creating an open, wall-less, and paperless educational environment that serves the needs of more citizens, especially the ones traditionally disadvantaged. The government needs to increase its support to both public and private organizations and stimulate the necessary competition among education providers. Governmental support is also necessary to achieve the main objective set by the European Council held in Lisbon in 2000. The European Council decided that by 2010 the EU should "become the most competitive and dynamic knowledge-based economy in the world." Reaching this goal implies a challenging program for modernization of the education and training systems, both in Cyprus and elsewhere in Europe.

Establishing a clear e-learning strategy is not an easy task, particularly when one deals with technologies that change so rapidly. The most critical challenge facing education systems is how to develop the capacity for change and remove the barriers built into their cultures which prevent change. In addition to increased funding, what will facilitate the development of advanced e-learning is the establishment of clear policies and support mechanisms in order to remove the barriers placed on attempts for change, innovation, and technology adoption. Therefore, framing a comprehensive e-learning strategy within which quality education and training will be offered is just one of the many ways in which Cyprus will be established as a regional center of excellence in education.

REFERENCES

Daniel, J. S. (1996). *Mega universities and knowledge media: Technology strategies for higher education*. London: Kogan Page.

Empirica (2006). *Use of computers and the Internet in schools in Europe 2006. Country brief: Cyprus*. Retrieved November 16, 2007, from http://ec.europa.eu/information_society/ eeurope/i2010/benchmarking/index_en.htm

European Commission. (2007). *Life long learning programme*. Retrieved December 3, 2007, from http://ec.europa.eu/education/ programmes/llp/index_en.html

International Institute for Educational Planning. (1997). *Appraisal study of the Cyprus education system*. Paris: UNESCO.

Kefalas, P., Retalis, S., Stamatis, D., & Kargidis, T. (2003, May). Quality assurance procedures and e-ODL. *Proceedings of the International Conference on Network Universities and E-Learning*, Valencia, Spain. Retrieved from http://www.city.academic.gr/special/ research /xcityng/papers/Kef-Ret-Sta-Kar-03.pdf.

Pawlowski, J. M. (2007). The quality adaptation model: Adaptation and adoption of the quality standard ISO/IEC 19796-1 for learning, education, and training. *Educational Technology & Society, 10*(2), 3-16.

Vrasidas, C. (2002). Educational technology in Cyprus and strategies for higher education. *Educational Media International, 39*(2), 123-132.

Vrasidas, C., & Glass, G. V. (Eds.) (2002). *Distance education and distributed learning*. Greenwich, CT: Information Age.

Education Leaders Perspectives

Pros and Cons of Distance Education in a Small Caribbean Island

Noverene Taylor

INTRODUCTION

Due to the rapid advance in computer technology and Internet access, the landscape of education has changed drastically over the years. Because of this dramatic change, many educational institutions today have realized that teaching, and learning are no longer confined to delivery models such as face-to face instruction, and are in the process or restructuring what goes on inside

Noverene Taylor, Grand Turk, Turks and Caicos Islands, B.W.I.
Telephone: (649) 946-1471.
E-mail: noverene@nova.edu

their school walls. As part of their restructuring effort, distance education plays an important role. Owing to the myriad of benefits for K-12 education offered by distance learning technologies, schools are using these technologies to reach all students, especially those in remote locations, and provide them with challenging and appropriate educational experiences.

This article examines education leaders' perspectives regarding the advantages and disadvantages of distance education in the Turks and Caicos Islands. In order to understand these, it is important that readers have a basic understanding of the islands' geography, people, and education.

THE TURKS AND CAICOS ISLANDS

The Turks and Caicos Islands consist of eight inhabited islands and about 40 cays. The islands are located at the southeastern end of the Bahamas chain, 575 miles southeast of Miami, and 90 miles north of the island of Hispaniola. The islands are accessible by aeroplanes and boats. The native people are of African descent. The expatriate community of British, American, French, Canadian, Haitians, Dominicans, and Jamaicans gives the islands some international influences.

Education is an important feature of the Turks and Caicos Islands and, as such, is provided for students up to the secondary level on most of the islands. With a student population of approximately 6,000 students, enrollment data shows that close to 3,000 students are from culturally diverse backgrounds for the 2006-2007 school year. Similar trends in enrollment were also observed for the 2005-2006 school year. Students completing their primary school education sit for the Grade Six Achievement Test (GSAT), while those after five years of secondary school sit for the Caribbean Secondary Education Certificate (CSEC) examinations.

Students who have completed elementary education and do not have immediate access to traditional high school would normally relocate to one of the other islands where the necessary facilities for education are provided. With only two community colleges on these islands, the same can be said for students who have finished high school and want to access college-level education. With the hassle of relocation, costly airline tickets, and the

islands being multicultural in nature, distance education technologies can offer a great deal of flexibility, and convenience as to when, where, and how education is distributed to students at the elementary school, high school, and community college in the Turks and Caicos Islands.

DEFINING DISTANCE EDUCATION

It is important that definitions that are associated with this approach to instruction be examined so that readers will have a better understanding of the pros and cons of distance education in the Turks and Caicos Islands. Distance education can be defined as: "institution based formal education where the learning group is separated, and where interactive telecommunications systems are used to connect learners, resources, and instructors" (Simonson, 2003, as cited in, Simonson, Smaldino, Albright, & Zvacek, 2006, p. 32). Traditionally, this includes a variety of activities from correspondence program using postal services; courses

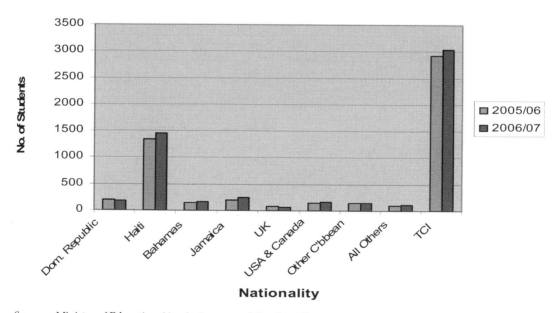

Source: Ministry of Education, Youth, Sports, and Gender Affairs (2007).

Figure 1. Enrollment by nationality in both government and private schools for the school years 2005/2006 and 2006/2007.

broadcasted using the radio, distributed video lectures, or other materials to enhance instruction. Today, with the rapid increase in technology, more attention is given to online distance education.

ONLINE DISTANCE EDUCATION

Distance education has been in existence for at least 160 years (Simonson et al., 2006), and the medium has changed from paper-and-pencil correspondence study to real-time online education. The development of this "subfield" of distance education has become a central focus of the field of education due to its flexibility, affordability, convenience, and attractiveness. It is distinguished from other previous paradigms of distance education by its ability to create critical communities of inquiry (Garrison, Anderson, & Archer, 2003). Many may still use distance education and online education interchangeably, but it is believed that the distinction is useful in helping us to see the development of this "subfield" of distance education in which technologies have played a major role.

Online education is delivered over the Internet. It may be synchronous, in which the teacher and the student interact with each other in "real time." For example, with two-way videoconferences, students interact with "live" video of an instructor. Telephone conversations are also considered synchronous. Asynchronous delivery, on the other hand, does not take place simultaneously. In this case, the teacher may deliver the instruction using video, discussion board postings, Web sites, or other means, and the students respond at a later time. While adult students are benefiting from online distance education programs, the young and traditional students have increasingly begun to realize the new opportunities that are available to increase their academic achievement.

DISTANCE EDUCATION VERSUS TRADITIONAL INSTRUCTION

Distance education's quality is often compared with that of traditional instruction. Most recent reports have shown that there are no significant difference between online learning and traditional instruction in terms of student grades, test scores, and other measures of student achievement (Worley, 2000). Phipps and Merisotis (1999) completed a review of distance education's effectiveness and concluded that no matter what technology is used, distance education courses are as favourable as traditional face-to-face learning.

ADVANTAGES OF DISTANCE EDUCATION IN THE TURKS AND CAICOS ISLANDS

In the Turks and Caicos Islands (TCI), education leaders consider some of the key strengths of distance education to rest in its capacity to provide "anytime" and "anywhere" education to students. According to the views expressed by some of the education leaders, distance education affords many adults on these islands the opportunity to access education that would not otherwise be possible.

The director of education, Beatrice Fulford, who is presently pursuing her doctoral degree, indicated that distance education is a great learning opportunity for individuals who have jobs and families, and do not want to interrupt their job to go back to school but really want to pursue higher education. While distance education is different from the face-to-face traditional setting, she noted that it is very convenient, flexible, and affordable. Convenience suggests that students do not have to spend time commuting to classes during the week or at a particular time of the day. As a distant learning student, she has great freedom to study at times that suit her, be it early morning or middle of the night, and completes her assignments when the time is convenient, whether during lunch hours or after work in the convenience of her home.

Thomas Joyner (personal communication, March 20, 2007), the education psychologist, stated that, in these islands, distance education is of tremendous benefit to adult learners who have difficult schedules because they can learn at their own pace and time. In other words, distance learners control their learning environment; school is brought to the student, and not the student to school. Joyner also noted that certain learners, for example those who are shy, will find distance education suitable to meeting their educational needs. Distance learning, he said, eliminates the need for some students to feel judged or embarrassed by their classmates.

Distance education can be a worthwhile experience for learners. It can provide convenient locations for both students and instructors because many of the technologies, such as the Internet, videotape, and telephone, can be easily accessed at home, noted the education officer for the literacy program, Kaydeen Miles. She also pointed out that when you look at the benefits of learning new technological skills in order to adequately prepare yourself for the virtual environment, distance learners are at an advantage above the traditional student. She noted that distance education offers great potential for alleviating educational inequity in these islands because the islands are multicultural in nature. Distance education she believes, can also be less costly than that of traditional education. Books, course content provided by the instructor, and other resources are only a click away.

In order for students to move on to high school, they have to achieve an average of 50% or more on the Grade Six Achievement Test. When results for the June 2006 examination were analyzed, it was found that of the 292 students who sat the exam, approximately 188 students received a

score of 50% or more. This clearly indicates that these students could have benefited from distance education, which could be used as a legitimate teaching method to provide appropriate instruction for students to enhance their academic performance. Students who did not achieve a score of up to 50% might not necessarily be weak students. They could be students with different learning styles, needs, and abilities. Placed in a different learning environment, such as a distance learning setting, where they can work at their own pace, they could show marked improvement.

Pass marks for the Caribbean Secondary Education Certificate (CSEC) examinations range from grade one to three, with one being the highest and three the lowest. On the May/June 2006 examinations, 88 students received a grade one, 226 students received a grade two, and 338 students received a grade three. Therefore, if these students were provided with a distance learning environment, where they can collaborate and work together, and be more actively involved in their own learning, the possibility exists that the number of students who receive a grade one could increase, thereby decreasing the number of students who receive a grade three.

Several teachers who were interviewed agreed that, while adult learners are using distance education programs to achieve higher education, in the Turks and Caicos Islands, elementary school students, high school students, and the traditional college students should have access to the new opportunities presented by distance education. Indeed, distance learning represents a network of technologies that can connect the public school systems, and provide greater motivation, reduced learning time, and higher achievements, among others.

The community college offers associate degrees to students who have completed high school education. Distance education could allow students studying at this level

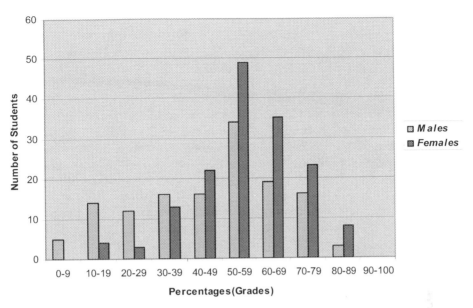

Source: Ministry of Education, Youth, Sports, and Gender Affairs (2007).

Figure 2. Grade Six Achievement Test Results for June 2006 (males = 135, females = 157).

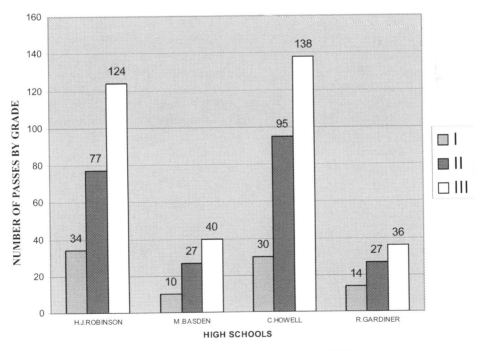

Source: Ministry of Education, Youth, Sports, and Gender Affairs (2007).

Figure 3. Caribbean Secondary Education Certification passes by grade and school for May/June 2006.

to pursue courses that are not available on these islands. This educational approach could also address growing populations, limited space, and permit students who have failed a course to take it again. This could eliminate the hassle of getting student visas, and transportation to and from campuses. In addition, students would not have to worry about housing accommodation or the expense of airline tickets to return home because they would not have to go overseas to study. And even if they do, traveling to the institutions campus would not be for any extended period. Distance education is not normally tailored around the schedules of traditional semester schedules. Therefore, students would be more flexible with their time in completing courses.

In a multicultural society where students may have language challenges, the distance education environment would be quite appropriate to make them feel more comfortable and relaxed using the English language without the fear of being embarrassed or judged by their peers. Additionally, distance education can afford traditional teachers the opportunity to move away from a mechanistic style of teaching where knowledge is imparted by the teacher to students, to a more active and creative process, one in which teachers design and facilitate activities that are geared towards students using technology to generate, discover, and build their own framework of knowledge collaboratively. Montgomery (1998) argues that not all students learn the same way, and so using multimedia allows students to take an active role in learning in ways that the traditional classroom cannot afford. This implies that distance education environments can be designed in ways that meet each student's needs.

Students' interisland interaction is limited to inter-island school events, where only the competitors from each school get to interact with each other. Having established a platform for distance education,

this would open up the gateway for complete interislands interaction. All of the schools in these islands would be able to interact with each other regardless of geographical location. The adoption of distance education here in the Turks and Caicos Islands, at the elementary, high school, and community college levels could also afford students the opportunity to interact with other students across the globe. Imagine students collaborating with each other, sharing research ideas, and forming study groups for the Grade Six Achievement Test or the Caribbean Secondary Education Certificate. This could be a great motivator and a wonderful learning experience!

Teachers believe that they could work collaboratively in developing online courses for students at the different grade levels and share resources for the benefit of the students. This could be seen as an advantage wherein, the teachers would not have to develop courses on their own. The design of distance education courses does take time, and much effort, and must be done properly for students to be successful.

Through the technologies of distance education, students would be at an advantage in interacting with first world countries classrooms that may be using cutting-edge technologies. Furthermore, the Turks and Caicos Islands, being a third world country, could be brought to modernization, in order to become more productive and inventive.

DISADVANTAGES OF DISTANCE EDUCATION IN THE TURKS AND CAICOS ISLANDS

Lack of vision and financial resources may be considered two of the major factors that can disadvantage elementary school, secondary school, and community college students from distance education opportunities on these islands. Other drawbacks include, but are not limited to, lack of face to face interaction, academic dishonesty, no campus atmosphere, stigma attached, and the requirement of new skills for both the instructor and student.

The director pointed out that, with her experience in a distance education environment, she believes that the "distance" aspect of distance education seems to have taken away much of the social interaction that is present in traditional instruction. She noted that distance learning may not be for everyone. Those who do not have a strong desire to learn on their own can become easily distracted, playing online games such as pool or simply chatting with friends. In addition, when a student needs assistance with a particular assignment, it can be very difficult for the instructor to assist without being physically present. A student working alone at times can also feel isolated and depressed. Therefore, it is important that distance learners feel connected one way or another to the learning environment.

The director stated that some students are at a disadvantage when participating in certain activities for their distance education program. For example, for her program of study, the university offers weekly and monthly on-campus workshops and seminars that are beneficial to her professional development. But as a student in the distance education environment she does not have these opportunities readily available at her "fingertips." She mentioned that even though students are able to interact with people across the globe, the interaction is not necessarily the same as when you are in a traditional setting. Mediated communication takes away a lot of cues and personalized attention. Fulford also stated that some employers might not value certification through distance education. They tend to believe that the reputation of distance education is questionable. Therefore, students pursuing distance education courses must ensure that the course or program is accredited by a valid educational agency.

According to Joyner (personal communication, March 20, 2007), when students pursue online courses, it can be very hard to detect cheating. In the privacy of one's home students can easily receive an A grade by submitting another student's work. Hence, this is a matter that must be dealt with by teachers who are considering teaching at a distance. Joyner added that teachers must ensure that instruction is designed so that each student submits authentic work.

Miles, the literacy officer, noted that if you are afraid of change or learning new technology skills, then online distance education might not be suitable for you. She further claimed that if the instructor is not adequately prepared to deal with the virtual classroom, learners can become frustrated and drop the course. Therefore, in order for distance education to be successful in these islands, technical barriers would have to be a nonissue.

Some teachers believe that the lack of exposure to distance education settings would put some students at a disadvantage. When asked the reason for drawing such conclusion, the teachers simply stated that some students are already accustomed to the traditional classroom, and so exposing them to a faceless classroom environment could prove difficult. They believe that the transition from a face-to-face classroom to a faceless classroom might not be an easy task for some students.

The teachers further indicated that students in the current school system who are not yet exposed to the technological skills needed to succeed in a virtual environment would have to be properly trained. Teachers would have to be equipped technically and be trained to develop online courses and implement them accordingly. Institutions would have to acquire and install the needed equipment, course management systems, and other resources required. This could be very costly for the institutions, especially those operating on a tight budget. The success of any distance education program is dependent on the efficiency and effectiveness of a distance instructor and how prepared students are for the virtual environment. Therefore, if adequate training and support are not provided, in the initial stage of participating in distance education programs the attrition rate could be very high.

It is also unrealistic to expect young children to attend distance education courses at their own time and convenience. Someone must be able to supervise them. Elementary school students would not have recess time to socialize and play, and of course, social development is vital to the development of the whole child, especially when preparing students to survive in a highly socialized work environment. Not being able to attend important workshops, seminars, and special functions on campus would disadvantage some distance learners, especially those students who are just leaving high school.

Students who are weaker academically may be at a disadvantage in the distance learning environment. Distance learners have to be self-directed and intrinsically motivated. They also have to have good reading and comprehension skills. The weaker students may not be disciplined enough to use their own initiative to be successful. These are usually the students who require face-to-face interaction in the traditional classroom setting. Therefore, online education may not be for all types of learners.

Being in a third world environment, access to computers may be difficult on the part of some students. This would certainly put some of these students at a disadvantage where distance education is concerned. The monthly cost of Internet access might not be affordable to some students.

Tradition affects a wide cross-section of society. Most recent research demonstrates that there is no significant difference in terms of students' course grades, rating of course content and the instructor, and other outcomes. Therefore, it is incumbent of educators to make it clear to parents, and the wider community that distance education has been proven to be just as effective as traditional face-to-face instruction. One point is of paramount importance; if distance education is successfully implemented at all levels of the education system in these islands, it will have a promising future!

SUMMARY AND CONCLUSION

Distance education can be just as effective as any other category of instruction here in the Turks and Caicos Islands because when used effectively, learning occurs and knowledge is gained, which is the objective of teaching. Distance education is also cost effective, flexible, and convenient for many adult learners on these islands. Even though distance learning courses originally catered to nontraditional students as its target group, students at the elementary, high school, and community college levels can benefit from the new opportunities provided by distance education. The teacher's ability to create an interactive environment is vital for quality online education. Not all students may benefit from distance learning opportunities. Students who are intrinsically motivated and self-directed are most likely to succeed. Distance education may create feelings of isolation, and depression for some students. However, the advantages of distance learning seem to far outweigh the disadvantages. Therefore, by carefully identifying, and dealing with drawbacks that are within their influence, institutions on these islands may very well find that such actions are sufficient to provide students with distance education opportunities so that they can become contributing citizens in a global, diverse, and technologically advanced society.

REFERENCES

Garrison, R., Anderson, T., & Archer, W. (2003). In M. G. Moore & W. G. Anderson (Eds.), *Handbook of distance education*. Mahwah, NJ: Erlbaum.

Ministry of Education, Youth, Sports, and Gender Affairs. (2007). Turks and Caicos Islands Education Statistical Digest.

Montgomery, S. M. (1998). *Addressing diverse learning styles through the use of multimedia* [online]. Retrieved March 25, 2007, http://www.vpaa.uillinois.edu/tid/resources/montgomery.html

Phipps, R., & Merisotis, J. (1999). *What's the difference? A review of contemporary research on the effectiveness of distance learning in higher education*, Washington, DC: The Institute for Higher Education Policy. Retrieved April 11, 2007, from http://eric.ed.gov/ERICDocs/data/ericdocs2/content_storage_01/0000000b/80/11/6f/e4.pdf

Simonson, M., Smaldino, S., Albright, M., & Zvacek, S. (2006). *Teaching and learning at a distance: Foundations of distance education* (3rd ed.). Upper Saddle River, NJ: Prentice Hall.

Worley, R. B. (2000). The medium is not the message. *Business Communication Quarterly, 63*(2), 93-103.

Distance Learning in Belize
A Benefit for Youths and Adults

Yvonne Palma

In today's changing world with its economic challenges, addressing the needs of underprivileged youths and adults becomes a growing challenge for any small nation such as Belize. Belize, a Caribbean country in Central America, is the only English-speaking country in the region. With a diversity of people, sites, and a democratically elected government, Belize has a population of 310,000 (Statistical Institute of Belize, 2007).

DEMOGRAPHICS OF BELIZE

As a developing nation, Belize suffers from many societal ailments, such as youths leaving school early with limited opportu-

Yvonne Palma,
2917 Albert Hoy Street, P O Box 2419,
Belize City, Belize.
Telephone: (501) 620-9256

nity for meaningful employment, and adults who are unskilled and unable to occupy job positions that are available to sustain their families. The problem of crime starts with youths dropping out of school; poor adults received little education, have big families, and are unable to meet their expenses (Crawford, 2010). A survey of the *Police Notebook* (Belize Police Department, 2010) shows crime and violence on the rise, and the age of criminals being youths 13 and 17 years and early 20s.

In 2007, the unemployment rate among youths was 24%. While female unemployment rate was 32.8% of 41.8% participation rate; males were 18.7% of a participation rate of 77.5% (Statistical Institute of Belize, 2007). The concentration of unemployment, according to the Statistical Institute of Belize (2007), has been in the rural area of the country, with high rates of unemployment recorded in the northern and southern districts. The highest unemployment rate for females was in the southern district. In 2009, the highest unemployment was concentrated in the northern district. This was credited to the decline in the sugar industry located in the northern districts and the economic downturn (Statistical Institute of Belize, January 2010)

PROFILE OF THE BELIZEAN STUDENT

Belize, aware of the global environment, is focused on guaranteeing quality education as a basic human right to all through "allocating public funding to schools equitably by funding schools on a per student basis" and "free tuition policy. We know that many of the students who do not attend secondary school because of poverty and limited access (United Democratic Party, 2008). Through the establishment of these policies, more students will have access to a quality education.

According to the Ministry of Education (2008), of 42,000 students who begin elementary school, 38,000 transition to secondary school, and 20% drop out of secondary school. According to Ingels, Chen, and Owings (2005) students perceive positive school experiences based upon the attitude and skills of their teachers, the degree of safety they feel within their school, their perception of victimization at a school, their perception of school rules, the importance they place on good grades and their reason for being in school. The secondary schools in the country with the highest student enrollment are the urban areas (Ministry of Education, 2008).

The Belizean student lives with mother and father, father, mother, stepfathers or stepmothers, relatives, on their own, boarding with boarders, grandparents or grandparent. The parents of these students have varying levels of education ranging from primary level education to postgraduate degrees. Based on the availability of distance education within the country, more and more parents are returning to school to pursue higher education (E. J. Lopez, personal communication, April 20, 2010).

DISTANCE EDUCATION: A POSSIBLE SOLUTION?

In attempting to address the needs of youths' and adults' unemployment or underemployment, Belize has over the years recognized that the traditional system of education no longer meets the needs of these learners. According to United Nations Educational Scientific and Cultural Organization (n.d.-a), conventional education systems are poorly prepared to deal with the challenges and opportunities that are present in the emerging information and communication technologies and little has been done to address the growing problem of social fragmentation, human frustration and disempowerment, cultural dislocation, and technological alienation (p. 2). According to Adaji, Salawu, and Adeoye (2008), distance education provides avenues for higher education for vast under-privileged population.

According to Simonson, Smaldino, Albright, and Zvacek (2009) distance education is institution-based formal education where the learning group is separated, and where interactive telecommunications systems are used to connect learners, resources and instruction. Furthermore, research has found no significant difference between distance education and traditional education in terms of student achievement.

According to E. Raymond (personal communication, April 21, 2010) learners in Belize have been participating in distance learning since 1964. This was in the form of examinations for teachers, where teachers attending the teachers' training school in Belize take qualifying examinations through correspondence. Two-way communication was between student and examination authority through postal services. Students from Belize also completed qualifying subject specific examinations from London's Royal Society of Arts and General Certificate of Education in ordinary and advance levels. Teachers were also able to obtain professional teachers' certification, advancing to the doctorate level through correspondence. Today, these examinations can be taken at a distance online, or via postal and courier services.

Telesecundaria. In 1999, the Ministry of Education through technical assistance from the Mexican government as part of the EDUSAT project embarked on a distance learning initiative. According to Ministry of Education (2009) the EDUSAT project was to establish secondary education through satellite and television throughout remote parts of the country of the country, to provide secondary education opportunities to students who otherwise would not receive the opportunity. Technical assistance from Mexico included the training of facilitators in the methodology and use of course materials, technicians to provide equipment support, donation of satellite dishes and televisions, as well as course materials for students. The telesecundaria was implemented in the northern district of Corozal at Escuela Secundaria Mexico because the language of the materials was in Spanish, and people in the northern districts were considered more competent in speaking Spanish and hence would immediately benefit from the training (D. Eck, personal communication, 2009).

Telesecundaria, which was launched in Mexico in 1968, provided lower secondary school learning with television support to remote and small communities; lessons corresponding to Grades 7 to 9 were transmitted live, through open public channels to television sets placed in distant classrooms where students listened and took notes in the presence of a teacher (United Nations Educational, Scientific and Cultural Organization, n.d.-b, p. 2). This program was operational from 2005 to June 2008. After being informed of the program being discontinued, the Ministry of Education conducting an investigation to determine the circumstances that led to the program being discontinued; upon completion of the investigation the explanation received from the principal was the need for additional classroom space (A. Castillo, personal communication, April 20, 2010). Although this program was accessed by many youths and adult learners, training time for the program was Monday to Friday between the hours of 8 A.M. to 2:30 P.M. The time factor also allowed for fewer individuals to access the program and restricted the benefit of utilizing existing

space and available teachers. Although the signal could be accessed in any part of the country, the program was never expanded to other areas within the country. An additional factor may have been language, as the language of course materials and instruction was in Spanish.

TECHNICAL AND VOCATIONAL EDUCATION AND TRAINING

Technical and vocational education and training has been recognized as an important element in a nation's development. According to Caribbean Secretariat (1990) TVET is looked upon by developing countries as "a vehicle for the development of marketable skills as an engine for development" (p. 1). As a measure of preparing countries within the region to become more competitive in the global economy, TVET is called upon to help unemployed young people, upgrade existing workers' competencies, reduce the burden of higher education, provide qualified labors to attract foreign investment, and any investment in human development draws return on the individual as well as the society as a whole (CARICOM, 2001). Individuals will benefit from a better career, increased earnings, and a better quality of life. What benefits the society is a skilled-workforce that enables global competitiveness and economic growth.

In an effort to expand and improve TVET in the country of Belize, and provide opportunities for its people, the government of Belize invested $4.4 million into the establishment and development of Institutes for Technical and Vocational Education and Training (ITVETs) (Caribbean Development Bank, 2001). The Institutes for Technical and Vocational Education and Training (ITVET) are government of Belize skills training institutions that provide training for employment. These institutions are located in each of the seven districts of Belize and provide training based on employment training needs in each district.

Stann Creek ITVET is located in the southern district of Stann Creek. The institution provides training in the area of tourism and hospitality, automotive, masonry, carpentry, and electricity. The main industries in the district are tourism, hospitality, and citrus. New resorts are being built in the district, requiring persons skilled in masonry, carpentry, and electrical installation. Once the resorts have been built, skilled persons will be required to provide services in tourism and hospitality. Automotive training was provided to address the needs of the citrus industry. According to S. W. Bowman (personal communication, February 26, 2010) work has began to expand training to secondary school students within the Stann Creek district. He hopes to provide more employment opportunities for the students with the inclusion of a TVET program as part of their training.

Similar to Stann Creek ITVET, Belize ITVET provides similar training with the addition of customized training to specific groups based on request. The institute provides customized training for the Belize Defense Force, along with courses offered at night in the area of air conditioning and refrigeration and auto body repair. Further, request for training has been received from several different organizations, and these programs are customized programs (K. Ellis, personal communication, March 11, 2010).

Orange Walk ITVET, located in the district of Orange Walk, provides training in the area of building construction trades, computer repair, and automotive repair. Orange Walk ITVET focuses on preparing trainees to become competent and excel in the Belize National Vocational Qualification examination. Beyond the entry level program offerings, the institution has moved to offering training in level two, which prepares employees to perform tasks requiring some level of autonomy.

The other four institutions provide similar training with the inclusion of training in the agricultural area in the Toledo district.

According to Bowman (2010, January) the enrollment for Stann Creek ITVET has experienced a decline in the student population. Twelve trainees dropped, out leaving 58 participating in training. Toledo ITVET has 35 trainees enrolled in the programs, which is very small to justify the expense in operating the programs. Bowman (2010, January) attributes the decline in enrollment to financial problems experienced by the trainee in meeting the cost of the program.

DISTANCE LEARNING IN TECHNICAL AND VOCATIONAL EDUCATION

As the economic situation of individuals continue to decline, the management of the various institutions recognizes the need to expand and increase access for persons who would otherwise be unable to access training. Distance learning in technical and vocational education can allow for underprivileged youths and adults to obtain skills that will make them employable. Although presently the institutions have only computers and Internet, with regards to technological capabilities to provide distance learning using telecommunications systems, the process of trying to provide training for youths and adults in other locations is considered a priority. Belize ITVET began implementing its first distance learning initiative in San Pedro, Ambergris Caye (K. Ellis, personal communication April 20, 2010). This town is approximately 45 miles outside of the city. This initiative provides training to electricians who are unable to travel to Belize City to attend classes. Students will be able to perform the practical aspect of the training by conducting installations within the workplace. This initiative falls within the category of traditional distance learning program that used postal services, and the EDUSAT concept, though without the technology of satellite and television. For the institution, this is a start and the intention is to expand the distance education program to more individuals through the use of the Internet and other communications technology. There are many open software and available support web-based sites that can be accessed by purchasing licenses or obtaining permission to use the resources.

It is anticipated that programs will be expanded to include students attending secondary schools within the district; satellite centers located in smaller communities would be able to transmit the course using satellite dish and television, as well as videoconferencing and the Internet. (S. W. Bowman, personal communication, February 26, 2010). Distance learning programs will expand opportunities for other students as well as for students at the Orange Walk ITVET (A. Gomez, personal communication, March 11, 2010). The advantage will be that students will be able to take course in programs not offered at that specific ITVET. With distance learning programs offered through the ITVETs, the youths and adults who are ultimately the clients that the ITVET targets will benefit from such an initiative. This will facilitate quality skills training being provided with the introduction of communications technology to persons who would otherwise be unable to access training offered using technology. According to Moore and Tait (2002), many countries have developed vocational and other types of short-cycle colleges, sometimes spanning both secondary and postsecondary levels to provide training to adults and youths. In this sector there are many examples of open and distance learning programmes that may be useful to the ITVETs.

A Coordinated Effort

In order to be successful, the plans and efforts of the ITVETs in providing distance education to clients requires coordination and funding. A distance learning division within the TVET system is required. The division will offer individuals the opportunity that would otherwise be inaccessible to them within their own location through a system of telecommunications and internet technology. This initiative will not only provide programs that will be offered through the distance unit, but also allow existing customers from the traditional face to face division, local community, and other targeted groups to access training from the convenience of their own location. According to Simonson et al. (2009), the unavailability of technical support creates a major barrier that discourages many faculties from teaching online course. The need to offer the relevant support to the institutions will also be required, and that will require the Ministry of Education to invest in infrastructure development and teacher training.

Benefit to Youths and Adults

According to the Commonwealth of Learning (n.d.), benefits of distance education include overcoming problems of physical distance, solving time or scheduling issues for learners and schools, expanding limited number of places available for learners, and it makes the best use of few teachers. In 2008, the Ministry of Education began a subsidy program, in which students entering secondary schools and those entering the second year receive subsidies to assist with cost of school. In 2010, students completing elementary schools from the Stann Creek and Toledo districts were automatically entitled to subsidies to offset the cost of schooling (A. Genitty, personal communication, April 22, 2010). With the availability of this program, underprivileged students living in remote areas will have the opportunity to obtain relevant materials required for schooling face-to-face or at a distance.

With its small population and high unemployment rate, Belize can benefit tremendously from distance education. The ratification of the free labour movement among Caribbean countries, now more than ever, highlights the need for Belizean youths and adults to become skilled, certified, and competent to meaningfully participate in employment. The vast amount of capital investment made by the government of Belize into infrastructure development in technical and vocational education and training can be further expanded with additional investments to include the development of distance learning initiatives. This will allow for the participation in distance education of more underprivileged youths and adults throughout the country.

REFERENCES

Ajadi, T. O., Salawu, I. O., & Adeoye, F. A. (2008). E-learning and distance education in Nigeria. *Turkish online journal of educational technology*. Retrieved from http://0-www.eric.ed .gov.novacat.nova.edu/ERICWebPortal/ Home.portal?

Belize Police Department. (2010, April). Police notebook. *Amandala*, p. 4.

Bowman, S. W. (2010, January). Monthly report. Stann Creek ITVET.

Caribbean Development Bank. (2001). *Appraisal document: Loan to government of Belize*. Bridgetown, Barbados: Author.

Caribbean Secretariat. (1990). *Regional strategy on TVET*. Georgetown, Guyana: CARICOM.

CARICOM. (2001). *CARICOM regional TVET strategy*. Georgetown, Belize: Author.

Commonwealth of Learning. (n.d.). *Advantages of open and distance learning*. Retrieved from http://www.commonwealth of learning.org

Crawford, J. I. (2010, April 25). Treasury lane car washers: "Its tough, but it's honest work." *Amandala*, p. 19.

Ingels, S. J., Chen, X., & Owings, J. A. (2005, March). A profile of the American high school sophomore in 2002; initial results from the base year of the education longitudinal study of 2002. *Statistical Analysis Report*. Washington, DC: U.S. Department of Education, NCES.

Ministry of Education. (2008). *Statistical digest*. Projects & Planning Unit.

Ministry of Education. (2009). *Report on Telesecundaria*. Belmopan, Belize: Author.

Moore, M. M., & Tait, A. (2002). *Open and distance learning: Trends, policy and strategy consideration*. Paris, France: UNESCO. Retrieved from http://unesdoc.unesco.org/images/0012 /001284/128463e.pdf

Simonson, M., Smaldino, S., Albright, M., & Zvacek, S. (2009). *Teaching and learning at a distance: Foundations of distance education* (4th ed.). Boston, MA: Allyn & Bacon.

Statistical Institute of Belize. (2010). *Annual report 2009*. Belmopan, Belize: Author.

United Democratic Party. (2008). *United Democratic Party manifesto*. Retrieved from http:// www.udp.org.bz/UDP-Manifesto9.htm

United Nations Educational Scientific and Cultural Organization. (n.d.-a). *Learning Without Frontiers*: Constructing open learning communities for lifelong learning. Retrieved from http://www.unesco.org/education/lwf/

United Nations Educational Scientific and Cultural Organization. (n.d.-b). Telesecundaria, Mexico. (Lower secondary school learning with television support). Retrieved from http://www.unesco.org/education/educprog/ lwf/doc/portfolio/abstract8.htm